The Law

Over **1,160** questions and answers on United Kingdom, Human rights Europe, international Law.

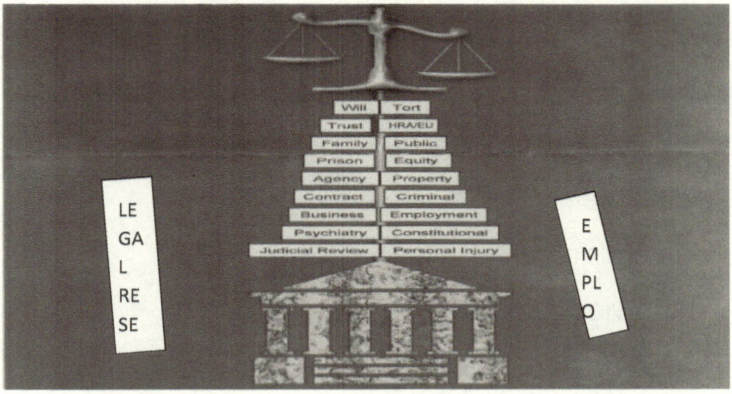

By James Safo

LLM (Master of Laws (0/g)), BA (Hons.) laws and accounts, Dip. Business law, Dip. Criminology. Cert. Acct, Cart. Ed ,Psy.N, GN. Dip: scrip writing, Business , computer, Safety management. etc.

Quick content search

Part 1

CONTENT

Disclaimer (Exclusive clause)

The author and all employees disclaim any incorrect interpretation wrong answers to questions or text, harm include emotional, psychological, and physical or any form of harm to the reader/listener or being given information by third parties. Furthermore, this disclaimer protects all contributory people, directors, employees, 3rd party,

and author and will not be liable for any injury caused.

Dedication

To my daughter Kiahna and son Elliot who worked very hard at School despite my miscarriage of justice to achieve good university education in Psychology

To my niece Danibelle Lartey whose father died when she was very young but managed to achieved distinction at A level and read Law, her dream in university

To my son, Elliot full over £450,000 scholarship to Harvard University USA to obtained Bachelor of Arts in Economics

Was Junior Olympic, Commonwealth, United Kingdom champion and world number 3 in Long Jump. Also brain of Britain for 2 year (GCSE and A level)

The above demonstrate Almighty God's powers to help those who believe, trust and have faith in Him.

Acknowledgements

I had pondered on this topic for months with no answer to who inspired me to write about ten books, plus my autobiography while in a constrained environment – prison. I had no hesitation to delete human beings from my list. The real author of all my books is Almighty God/Allah/Parama Ananba through his messengers. I was not capable of neither writing books or achieving those high-powered qualifications: physically, 75% of my bones are in the advanced stage of arthritis, I have the worst type of cardiovascular disease, a large heart (hypertrophy), chronic depression and anxiety and, worst of all, three out of four of my brain lobes have been damaged since 1998 as a result of a serious car accident. Yet I rose to be one of the most successful international entrepreneurs in the world.

Preface

The aim of this book is to provide knowledge and understanding of the various categories of the laws in United Kingdom, Europe and international. It is not meant to be legal advice which one needs to obtain from qualified lawyer or solicitor

It is for both non-lawyers and law students and refence for practicing lawyers. The laws in the United Kingdom are like a maze and when combined with European and international treaties it becomes a no-go area for non-lawyers. No wonder there has been so many miscarriages of justice in the United Kingdom. Since laws are always being amended, enacted and common law being made, I will encourage my readers to check the situation of specific law.

I have deliberately listed all the 1,160 questions separately so that individuals (especially) might test themselves if they so wish before would refer to the questions and answer. Some of the questions are short, long, scenario

To make case strong, search for similar case and quote it, this could be common law or statute, criminal or judicial review decision.

Lawyers' fees are expensive so it would be for your interest to prepare your own case in chronological order

A good lawyer will appreciate this before interview, and can spend more time to discuss the issue.

To protect any statement you make write at the top "Without prejudice\subject to contract" so that it cannot be used against you without your written consent. There is exception in this privilege such as security of the country

Part 2

Chapter 2.1

About the Author

I was an abandon child at the age of four. As an adult I became a high-profile international entrepreneur based in England for over twenty-five years and owned ten different businesses at the same time, including an international college, etc. I was arguably one of the most successful black people in Europe at the time, before my miscarriage of justice. After writing the books, three medical experts cast doubt on my conviction (miracle). My autobiography reveals my extraordinary journey as a Slave of God. My autobiography confirms that my pain and suffering was equivalent to the Prophets Job and Joseph together (found in the Holy Bible and Holy Quran), which are true events and not fictional as most of the unbelievers thought. Please read my autobiography to see how God has answered doubters as history has been repeated. I am severely disabled physically with mental health and neurological problems, I was brought down from being a millionaire to penniless due to my miscarriage of justice, but the conspirators could not take away my faith which resulted my achievement as evidence of Almighty God. Miracles.

Chapter 2.2

Qualifications

I left college with A in physics, Chemistry, Biology, applied and pure Maths. B in English language, Latin and English literature and C in Geography

I am probably one of the oldest men to achieve an Honourable Open degree in Law and Accounts (Financial and Management), as well as Psychology and Social Sciences at University level

My areas of Qualification

1. BA (Hons) , Law: **include** Criminal, Tort, damages, Contract, Property, Equity and Trust, European law, Public, Constitutional, Judicial Review
2. On Master of Law level; which is on -going, but I have passed the module " legal research", and "business, CSR Corporate social responsibility and human Right law"

3. Advance Dip. Business Law, Level 4: include Employment, Agency, Damages, Tort, Contract, employment tribunal etc.
4. Dip. Criminology
5. BA (Hons)op. Account: Financial Accountant and Management Accountant
6. Cert. Acct; Professional Certificate in Financial and Management Accounting
7. Dip. Book-keeping, Level 3
8. Nursing: RMN Psychiatry trained nurse
9. General Trained Nurse
10. Cert. in Education (Lecturer)
11. Business Certificate in Advanced Management
12. Cert. Business Enterprise
13. Advanced Food Hygiene
14. Intermediate Health and Safety
15. Dip. Safety Management
16. International Entrepreneur for over 25 years
17. Computers: Cert. Cisco Level 2 Technician, (build, repair, networking)
18. Dip. Clait Plus (in all software)
19. New Clait Dip. Level 2
20. Microsoft Specialist
21. ECDL Level 2
22. Script writing: Dip. TV, radio, stage and film

23. Non-fiction writing: Dip. Autobiography, Biography and Family History

24. Cert. in Counselling

25. Author/Self-Publisher: Over 12 books (with some yet to be published)

26. Plumbing: Level 3 City and Guild

27. Theology: Cert. Bible studies; researched Theology for my PhD (most faiths)

28. Psychology and Social Science (Level 1 at university)

29. Photographer: Portrait, Glamour and Figure Photographer (PGFP).

30. Dip. Hypnotherapy

31. National Vocation Qualification (NVQ); Internal Verifier, Trainer and Assessor

32. 2018-2020: University Student of LLM (Master of Laws) NVQ

33. Author Publisher of over 22 titles books by June 2019

34. I am currently (2019) self-employed author, accountant, lawyer etc.

Chapter 2.3

My Completed and Published Books and Books in progress

Fifty percent of my books relate to all major faiths with one mission, “to unit them under one God”; the rest has been the way of life.

During my research, it was sad to hear that some people do not wish to read any other religious holy books, either by their own choice or because of influence from others who do not want them to be confused.

It is also sad to learn that most Christians do not know the Bible well, having different interpretations to Jesus Christ’s parable teaching. This has unfortunately caused splits into thousands of different Christian denominations.

My original book on faith, covered most of major faiths consisting of over 2,000 pages. Due to the book’s size, I created four main books including *Faith Unity* (over 980 pages) and *Love all Faith* which covered over 1,300 questions and answers of all faiths (over 450 pages). I further created another book named *God Messengers before Christ* (400 pages). All these books have valuable information on various faiths, designed for the 20% of believers who, for whatever reason chose not to read about other faiths, to read them.

The world population consists of about 75% of believers who are Muslim or Christians. My research revealed that these two faiths are descendants of one father (Abraham), whose wives Hagar (Islam: Prophet Muhammad) and Sarah (Christianity: Jesus Christ). Both the Bible and the Quran feature the Ten Commandments, and both believe the story of the Prophet Moses. It is sad that both faiths appear to dislike each other without reading the other's doctrine.

To address this, I have written the book *Islam v. Christianity* (over 450 pages), quoting from both the Bible and the Quran to support my call for Unity among these two faiths. I also hope to promote world peace on earth and to march to Heaven with Muslims and Christians as brothers, who after accepting their differences, are able to live in peace. I am prepared to offer my life as sacrifice for this mission. I sincerely believe that God wants the two faiths to live in harmony and wants them to direct or publicly dissociate themselves from people who fail to abide by the Ten Commandments.

My books encompassed all the revelations to God's messengers/prophets namely: the first five books of the Bible; the Ten Commandments given to Moses, the Old Testament, David when he received the revelation to write the book of Psalms and Jesus Christ who came with the teaching from God as prophesied in the Old Testament. Over five hundred years later, humans continue to disobey God's commandment to "love" and "forgive". God has given humans a last chance when He sent his last revelation, "The Quran", through his last prophet Muhammad, as the way of life for all humans in the whole world.

I would like to remind the whole world and nations, that all God's revelations through his special messengers including Moses, David, Jesus Christ, Prophet Muhammad, Lord Krishna, the 10 Gurus and Indian messengers, resulted in the writing of the holy scriptures. These scriptures include The Tora, the Old and New Testament, the Quran, Bhagavad Gita; all of them are for the whole world to adhere to. The fact that God chose different people of different origins does not matter. God created all of us with the same organs, red blood and we all breathe the same air. The colour of the skin is only to differentiate which part of the world one comes from, and in the eyes of God must not form barriers to love and living in harmony.

God loves and accepts the way that all faiths worship and praise Him; that is why He gave all humans freewill. So please, learn to live with your differences and leave judgement to God.

My books are just to remind you once again, what God wants, which has not changed since Moses delivered the Ten Commandments to all nations. I sincerely hope all believers will pray for increase in faith, trust and belief in God; to love and forgive one another irrespective of one's faith. Lastly, the aim of my books is to encourage unbelievers who wish to practice a faith to do so. Never attempt to persuade anyone to change his faith, as this will upset God.

Let us all work hard to bring world peace; do not be a hypocrite and be genuine when partaking in God's mission and way of life.

During the last stages of my draft of this book, my conscience reminded me of the prodigal son in the Bible, who took all his inheritance and went away spending the whole lot. He became penniless and when he came back to his father he was warmly accepted. He was forgiven.

I am also reminded of the Prophet Muhammad's next-door neighbour who insulted him and poured rubbish onto his property. Yet when she became ill, it was only the Prophet who attended him. Guru Nanak's four boys were murdered. All these messengers forgave their enemies. This reminds me that we are all God's children and God is merciful. Therefore, we must not pray to God to punish our enemies, because The Almighty God hopes that one day, they will repent and come back to follow his commandments by their own freewill - not by force or punishment. For those of you who pray for their enemies to die, would you pray for your children to die if they stole from you?

2.3

List of my published Books

In June 2019, I published the following books plus other books translated into Arabic, Spanish, French and Chinese, plus different formats such as eBooks, Audiobooks, paper and hardback etc.

1. *"The One" Over 130 Poems* Copyright © 2019
2. *Allah Loves Islam* Copyright © 2019
3. *Faith United* Copyright © 2019
4. *Faith Unity* Copyright © 2019
5. *God Enlighten (Awaken) Buddhism* Copyright © 2019
6. *God Loves Christianity* Copyright © 2019
7. *God/Allah Messengers* Copyright © 2019
8. *In Search of Wisdom in Freemasonry* Copyright © 2019
9. *Islam v. Christianity* Copyright © 2019

10. *Love All Faiths: Over 1,300 Questions and Answers* Copyright © 2019
11. *Mood Disorder* Copyright © 2019
12. *Parama Ananda Loves Hinduism* Copyright © 2019
13. *Sweet and Sour Women* Copyright ©2019
14. *Autobiography* Copyright © 2019
15. *The Law (Over 1,000 Questions and Answers)* Copyright © 2019
16. *Business Law* Copyright © 2019

The following are Translated completed and published books in June 2019.

The following translated in Spanish

1) Dios ama el Cristianismo (God loves Christianity)

2) V. Islamites Cristianismo (Islam v Christianity)

3)) De la Sabiduria En la Masoneri

(In search of Wisdom in freemasonry)

4) Ame todas Las creencias (love all faiths)

5) Mensageros De Dios (God's Messengers)

6)) Allah ama elIslam (allah loves Islam)

The following translated in French

1) Messagers de Dieu (god messengers)

2) Islamisme. v. Christianisme (Islam v Christianity)

3) A la recherche de la sagesse dans la franc-maçonnerie (In search of wisdom in freemasonry)

4) Aime Toutes les Fois (Love All faiths)

5) Dieu Aime Le Christianisme (God loves Christianity)

6) Allah aime l'Islam (Allah loves islam)

The following translated in Chines

上帝爱伊斯兰教 (Allah loves Islam)

伊斯蘭教訴基督教(Islam v Christianity)

The following translated in Arabic

1) إل التشكل من الإسلام الاكتمال

2.4

Chapter1.4

My Books in Progress

The following books are in progress. I had been working and living in homeless accommodation on benefits. I have saved every penny in order to obtain suitable resources to write these books, have hot water and do my shopping at the pound shop. Prior to my miscarriage of justice, I shopped in Harrods, stayed in expensive hotels, lived in a mansion, drove a sports car etc.

1.You Don’t Need Money to Start a Business

2. Criminology Copyright

3. Great Blacks Copyright

4.Financial Account Copyright

5.Management Account

6. Christmas Jesus is coming back

Part 3

OVER;1,160 (one thousand one hundred and sixty) LAW QUESTIONS.

This is for you to test your knowledge before view the questions and answers in part 4 of this publication.

Due to frequent amendments, abolished, new laws etc. Please check current situation on specific law or seek lawyer advice before applying.

Chapter 3

Criminal Law

Chapter 3.1

ACCOMPLICE AN;D LIABILITY(accomplice, principal, aid, Abert, procure, actus reus ,mens rea.)

1) **Q;** what is accomplice;
2) **Q:** How can accomplice be successful prosecuted?
3) **Q;** Who is principal offender?
4) **Q**; what law support accessories?
5) **Q;** What is Actus reus of accomplice
6) **Q:** What Act can the Aid, Abert Counsel or procure be found?

7) Q; what does Aid and abet mean?

8) **Q**; what is Counsel?

9) **Q;** What is procuring?

10) **Q;** Which law support accomplice liability?

Chapter 3.2

MENS REA

11) **Q;** What is mens rea**?**

12) **Q:** Does it matter if defendant claim insane and why?

13) **Q** What is the mens rea of accomplice?

14) **Q:** Explain mens rea of intention?

15) **Q**; Explain mens rea of knowledge?

16) **Q;** Explain this what Lord Devlin might mean?

17) **Q**; How did Lord Goddard explain knowledge?

18) **Q;** What must accomplice do to be convicted?

19) **Q;** Give an example of just stood and watches?

20) **Q**: What about non-accidental presence?

21) **Q:** Is it a crime to fail to act?

22) **Q**: What is sentence difference between principal and accomplice?

23) **Q:**What about the actus reus of both accomplice and principal?

24) **Q:** Give two cases on accomplice?

25) **Q**: How can owner of a car be charged as accomplice?

26) **Q;** Give example of duty to Act in accomplice?

27) **Q:** What case that a bar owner charged as accomplice?

28) **Q;** What is the actus reus element of accomplice liability?

29)**Q:**What difference if accomplice action is before or after the crime?

30)**Q:** What is the accomplice position after the crime?

31)**Q;** How can insanity (lacked mental capacity) be used as defence)?

Chapter 3.3

ACTUS REA

32)**Q**: what is actus reus (guilty conduct)

33)**Q;** How do you know what the Actus REUS of a particular crime is?

34)**Q:** How does one find out the element of crime?

35)**Q:** How do you know whether certain circumstances have existed?

36)**Q:** What does actus REUS of criminal damage?

37)**Q:**Give an example of actus reus criminal damage?

38)**Q:**What is positive conduct of actus Reus?

39)**Q:** Are there some crimes that only need actus reus to convict?

40)**Q**: What is the test or judgement for this liability/?

41)**Q**: What is the objective standard required for such strict liability?

Chapter 3.4

DURESS (duress, necessity, circumstance**)**

42)**Q;** what is Duress?

43)**Q** Is duress a defence for murder?

44)Q; What crime can duress be used as defence?

45)**Q**; Give an example of cases on duress.

46)**Q**; Can duress be defence for attempted murder?

47)**Q:** Can threat be used as duress in defence?

48) **Q;** What is duress necessity

49)**Q**: What are the elements of duress necessity?

50)**Q:** Give a case in duress necessity?

51)**Q;** What is duress of circumstances?.

52)**Q:** How is the defendant expected to act in duress circumstances? And give case example?

Chapter 3.5

Driving

53): What used to be the maximum find for careless driving and kill someone?

54)Q: Can this be increased?

55)Q: How are motor accident assessed or judged?

56) **Q;** How would you describe a driver who is drunk?.

Chapter 3.6

INTOXICATION (Voluntary, involuntary, basic intent, strict intent, negligence)

57)**Q;** What is intoxication?

58)**Q;** How easy to use intoxication as defence?

59)Q; What is involuntary intoxication or misbehaviour

60)**Q:** Can involuntary intoxication be used as defence?

61)**Q** Does this include specific and basic intent?

62)**Q;** Give example of cases of on involuntary intoxication?

63)**Q**; Give another example of involuntary intoxication case?

64)**Q:** What is voluntary intoxication?

65)**Q:** How can voluntary intoxication be used as defence?

66)**Q**: What is specific intent voluntary intoxication?

67)**Q**: What is basic intent (voluntary)?

68)**Q:** What has the prosecutor have to proof?

69)**Q:** Is voluntary intoxication a defence to basic intent crimes?

70)**Q;** Give some cases of voluntary intoxication?

71)**Q;** in what situation that voluntary intoxication not defence?

72)**Q;** what about negligent due to voluntary? intoxication?

73)**Q:** what about basic intent crime in relation to voluntary intoxication?.

74)**Q;** what case relates to voluntary intoxication?

75) **Q**; in what situation can voluntary intoxication be used as defence?

76)**Q** what case relate to this exception in voluntary intoxication as defence?

77)**Q**: In what other way can voluntary intoxication be a defence?.

78)**Q;** what is Dutch courage?

79)**Q;** Give an example and can the defendant plea insanity?
80)**Q;** What about drinking in moderation?. If one is drinking alcohol in moderation but unknown that that it was spiked with vodka and get drunk more than he would have?
81)**Q;** Can involuntary intoxication is used as defence?
82)**Q;** what happens if two people were drunk and one kills the other?

Chapter 3.7

LIABILITY (Strict Liability, Absolute liability, Lawful excuse)

83)**Q:** What is Absolute liability;?
84)**Q:** What is strict liability;?
85)**Q**: Give example of strict liability?
86)**Q;** Explain crime of strict liability?.
87)**Q:** Where do you find strict liability? Give example
88)**Q:** What does strict liability use for?
89)**Q;** Does strict liability breach European article?
90)**Q;** What is crime of absolute liability?.
91)**Q:**What is lawful excuse? and give an example

Chapter 3.8

OMISSION (Fail to Act)

92)**Q:** What happen if someone fails to act?
93)**Q:** What happen if you are a career or exception case?.
94)**Q;** what other liability for omission to act.?
95)**Q**; what happen in dangerous situation?

USING FORCE

96) **Q:** What happen if you prevent crime using force?

Chapter 3.9

MISTAKE

97)**Q** What if the defendants claim to be making mistake? Or if the defendant claim of making A: mistake about the need to prevent crime?

98)**Q:** What about if the defendant was intoxicated when he \she used the force?

99) **Q;** What about if the defendant was involuntary intoxicated?

100) **Q;** If a say to B, "kill my friend" but B did not can A be charged of accomplice.?

101) **Q:** What can A be charged?

Chapter 3.10

Miscellaneous (rape innocent agent)

102) **Q:** When did husband can rape his wife started?

103) **Q:** Who is an innocent agent?

104) **Q:** What happen to the instigator?

105) **Q:** What happen if Actus reus had been committed who can be convicted?

106) **Q:** What is the appropriate charge in sexual offence

107) **Q:** What about female using a male to commit rape?

108) **Q;** Will the girl be charged?

Chapter 3.11

Murder **(** types, death, homicide, unlawful killing, felony, euthanasia, malice, mercy killing. GBH, provocation**)**

109) **Q;** How many types of murder?

110) **Q** What is first degree murder?

111) **Q;** what is second degree murder?

112) **Q;** what is Actus reus of murder.?

113) **Q**; what is mens rea of murder?

114) **Q:** What is legal definition of death?

115) **Q:** Name the three main homicides?

116) **Q;** What is the common element on Homicide?

117) **Q:** Why was a year and one day rule introduced in1994?

118) **Q;** Define Homicide?

119) **Q;** What is the main element to replace " A year and a day"?

120) **Q;** what **i**s Felony**?**

121) **Q;** What is voluntary **Euthanasia**?

122) **Q;** what law does murder comes under?

123) **Q;** what are the elements of murder?

124) Q: give an example of mercy killing?

125) **Q:** What case support mercy killing?

126) **Q;** Name some partial defence available for murder or GBH (gracious bodily harm)

Chapter 3.12

SUICIDE PACT (Diana Pretty, Mr. Purdy)

127) **Q:** What law does the suicide Act 1961 under?

128) **Q:** What are the main element of suicide pact?

129) **Q:**What will the defendant be charged

130) **Q;** What is a suicide pact based on?

131) **Q;** name case law to support suicide pact?

132) **Q;** What law can the court use to refuse application for suicide pact?

133) **Q** Explain the case of Diane Pretty (2001)

134) **Q;** Explain the case of Mrs. Purdy (2009)

Chapter 3.13

MANSLAUGHTER (voluntary, involuntary, domestic violence, vulnerable adult, self- defence, aggressor, excuse of homicide)

135) **Q:** What is manslaughter?

136) **Q**; What is voluntary manslaughter?

137) **Q;** What is involuntary manslaughter?

138) **Q;** What was the sentence for manslaughter

139) **Q;** When and what was abolished in the Corona and Justice Act 2009?

140) **Q;** What is the hierarchy of homicide cases?

141) **Q;** which law protect the vulnerable persons?

142) **Q** Explain section 5.1 (I)?

143) **Q**; Explain section 5.d (ii)

144) **Q:** How will you define vulnerable adult?

145) **Q:** What is self-defence in homicide and give an example?

146) **Q;** Use case law to explain self- defence?

147) **Q;** What are the two reasons for self-defence?

148) **Q;** What rule can be used as "Excuse of Homicide"?

149) **Q;** Explain "the theory of Excuses"

150) **Q;** Give another case to support "excuse of homicide"

Chapter 3.14

ASSIST to prevent or commit crime (trespass, assassin, ignorance, GBH, EU)

151) **Q;** What happen to one who assists against assassin self-defence?

152) **Q;** using case law, explain rule on self-defence?

153) **Q;** What happen if someone helps to fight and\or cause injury to another?

154) **Q:** Give an example of landlord tenant in self-defence?

155) **Q;** What law did the landlord breach?

156) **Q;** What does the criminal law say about the self-defence ?

157) **Q;** is ignorance a defence?

158) **Q:** what happen if the person have no insight in the criminal action? Give example

Chapter 3.15

INSANITY (special verdict, non-insane automatism)

159) **Q;** Can one use insanity as defence

160) **Q;** What does the defendant have to prove for insanity?

161) **Q:** If accused is found guilty what powers under the criminal procedure (insanity and unfitness to plead) Act 1991 to order

162) **Q;** What is special verdict?

163) **Q:** What is the disease of the mind? (NOT the Brain)

164) **Q;** what is Non-insane automatism?

165) **Q;** Name some diseases of the mind under none-insane automatism?

166) **Q:** Describe non- insane automatism.

167) **Q:**Give case example of non-insane automatism?

168) **Q;** Can one claim non-insane automatism after the act?

Chapter 3.16

DIMINISHED RESPONSIBILITY:

169) **Q**: Explain Diminish responsibility

170) **Q** Explain the Corona and Justice Act 2009?.

171) **Q;** How could this be argued with someone with concussion?

172) **Q;** What happens if the defendant was drunk?.

Chapter 3.17

SOME CRIMINAL TERMINOLOGY(civil matter, summary, either way, Indictable, truly criminal, outlandish, exonerate, weakness, protagonist, intervene event, But for,)

173) **Q;** what are the two main elements in criminal case?

174) **Q;** How is criminal action viewed?

175) **Q;** What is a civil matter?

176) **Q;** Name some criminal punishments?

177) **Q**: What is the first thing that a lawyer to do in a case?

178) **Q;** What do the type of offence prescribe by parliament?

179) **Q:**What precaution must the judge consider in common law?

180) **Q**; Which court does criminal cases start?

181) **Q**; How are criminal offences classified?

182) **Q;** What is truly criminal?

183) **Q;** What is quasi- criminal?.

184) Q; Give an example of **quasi-criminal**?

185) **Q;** What is Outlandish?. And what test can be used?.

186) **Q;** What is Protagonist?.

187) **Q;** what is Exonerate?.

188) **Q:** Give example of Exonerate

189) **Q:** Explain Weakness/Vulnerability?

190) **Q;** Give example of outlandish?

191) **Q;** What is Intervening event?.

192) **Q;** Give example of intervening event?

193) **Q:** What is needed to establish guilty in intervening event?

194) **Q;** What is the "But For" test?

Chapter 3.18

BURDEN OF PROVE (civil liberty, evidential burden, rule of law, appropriate

195) **Q**; who has to proof what;

196) **Q;** Give an example of case on burden of prove is on the prosecution?

197) **Q;** How must the burden be proven?

198) **Q:** Why the standard of is prove so high?

199) **Q;** What is evidential burden?

200) **Q**; On what can the defendant use to challenge?

201) **Q:** What is the "rule of law"?

202) **Q;** Where do one find the offence law?

203) **Q;** can defendant give any reason for offence?

204) **Q;** What do you understand by appropriate in law?

205) **Q;** give example of appropriate?

Chapter 3.19

DIRECT AND INDIRECT INTENT

206) **Q:**What is Direct intent?

207) **Q;** Q; what is Indirect or Oblique intent?

208) **Q;** In what circumstances can one be found guilty in indirect intent?

209) **Q;** What is incapacitation?

Chapter 3.20

DISHONESTY (theft, subjective, objective Ghosh test), oblique intent, incapacitation)

210) **Q;** How is dishonesty defined?

211) **Q;** How do one judge dishonesty?

212) **Q;** how can one use theft Act to understand dishonesty?

213) **Q:** What are these situations in the theft Act?

214) **Q;** what can Ghosh test be applied?

215) **Q;** what are the procedure to us Ghosh test?

216) **Q:** What two important questions a judge direct the July to as themselves to for honesty?

217) **Q:** Give an example of subjective question/test?

Chapter 3.21

INFANTICIDE.

218) **Q;** what is infanticide?

219) **Q;** What diagnoses or circumstance to lead to infanticide?

220) **Q:**Give another example of infanticide?

221) **Q;** What is the amended infanticide act of 1938 s. 36

Chapter 3.22

LOSS Of CONTROL

222) **Q:** What offence can loss of control are used?

223) **Q;** What is the test to establish loss of control?

224) **Q;** What are elements of loss of control?

225) **Q;** What might trigger loss of control?

226) **Q;** What is Recklessness?

227) **Q**; What was the House of law verdict on these cases.?

228) **Q;** What did the House of Lords decision on Caldwell case?.

229) **Q;** What happen in R. v. Cunningham case?.

230) **Q:** What is transferred Malice?

231) **Q:** Give another example of transfer malice?

232) **Q;** What is the exception to transferred malice?

233) **Q;** What is the manse rea of transferred malice?.

234) **Q** What is subjective test?

235) **Q;** How do Jury be sure using subjective test.?

236) **Q;** Name the section of Offence against person's Act 1861?.

237) **Q;** What is section 18of offence person Act 1861?

238) **Q;** What is section 20 of the Act 1861?

Chapter 3.23

CRIMINAL ATTEMPT (inchoate crime, substantive offence)

239) **Q;** What law relate to criminal attempt?

240) **Q;** What does Inchoate offence means (inchoate crime)

241) **Q:** What are the three main offence under attempt?

242) **Q;** What is substantive offence?

243) **Q;** What is the principal feature of Inchoate crime?

244) **Q;** What is the definition of attempt under criminal Attempt s.1 (1),2,3,4, 1981?

245) Q; Which court can section 1 (1) be triad?

246) **Q;** Give an example of complete attempt.?

247) **Q;** Give a case that support actus reus of attempt.?

248) **Q;** Give another case to support attempt.?

249) **Q;** Give an example of manse rea of attempted (intend to commit the offence)?

250) **Q;** Give an example of attempted offence?.

251) **Q**:What must prosecutor has to show in attempt offence?

Chapter 3.24

ATTEMPT IMPOSSIBLE

252) **Q;** what law covers attempt impossible?

253) **Q;** what does the criminal Attempt act 1981 section 1 (3a) state.

254) **Q;** What is section 1 (b).?

255) **Q;** Give an example of attempt impossible.

256) **Q;** Give another example of attempt impossible.

257) **Q;** what law covers attempt which cannot be attempted.?

Chapter 3.25

CONSPIRACY **(** justification, recklessly, aiding, abetting, procuring)

258) **Q**; what statute law on attempt which cannot be attempted.

259) **Q;** what is justification.

260) **Q;** what is recklessly.

261) **Q;** what is unlawful/strict liability.

262) **Q;** How do you define maliciously

Chapter 3.26

THEFT

263) **Q;** what is theft?.

264) **Q;** what is Actus reus of theft?

265) **Q;** what is manse rea of theft?

266) **Q;** what must be concise in prosecuting someone for theft?

267) **Q**; what is the definition of "appropriate"?

268) **Q;** How does the law define Appropriate?

269) **Q;** what is property?

270) **Q;** Summarise Theft Act 1968?

Chapter 3.27

"MAKING OFF WITHOUT PAYING" battery

robbery

271) **Q;** what law covers making off without paying?

272) **Q**; Explain with reference to Actus Reus, making off without paying?

273) **Q;** What is payment on the spot in "making off without payment"

274) **Q;** what is mens rea of making off without payment?

275) **Q:** Name some Act that came into force in 1861?

Chapter 3.28

BATTERY

276) **Q;** what is the Actus reus of battery?

277) **Q;** what is the mens rea of battery?

Chapter 3.29

ROBBERY

278) **Q;** Explain robbery?

279) **Q**; When is no robbery?

280) **Q**; what is Actus reus of robbery?

281) **Q;** Name two cases of robbery

Chapter 3.30

BURGLARY/ GBH

282) **Q;** which law covers burglary?

283) **Q:**define section 1 (a) of the theft Act 1968.

284) ; **Q;** Explain conditional intent?

285) **Q;** Define section 9 1 (b).

286) **Q;** What is the deference between (.1(a) and 9 (2) of the theft Act 1968?

287) **Q**: Explain inflicting GBH in both Section 9 1 am and section 9.1 b of the theft Act 1968?

288) **Q**; What defence can be used in Burglary?

289) **Q**; what is the Actus reus of Burglary?

290) **Q**; what is the Mens rea of Burglary?

291) **Q**; what does the court say about consent to burglary?

Chapter 3.31

ARSON

292) **Q;** Define Arson?

293) **Q**: What is Arson under the law?

294) **Q**; why is Arson trial as indictment?

Chapter 3.32

SELF-DEFENCE (reasonable force, consent, coward, gang, smacking)

295) **Q;** When can a defendant use self-defence as defence?

296) **Q**; what is the condition in using reasonable force.

297) **Q;** What about if the defendant has made a mistake?

Chapter 3.33

CONSENT

298) **Q**; in offence against person Act 1861, when can consent be used?

299) **Q**; When can consent be varied?

Chapter 3.34

COWARD as defence

300) **Q;** when can one use weak willed or coward as defence?

Chapter 3.35

CRIMINAL GANGS

301) **Q;** what happen if a person belonging to criminal gangs commit a crime?

302) **Q;** what does the law say about smacking children?

Chapter 3.36

SEXUAL OFFENCES (Assault, rape, consent intoxication, presumption)

303) **Q;** what was the date of sexual offences Act?

304) **Q:** What section of the sexual offence covers rape?

305) **Q;** what section covers assault by penetration?

306) **Q;** what section covers sexual assault?

307) Q; what section covers where children are victim?

308) **Q;** what did the old law said about husband and wife?

309) **Q;** When and what section can law on rape and was extended to men and women.

310) **Q:** What is the element of rape?

311) **Q;** Can a woman rape? If not then how can he be charged?

312) **Q:** What is penetration in the Act 2003?

313) **Q**; at what stage is consent?

314) **Q**; Define consent as in SOA 2003 s.74.

315) **Q;** what happen if the defendant put pressure or deceive the victim?

316) **Q**; what are it and how many elements in mens rea for rape?

317) **Q**; Define sexual assault by penetration?

318) **Q**; what is Actus REUS of sexual assault?

319) **Q:** What is the mens rea of sexual assault;

320) **Q;** What is the definition of sexual assault under section 3 of the sexual offence Act 2003?

321) **Q**; Define sexual as in sex offence Act 2003?

322) **Q;** Define purpose

323) **Q;** Define torching under section 78 (8

RAPE

324) **Q**; what is Actus REUS of rape? (assault by penetration)

325) **Q;** what is the mens rea of rape? (assault by penetration)

326) **Q:**What statute define attempted rape

327) **Q;** What is the Actus REUS of attempted rape?

328) **Q**; What is manse rea of attempted rape

329) **Q:** What is the leading case in attempted rape?

330) **Q**; what is the definition of consent under the sexual offence Act?

331) **Q**; what did the High court advice where the torching is not by nature "sexual" to consider?

332) **Q:** What is the difference between defendant and victim of sexual offence in intoxication?

333) **Q:** Which section is specific intent?

Chapter 3.37

PRESUMTION

334) **Q;** what is presumption?

335) **Q:** What does 76 (2a) state? Of the sexual offence Act

336) **Q:** What does 76.s 2b of the sexual offence Act?

337) **Q**: What does section 75 say about consent?

338) **Q:** What are the circumstances in section 75 to support evidence presumption?

339) **Q;** what happens in intoxication in sexual assault?

340) **Q;** Can defendant rely on intoxication for sexual offence?

Chapter 3.38

CHILDREN UNDER 13 IN SEXUAL OFFENCE

341) **Q;** what is the differing between section 1-3 and 5-7 of the sexual offence Act 2003.?

342) **Q;** what are mens rea for children under section 5-7 for children under 13 years of age?

343) **Q;** what are the Actus REUS for children under 13 (s.5-7)?

344) **Q**; Explain section 9 of the sexual offence Act 2003?

345) **Q**; What does section 9 (2) of the sexual offence Act 2003 say?

346) **Q**; Who can commit offence under section 9?

347) **Q;** What about defendant who is 18 or under

348) **Q:** Can a child of 12 be guilty of sexual offence?

349) **Q:** What was the rule of thumb?

Chapter .3.39

Fraud

350) **Q**; What is the Fraud Act?

351) **Q;** When does fraud occurs?

352) **Q;** In the 2006 Act what replaces by fraud?

353) **Q**: What did the law commission comment?

354) **Q**; What happened to the common law?

355) **Q**; What is the important of Fraud Act 2006?

356) **Q**; What happen if the gain or loss is temporary?

357) **Q**; What was repealed after the 2007 fraud Act?

358) **Q;** What is the meaning of false representation?

359) **Q**; What is Actus reus of fraud by representation?

360) **Q;** What is the mens rea of fraud by misrepresentation?

361) **Q;** Does the defendant mens rea only needed?

362) **Q;** Summarise the element of fraud by false representation?

363) **Q**; How are the law deals with cheque and credit cards?

364) **Q;** What about using the pin of credit card to withdraw?

365) Q: How is property covered in fraud?

366) Q; How does being silence relate to fraud?

367) Q; Give an example of the right to be silent?

Chapter 3.40

Police (Pace, silence, Act)

368) **Q;** What happened in PACE (police and criminal evidence) section 34 (to remain silent)

369) **Q;** What does the European Article on silence?

370) **Q;** What can lead police to abuse their power?

371) **Q:** What can give rise to police being challenged?

372) **Q;** Give an example of defendant being given access to solicitor?

373) **Q;** What happens to escape unlawful arrest

374) **Q**; Give an example of unacceptable police statement?

375) **Q**; What police order control Marching?

376) **Q**; What European article can police rely on protesters?

377) **Q;** What else does Article 10 (20 and 11(2) give to police.

378) **Q**; What does Police Order Act 1986 section 14?

Chapter3.41

Scenario (**criminal liabilities**)

379) **Q**; Name three cases of criminal liability by omission?

380) **Q**; Summarise ; R v Instan (1893)1 QB 450

381) **Q;** What was the verdict in the above case (R. v. Instan (1893)

382) **Q;** What was the reason of the court decision on R.V**. Instan** (1893)

383) **Q:** Why was the judge in favour of moral obligation?

384) **Q:**What was the court of appeal findings?

385) Describe similar case:

386) Q: Summarise R .v. Stone and Dobinson

387) **Q:** What was the court verdict?

388) **Q;** Summarise R. v. Ruff ell (2003) EWCA Crim 122

389) **Q:** What was the Appeal court decision (r. v. Ruffell) (2003) EWCA crim. 122.

390) **Q:** Summarise the case of R. stone and Dobinson (1977) IQ .B.354

391) **Q:** What is the decision and why on the case of R. stone and Dobinson (1977) IQ .B.354 (summary)

392) **Q;** Summaries for all the three cases and the effect of R. v. Instan (1893) 1qb

Chapter 3.42

GANG

393) **Q** : summarise this scenario on gang?

394) **Q;**_Discus the criminal Liabilities of Jake only

395) **Q:** How did the court view Jake with flicker knife?

396) **Q** : How is Jake likely to plea?

397) **Q:** What will be Jake argument?

398) **Q:** What will be the charge?

399) **Q** ; What will be likely defence for Jake?

400) **Q;** Why was his plea on necessity failed

401) **Q;** What sentence Jake likely to get?

402) **Q:** Give similar case and the reason of the court decision?

403) **Q;** Why was the appeal court not sympathetic

with Jake predicament?

404) **Q;** What did criminal law review think of Lord Bingham **decision?**

Chapter 4

PSYCHIATRY

405) **Q;** How is psychiatry injury classified?

406) **Q;** Explain the two conditions?

407) **Q;** what happen when these two are established:?

408) **Q**: How does the law classified psychiatry injury?

409) **Q;** what condition one has to satisfy before claim of psychiatric injury without physical injury.

410) **Q**; What was the reason of rule on psychiatric claim

411) **Q**: Name some cases relate to psychiatric injury?

412) **Q;** Summarise the case in McLaughlin v. O'Brian (1982)

413) **Q:** What was the court's decision and why?

414) **Q:** What was the appeal court decision?

415) **Q:** What was the house of lords decision?

416) **Q;** Summarise the case in Alcock v. Chief Constable of south Yorkshire (1992)

417) **Q;** what was the court's decision?

418) **Q:** What condition for The House of Lords allowed the claim.

419) **Q;** Summarise the case in Page v. Smith (1996) Ac 155

420) **Q:** What did the court do in this case?

421) **Q;** An what did the judge said about actual bodily harm in these cases Hobhouse. L.J in R.V .Chan-Fook (1994)1W.L.R.689 CA?

422) **Q:** Can symptoms of nervous system be regarded as a psychiatric assault?

423) **Q;** What was the court decision and why?

424) **Q;** What did Lynskey .J. said about actual bodily harm in R. V. Miller (1954)2 Q.B 282)

425) **Q;** What did LORD WELBERFORCE said about the body and mind in McLaughlin .O'Brian (1983) 1 AC 410,418?

426) **Q;** What case did the court dealt with distress and grief?

427) **Q;** Comment on case In R.v.Robert,56 Cr App. R.95?

428) **Q**; Comment on case In Morris (1998)1 Cr.App.R.386.?

429) **Q;** What happened when both Savage and Parmenter?

430) **Q;** What did Lord Acker said about assault occasioning actual bodily harm?

Chapter 5

VICARIOUS LIABILITY

431) **Q:** What is the definition of Vicarious liability?

432) **Q:** When will the employer be vicarious liable?

433) **Q:** What three elements that make employers liable?

434) **Q;** What is the general rule to make employer liable?

435) **Q;** What about if the employee act is not authorised by the employer?

436) **Q;** What did the courts view on vicarious liability on manner and scope? And give example.

437) **Q:** what is Lord Phillip view on vicarious liability?

438) **Q:** What test did the House of Lords introduce in relation to employees?

439) **Q** ; Give reasons for the court's decision?

440) **Q:** What are the three reasons for vicarious fairness?

441) **Q;** Why must employee take full responsibility of employee action?

442) **Q;** Why is it unfair to impose vicarious liability on employer?

443) **Q;** Give example of vicarious liability?

444) **Q;** What is the author (my) view on vicarious liability?

445) **Q:** What is the reason why hospital liable for doctors/employee negligence?

446) **Q;** What about if the employees act is not authorised by the employer?

447) **Q;** what did the courts view on vicarious liability on manner and scope? And give example.

448) **Q:** what is Lord Phillip view on vicarious liability?

449) **Q;** Give reasons for the court's decision?

Chapter 6

TORT and Vicarious liability

450) Q: What is the purpose of tort?

451) Q: What must claimant satisfy?

452) Q; Name other types of harm that comes under tort negligence?

453) **Q:** Name the types of defamation?

454) Q: Are there overlaps in tort and crime

455) Q; Give an example of where tort and contract law can be used together?

Scenario on tort

456) Q: Advise Edward as to his potential claim in facts explaining the issues which have arisen on the facts.

457) **Q:** What will be Edward claim under?

458) **Q:**What will Edward be advised to do and why?

459) **Q:** Summarise in table form the potential claim.

460) **Q;** Give brief account of Duty of care?

461) **Q;** Name two cases to support duty of care?

462) **Q:** What can Edward claim from the fire service for the injury he sustained?

463) **Q:** What can Edward claim from Morgan with reference to duty of care?

464) **Q:** : What can Edward claim from Morgan with reference breach duty of care?

465) **Q:** What can Edward claim from Morgan with reference to causation.

466) **Q:** What can Edward claim from Morgan with reference to remoteness

467) **Q;** what defence can Morgan raise?

468) **Q;** Explore the possible claim by Edward from the hospital and the doctor?

469) **Q:** Was there duty of care for Edward?

470) **Q;** Was the duty breached?

471) **Q:** What must the claimant proof with regard to Causation in the fact of the case?

472) **Q:** How was remoteness of the injuries?

473) **Q:** How would you summarise the claim?

474) **Q:** Are there any defence?

475) **Q:**What conclusion will you reach in this case?

Chapter 7

PURE ECONOMIC LOSS

476) **Q;** Define pure economic loss?

477) **Q:**Define negligence in relation to pure economic loss?

478) **Q;** What are the rules when considering pure economic loss?

479) Q; Name a test in considering duty of care?

480) **Q;** Define psychiatry injury in relation to pure economic loss given case laws in support?

481) **Q;** What is reasons rules on pure economic loss in relation to Psychiatry injury ?

482) **Q;** Give reasons why pure economic loss is not recoverable in tort of negligence?

483) **Q;** Explain consequential economic loss, give case law in support?

484) **Q;** Explain pure economic loss by in relation to property?

485) **Q;** Give example of fairness in implementing pure economic loss?

486) **Q:** Who does the rules protect?

487) **Q:** What has been the advantages?

488) **Q:** What did Lord Atkins warned about duty of care?

489) **Q**; What are the restriction or unfairness in pure economic loss?

490) **Q:** What did the court decided in Murphy case?

491) **Q:** What did Lord Lloyd said I Aswan case?

492) **Q:** How has policy or politics plays part in decision\judgement?

493) **Q**:What do you think of the inconsistent in some judgement?

494) **Q:** What do you think of terminology used in the judgement?

495) **Q;** Do you ting the law is fair on economic law policy?

496) **Q:** What did the law say about the emergencies team?

497) Q; What do you think must be done in relation to the rules?.

498) **Q:** Do you entirely agree with the law on pure financial loss not revocable?

499) **Q;** who does the pure economic law favours?

500) **Q:** Give an example in relation to pure economic?

501) **Q:** What do you think the law should be?

Chapter 8

PROPERTY LAW (exclusive, estoppels, lease, licence, deeds, overriding, equitable registration of property, easement, TOLATA, estate, tenancy, unities possession, title, interest time. Etc).

502) **Q:** What is Easement?

503) **Q**:What is Licence?

504) **Q;** What is Express licence?

505) **Q;** Explain Easement in relation to electric cable?

506) **Q:** Distinguishes licences and lease?

507) Q; Distinguished licence from easement?

508) **Q;** What is the factors used by the judges ?

509) **Q;** What are The "exclusive" possession factors?

510) Q: Explain Exclusive possession?

511) Q; Explain exclusive possession of easement as per the house of Lords?

512) **Q:** what is exclusive possession?

513) Q; Explain licence given case laws support?

514) Q; What is express licence?

515) Q: What is Bare licence ?

516) Q: What is licence couple with interest?

517) Q:Distinguished licence from easement?

518) **Q:** What is the function of Easement?

519) **Q;** What must be satisfied for right of easement terms?

520) Q: Distinguished licences and lease and give the factors to be considered

521) **Q:** Distinguished licences and lease and give the factor in relation to tenancy?

522) **Q:** Distinguished licences and lease and give the factor in relation to exclusive possession?

523) **Q** Use another case law to explain exclusion?

524) **Q;** Distinguished licences and lease and give the factor in relation to agreement?

525) **Q:** Give a case law of how words might be interpreted?

526) **Q:** Distinguished licences and lease and give the factor in relation to period of tenancy

527) **Q:** Distinguished licences and lease and give the factor in relation to avoid granting exclusive tenancy?

528) **Q:** How can the landlord be successful?

529) **Q:** Give a controversial case in licence?

530) **Q:** Is estoppels unfair?

531) **Q**; Is the law fair on landlord?

532) **Q;** Explain Legal and equitable leases

533) **Q**; Briefly explain licence

534) **Q**; Explain legal a; creation of lease?

535) **Q:** Explain if landlord sell the property the rule needs to be followed?

536) **Q:** What is the rule on registration of property?

537) **Q:** Explain the characteristics for the creation of lease?

538) **Q** What are the main types of leas?

539) **Q**; Explain fixed term lease as per agreement

540) **Q:** What right to forfeit the lease?

541) **Q**; What is periodic lease?

542) **Q:** What is exception to the rule?

543) **Q:**What is Payroll lease?

544) **Q;** Explain not legal lease?

545) **Q;** What is equitable lease ?

546) **Q;** Name four characteristics according to Ellenborough Park (1956) CH 131 for easement to exist?

547) **Q;** What are the rules for easement to exist?

Scenario on joint ownership

548) **Q**: What was created when the five friends

549) **Q:** How can legal estate be held

550) **Q;** How can equitable interest be held?

551) **Q;** How can tenant in common be supported?

552) **Q:** What factors to be considered in equitable interest?

553) **Q** What happen when Dianna died in June 2010

554) **Q:** What happen to Carol mortgage to Rob in February 2011?

555) **Q:** what happened to the equitable interest when Carol repaid the loan in September 2011

556) **Q:** How important is Belinda letter served on March 2012

557) **Q:** Will the notice varied?

558) **Q:** Who hold the legal estate after June 2016

559) **Q**: What is the end result of this saga

560) **Q**: Can Ellen stop Carol selling

561) **Q:** What would have been placed on the deeds and why?

Scenario

562) **Q;** What must property have for easement to exit?

563) **Q;** Give implications of using Electricity cable.

564) **Q;** Give an implications of Drive way?

565) **Q;** Give example of Building flats?

566) **Q:** How will Reena be advised?

567) **Q:** Described prescription Act 1832?

Chapter 9

CO-OWNERSHIP (joint tenancy, tenancy in common, express, declaration, legal estate, Co ownership)

568) **Q:** What is co-ownership?

569) **Q:** Explain co-ownership in relation to trust?

570) **Q**: What are the four tests to establish co-ownership?

571) **Q**; What is express declaration in co-ownership?

572) **Q:**What does title mean?

573) **Q;** What does interest mean?

574) **Q;** What does possession mean?

575) **Q:** Explain Co-ownership?

576) **Q**:Explain Characteristics of tenancy in common?

Chapter 10

EQUITY AND TRUST(trustee, trust, Duress, gift, undue influence, shares, charity

577) **Q;** As the court cannot supervise the activities of every trustee,

578) **Q;** What is the reason for beneficial principle?

579) **Q;** Who is the rear owner of trust?

580) **Q**; who enforce trust with a lot of beneficiaries?

581) **Q;** Explain Purpose trust?

582) **Q:**What are some duties of trustee?

583) **Q**: What can beneficiaries do to incompetent trustee?

584) **Q:** What are exception to the monitoring

585) **Q;** what is the beneficial principle?

586) **Q;** How did Equity originate ?

587) **Q**; Initially What was the judge based?

588) **Q;** How do you define Duress?

589) **Q**; briefly explain economic duress?

590) **Q:** How will you describe Equity?

591) **Q;** Give Example cases of laws to support duress;

592) **Q:** How can agreement be changed?

593) **Q**: Define undue influence?

594) **Q**; Give example of actual undue influence?

595) **Q;** why are some rules in equity judgement.?

596) **Q;** what is some exception to equity rules?

597) **Q;** what are the three conditions relate to a life time gift made in contemplation of one's death in DMC.?

598) **Q;** what are the Fortuitous vesting four conditions?

599) **Q**: What is the condition for transfer of shares?

600) **Q;** what are remedies in duress and undue influence?

601) **Q;** What can equity do?

Scenario

602) **Q:** Advice Ghazi whether the above disposition were valid and, if not what will happen to the property. Advice to executor (Ghazi)

603) **Q:** What was his intention with regard to Granddaughter?

604) Q: is this a varied trust?

605) **Q**: What was the intention regarding the shares?

606) **Q:** Why is Emmanuel bound by the trust?

607) **Q;** what was the intention regarding the shops?

608) **Q:** What was the intention of the company shares?

609) **Q;** Will equity rule suffice?

610) **Q;** When Emmanuel died, will equity take his share?

611) **Q;** what was intention regarding property?

612) **Q:** What is the intention on charity?

613) **Q:** What was intention on the chattels?

Chapter 11

JUDICIAL REVIEW (traditional, proportional, Grounds Impropriety, remedies, irrationality, proportionality, hybrid, narrow, mixed)

614) **Q;** "The difference in approach between the traditional grounds of Judicial Review and the proportional approach may

615) **Q;** What are the Grounds to challenge in Judicial Review?

616) **Q:** What is the procedure for procedural impropriety

617) **Q;** What is the remedies

618) **Q;** Explain irrationality

619) **Q;** Comment on proportionality

620) **Q;** What are the test for proportionality?

621) Q; Compare Irrationality and Proportionality

622) **Q**: What is the requirement for procedural fairness.?

623) **Q:**What is the leading case in proportionality?

624) **Q;** what is mixed case?

625) **Q;** name public departments which can be review?

626) **Q;** name cases where private bodies could be review?

627) **Q;** explain citation comparing traditional and modern

628) **Q:** Who used to be called respondent?

629) **Q**; who does statute provide for appeal?

630) **Q;** what is the function of the judicial by Eminent Lords?

631) **Q;** what has changed between the state and individual since Dicey era (1866)?

632) **Q;** what can the judicial review do?

633) **Q;** what is "standing" in judicial review?

634) **Q;** who can apply judicial review and quote case law?

635) **Q;** what are the requirements to challenge decision of public authority?

636) **Q;** on what grounds are claimant applications refused?

637) **Q;** Quote one case of judicial review by Lord Lane?

638) **Q**; how and what procedure is judicial review known as?

639) **Q;** what other way can judicial review obtain?

640) **Q;** name the two main procedures in judicial review?

641) **Q;** what is the difference between private and public law?

642) **Q;** what is the judicial review concern?

643) **Q;** which bodies are subject to judicial review?

644) **Q;** how could you recognise cases of judicial review?

645) **Q;** what and give example of the new citation?

646) **Q;** what procedure one has to follow?

647) **Q;** name the three requirements for challenging a decision by public bodies?

648) **Q;** what is the different in procedure between judicial review and private law, the judicial review?

649) **Q;** what document one need to lodge formal complaint?

650) **Q;** what else must be in the statement?

651) **Q;** why statement use?

652) **Q**; what are the remedies under public law?

653) **Q**; what are the remedies under private law (before 1978)?

654) **Q;** name decision makers subject to judicial review?

655) **Q**; what is a hybrid authority?

656) **Q**; how is a civil procedure rule?

657) **Q;** why are judicial review not available to others?

658) **Q;** cite the case to support delay prevent judicial review?

659) **Q;** what entails revision of judicial review in 1978?

660) **Q**; what case resulted private law remedies and what were they?

661) **Q;** why was judicial review procedure reformed in 1977/8?

662) **Q;** in O'rielly .V. Mackman (1983) 2 AC 237 what significance?

663) **Q**; explain exclusivity rule (modern

664) **Q**; name the two exceptions to exclusivity rule?

665) **Q;** what is the broad approach of judicial review on exclusivity?

666) **Q;** what is the narrow approach?

667) **Q;** name mixed cases which can be bought to judicial review?

668) **Q**; in modernised J.R, there had been an increase of reason to refuse compared to tradition, name some?

Chapter 12

CONTRACT LAW (offer, Acceptance, consideration, clauses, UCTA, test, express)

669) **Q**: Name the three elements for formation of contract.

670) **Q**; Explain offer

671) **Q**; Explain Acceptance

672) **Q**; Explain the three ways to terminate offer?

673) **Q;** Explain intention to create legal relations

674) **Q**: Explain consideration?

675) **Q;** What is Adequacy of consideration;

676) **Q;** What is sufficiency of consideration?

677) **Q:** Give brief explanation of exception clauses

678) **Q:** Explain UCTA (unfair contract trade Act 1977)?

679) **Q:** What is reasonable test

680) **Q:** What Factors considered in reasonable test

681) **Q;** Who does the Unfair terms Act 1999 applies?

682) **Q;** Outline how the Act prevent unfairness?

683) **Q;** Explain consideration?

684) **Q;** Explain timing?

685) **Q:** Explain Consistence?

686) **Q**: Explain contra preferential rule?

687) **Q**: In relation to terms of contract what does consideration mean?

688) **Q;** What does Express mean in term of contract?

689) **Q;** When is reasonable term use?

690) **Q**; Name one problem with regard to express terms of contract?

691) **Q;** Name another problem with express contract?

692) **Q**; What does Incorporate mean in contract?

693) **Q;** What is reasonable notice in express terms?

694) **Q;** What are the four main categories of implied terms of contract ?

695) **Q;** What is customs?

696) **Q**; What is necessary in contract?

697) **Q;** What is persistence in implied contract?

698) **Q;** Give an example of statute?

699) **Q;** What do one mean by intention of the parties?

700) **Q;** Briefly explain some contract obligation of the parties?

Chapter 13

WILL

Question from scenario

701) **Q:** How do one view this ?

702) **Q:** What is the starting point?

703) **Q:** Explain the terms for a will to be varied?

704) **Q:** How do you check the ethnicity of the Will?

705) **Q**: What happen if it is prove that the testor signature been forged?

706) **Q;** Is there any suspicion?

707) **Q:** Give a case law on suspicion?

Chapter 13.1

Mental Capacity (WILL)

708) **Q;** How do you deal with the mental capacity aspect?

709) **Q**; Give a case law relate to mental capacity to sign a will?

710) **Q:** Give any difference between statute and common law?

711) **Q;** What is the test use in assessing mental capacity?

712) **Q**: How do you use the bank test in assessing this scenario?

713) **Q**: What is the golden rule for mental capacity testor?

714) **Q:** How would you conclude this case might be?

715) **Q**: How do you deal with lack of knowledge and approval ?

716) **Q;** How will conclusion might be?

717) **Q;** What do you think of any undue influence?

718) **Q;** Explain how undue influence could be inferred?

719) **Q:** What is likely argument by the next of kin (John and Kiana)

720) **Q;** What might be possible conclusion?

721) **Q;** What about inheritance (provision for family and dependants?

722) **Q:** What is your conclusion on this scenario?

Chapter 14
Theft/ Honesty

723) **Q:** What is dishonesty?

724) **Q:** Explain Gosh test?

725) **Q:** How does the Julie use the Gosh test?

726) **Q:** What is the initial test in Gosh?

727) **Q;** Explain theft Act?

728) **Q:** What does the theft Act section 2a,b,c, relate

729) **Q;** what is lie test use for?

730) **Q**; what problem is with Gosh?

731) **Q:** How is honest judge?

732) **Q;** what does the Law commission say about the Gosh?

733) **Q;** what does professor Glanville think of dishonesty?

734) **Q**: What is the Supreme Court definition of dishonesty?

735) **Q;** what did professor dicey regard dishonesty?

736) **Q**; what is your view of dishonest test?

Chapter 15

Public Law, European Law

Scenario

737) **Q;** Outline the approach that the High court will take when considering the claim

738) **Q;** what argument might James present?

739) **Q;** What might the newspaper defend the claim?

740) **Q:** What will the court consider?

741) **Q:** what is the likely Judgement in court?

742) **Q:** What will be the aim of the court?

743) **Q;** what consideration the court will take regarding the press?

744) **Q;** what cases might be used by the court in making decision?

745) **Q;** Outline the jigsaw of judgement?

746) **Q:** what does Article 8 protect in this case?

747) **Q;** what does the court consider press code?

748) **Q:** How will they consider children involvement in this case?

749) **Q:** Discuses this statement. In the scenario

Chapter 16

Police

750) **Q;** Name some police powers?

751) **Q:** How are police treated if they break the law

752) **Q;** Give example of police and protesters?

753) **Q**; Give an example cases involve protestors and the police?

754) **Q;** Do the court sometimes compromise?

Chapter 17
CONSTITUTIONAL

755) **Q;** what do you understand by convention?
756) **Q**; Explain how convention is linked to UK constitution?
757) **Q**; Give an example of how tradition is link to convention?
758) **Q;** Is convention legal?
759) **Q**; Are there some element of legal and politic?
760) **Q**; How did Marshal and Moodier define constitutional convention;
761) **Q:** What is Characteristic of constitutional convention?
762) **Q;** what source is U.K constitution convention?
763) **Q;** what is the purpose of convention?
764) **Q**; Name some function of constitutional convention?
765) **Q:** Give example of convention relating to international law?
766) **Q:** What part is play by UK monarch and the parliament?
767) **Q:** why must convention rules is observed?
768) **Q**: What will happen if convention rules are disregarded?
769) **Q;** what happen if member state failed to observe the convention rules?
770) **Q;** what are Royal prerogative powers?
771) **Q;** Give example of how the parliament deals with issue of convention

772) **Q:** Can the court change Legislation?

773) **Q:** What happen when there is link between member state laws and convention rules?

774) **Q;** how is convention rules protected?

775) **Q:** What happen if there is conflict between member state and convention?

Chapter 18

HUMAN RIGHT

776) **Q;** When do the courts take notice of EU treaties?

777) **Q:**What happen to Magna Carta?

778) **Q;** Explain rule of law?

779) **Q;** Explain constitution of a country

780) **Q;** Explain Bills of Right in constitution?

781) **Q:** When European convention was first created?

782) **Q:** What is Standpoint?

783) **Q;** what approach was convention drafted?

784) **Q**; what does open ended constitution means?

785) **Q:** How can one repeal law in UK?

Chapter 19

EUROPEAN LAWS

786) **Q**: Name types of Human Rights?

787) **Q**: What is absolute right?

788) **Q**: What are impose to member state in Human Right?

789) **Q;** Give example of absolute rights?

790) **Q**; what is qualified Right?

791) **Q:** Give example of qualified rights?

792) **Q:** How many rights are qualified rights divided?

793) **Q:** Using Article 8, explain the part of qualified rights?

794) **Q:** Explain the part of Article 8?

795) **Q;** what does the first part of the second part of Article 8 state?

796) **Q;** what does the second element of second part of section 8 state?

797) **Q;** what does the third element of second part of section 8 state?

798) **Q**: What are the legitimate aims might consist of?

799) **Q;** What happen in Judicial Review

800) **Q**: Who decide the article?

801) **Q;** What are protocols?

802) **Q;** What does HRA section 3 allow member state?

803) **Q:** What happens when there are conflicting HRA Articles?

804) **Q;** what does the EU law section 4 allows?

805) **Q:** Give example of the House of Lords on compromise on EU law?

806) **Q;** Explain what powers the police have in English law to control the conduct of protesters.

807) **Q:** What are the powers to control protestors?

808) **Q:** How are freedom of expression protestors protected

809) **Q:** Why are some UK laws not repealed when new laws are enacted?

810) **Q**: What does UK stand with regard to Bill of Right in EU?

811) **Q:** When was UK Bills of Right?

812) **Q:** Are EU member state legally bound member states?

813) **Q:** Which Article deals with EU interpretation?

814) **Q:** What does the court have to consider during interpretation of HRA laws?

815) **Q:** What is the last result for member state if they cannot agree with the EU laws?

816) **Q:** What must member state minister do with incompatible law?

817) **Q:** Who is allowed to use section 4?

818) **Q**: What happen if verdict is declared unlawful?

819) **Q**: Does HRA gives right for state to abode?

820) **Q**: Which Article can be summoned when dealing with convention right?

821) **Q:** Name some of the legitimate aim for interference with EU Articles

822) **Q**: Name the 4 elements in Article 8?

823) **Q:** What are the related rights?

824) **Q**: Give example of case laws?

825) **Q**: What is the limitation or interference of qualified right such as Article 8, 10, 11?

826) **Q**; Explain Article 10 of EU.

827) **Q**: How does Article 10 affect moral? Give supporting case law

828) **Q**; Give example of how Article 10 affect moral?

829) **Q;** What Article direct or indirect relates to Article 10 (freedom of expression)?

830) **Q;** which section of the Article has restriction?

831) **Q;** Give example of the restriction of qualified right?

832) **Q:** How can EU members use the convention Rights?

833) **Q:** How is some of the member state court decision base?

834) **Q;** what section support remedy?

835) **Q**: What is the aim of award?

836) **Q:** what is the recommended way to deal with answering legal question?

837) **Q:** When was EU laws incorporate to UK.

838) **Q:** Name the two approaches in interpreted the law in EU?

839) **Q**: What effect is EU treaties have on member state?

840) **Q:** What must member state do if EU law don't have legal effect on member?

841) **Q**: How do member state interpreted EU laws?

842) **Q:** What advantage is section 2(2) of EU?

843) **Q:** What is the disadvantage of delegated legislation on UK ?

844) **Q:** What is the source of EU laws?

845) **Q**: What is directive using direct effect?

846) **Q;** Explain section 2(1) of HRA?

847) **Q:** Explain section 3(1) of EU?

848) **Q;** Explain section 3 (2) of HRA?

849) **Q;** Explain section 4 of HRA?

850) **Q;** Which Article or section specifically formulated to protect freedom of expression of media?

851) **Q:** how do we consider Right in EU?

852) **Q**: Explain Article 8 and give supporting case law.

853) **Q**: What consideration with regard to Article 8 and 10?

854) **Q**: What happen when Article 8 is breached? Give example

855) **Q;** Give case law of press breached Article 8?

856) **Q:** What happens if photograph is taken when the person is not in an official role?

857) **Q:** What about taken pictures of children?

858) **Q:** What does engagements of Article 8 & 10 depend?

859) **Q:** How can Article 8 be used in Tort Claim?

860) **Q:** How can European directive be interpreted?

861) **Q:** What is horizontal direct?

862) **Q:** Compare ECA (European Community Act 1972) and HRA Human Right Act 1998?

863) **Q**: What happen if there is conflict between the EU and UK laws?

864) **Q**: What is the aim and how EU laws are abided by member state?

865) **Q;** Why was the EEC established?

866) **Q:** When was the first attempt of economic

867) **Q:** What happened?

868) **Q:** Who were the countries involved?

869) **Q:** Who were the most influential in the formation of the first EEC?

CHAPTER 20

LEGAL RESEARCH

870) **Q:** How has legal research evolved

871) **Q**: Describe Doctrinal Research Method with some argument

872) **Q:** How do you view doctrinal research historically?

873) **Q:** What is the main structure of doctrinal research?

874) **Q:** Has there been criticism of doctrinal research?

875) **Q**: How has the doctrinal process been defined?

876) **Q:** How has the doctrinal researched been supported?

877) **Q**: How is the doctrinal research carried out?

878) ***Describe Comparative Method of Legal Research and argument***

879) **Q**:How will one argue for comparative research?

880) **Q;** How is comparative research helps advancement?

881) **Q:** How has rules affected comparative research?

882) **Q:** What happen when international laws compare to domestic?

883) **Q:** How can comparative research be made more effective?

884) **Q;** When was the Crime and Disorder Act

885) **Q:** In Republic of Ireland when was Children Act

886) **Q**: when was the Criminal Justice Act

Describe Historical Research Method with some argument

*887) Q: What does historical research incorporates**?***

888) **Q:** What is the objective of historical research?

889) **Q:** What is better way to understand historical research?

890) **Q;** What date was Abortion Act?

891) **Q**: What date was Human Fertilisation and Embryology Act?

892) **Q**: What date was Infant Life (Preservation) Act?

893) **Q;** What date was Malicious Shooting or Stabbing Act?

894) **Q**: When was the Mental Capacity Act ?

895) **Q**: What date was Offences Against the Person Act?

896) **Q;** What date was Offences Against the Person Act?

897) **Q;** What date was Offences Against the Person Act?

Describe Social-Legal Method with argument

*898) **Q:** Does socio- legal research only relate to societal facets?*

899) **Q:** What can socio-legal be link to?

900) **Q;** What other method could be used in conjunction with socio-legal?

901) **Q:** When was Children Act

902) **Q:** Children, Schools and Families Act

903) **Q:** When was the Family Procedure Rules

904) **Q;** Family Proceedings (Amendment) (No.2) Rules

905) **Q:** Human Rights Act

906) **Q:** When was the Mental Capacity Act

Chapter

Legal Research

907) **Q:** Name few cases to support social legal

Describe Feminism legal approach with argument

908) ***Q:** Does this involve more than feminist?*

909) **Q:** Has feminist theory been criticise

Describe Transnational legal method with argument

910) *Q: Describe transnational legal research*

911) **Q:** What does transitional legal research consider?

Describe Scientific Method with argument

912) ***Q:** what does scientific method involve?*

913) **Q:** What else is considered in scientific research method?

914) ***Q:** How will one conclude legal research finding?*

Chapter 21
Agency/contract/agreement

915) **Q**; Defined Agency
916) **Q**; Name some typed of agency
917) **Q;** What is special Agent?
918) **Q**; what is the duty of General agency?
919) **Q**; What is commercial agency?
920) **Q;** what is universal agent duties
921) **Q;** What is Contract?
922) **Q;** Give example of agreement in business?
923) **Q**; what is consolidation?

Chapter 22
Companies/business

924) **Q**; What are the statutory Books for companies?
925) **Q;** What must be done with company annual return?

926) **Q** What must the annual return consist of?

927) **Q:** What is United Kingdom company Act 1985 section 349?

928) **Q**; What is company constitution?

929) **Q;** what is company memorandum.?

930) **Q**; What is company association and article of association?

931) **Q;** What does section 14 of Company Act 1985 state?

932) **Q;** What is non-contractual obligation?

933) **Q:** Name some categories of non-contractual obligation?

934) **Q**: Do sellers have direct contact with customers?

935) **Q**; What Act govern these.?

936) **Q**: What is the rule of privet?

937) **Q**: What does negligence covers?

938) **Q**: Name four laws in business management?

939) **Q;** What must one look for in financial statements?

940) **Q** What do we mean by business environment?

941) **Q**: What do we mean by accounting system?

942) **Q:** What is control test?

943) **Q;** Give a case law in support

944) **Q;** What is integration test/

945) **Q** Give a case in support of integration test.

946) **Q;** What is economic reality test?

947) **Q;** Give a case law to support this?

Chapter 23

Employment

948) **Q;** What date is Employment Right Act?

949) **Q;** what date was the working time regulation?

950) **Q:** what date was Employment Act?

951) **Q:** What date was Equal pay Act?

952) **Q**:What date was National minimum wage?

953) **Q**; What date was unfair contract Terms Act?

954) **Q** what date is Unfair Terms in consumer Contracts Regulations?

Chapter 24

955) **Q:** Brexit Relevant Legal Consequences ?

956) **Q:** When did UK vote to leave EU?

957) **Q**; What was result of Brexit vote?

958) **Q**; When did Britain serve notice to leave EU?

959) **Q**: What is the problem?

960) Q; What is the Legislating for Brexit?

961) **Q**: What is the consequences for Civil justice cooperation?

962) **Q;** What is likely to happen?

963) **Q;** What Methods of legal research that could be used to research on Brexit?

964) **Q**; What is the purpose of research?

965) **Q**; What is Legal Research in General

966) **Q**: What is the Objectives of research into Brexit?

967) **Q**: Name one main reason for carrying out legal research ?

968) **Q;** Why using Historical Research in Brexit?

969) **Q:** What is one advantage of using historical research in Brexit?

970) **Q**: What is the Effectiveness of historical research method in Brexit?

971) **Q**; Why using Doctrinal Research Method in Brexit?

972) **Q**: What are the sources of doctrinal research?

973) **Q:**What is the Role of Hypothesis in doctrinal research?

974) **Q:** Describe effectiveness of doctrinal research in Brexit

975) **Q:** Name two prime ministers who resigned over Brexit

976) **Q:** Name other ministers who resigned over Brexit

977) **Q:** How is doctrinal research base on Brexit?

Chapter 25
BUSINESS/INCORPORATION

978) **Q**: Briefly explain the consequences of incorporation.

979) **Q**: What terminology used

980) **Q:** What is the advantages of corporation?

981) **Q**: What is the disadvantages of corporation?

982) **Q**: What happen to corporate fail to be honest.?

983) **Q**: How is criminal activities of corporation dealt with?

Chapter 26

CSR (MNEs, verification, auditing)

984) **Q**: What are some objective of corporate? CRS

985) **Q**: What does CSR stand for?

986) **Q;** How does CSR operate in corporation?

987) **Q**: Do some corporate breach CSR codes?

988) **Q**: How is breach of CSR code deals with?

989) **Q;** What action did United Nation taken to avoid abuse?

990) **Q:** Name some prominent people adhere with CSR?

991) **Q;** How are corporate involves in CSR?

992) **Q:** Does Human Right plays part in CSR?

993) **Q:** How is equality in terms of Human Right?

994) **Q:** Can Human Right be enforced on Corporation?

995) **Q:** Why is Human Right important in CSR?.

996) **Q;** How do international treaties protect Human Right?

997) **Q;** Is CSR obeyed by all corporate?

998) **Q**: Name example of how CSR been breached?

999) **Q**: How do one relate business to CSR

1000) **Q**; What is important of CSR in MNEs (Multinational enterprise)

1001) **Q**: Briefly discus branding

1002) **Q**: What is the rationale behind using CSR verification and auditing?

1003) **Q**; What is the reason for Verification?

1004) **Q**: What is the method for CSR verification?

1005) **Q**: What is the advantages of Verification?

1006) **Q**: What is the reason for auditing CSR?

1007) **Q**: What is the method for CSR Auditing?

1008) **Q:** What document used in auditing CSR?

1009) **Q**: What do we mean by company tour in auditing?

1010) **Q:** What parts do employees play in auditing?

1011) **Q:** What part do the auditor plays in auditing?

1012) **Q:** How significance is CSR to business

Chapter 27

ILO (**International Labour organisation**)

1013) **Q:** What does ILO stand for?

1014) **Q;** What does ILL stand for?

1015) **Q:** What is the Background of the formation and development of International Labour Law?

1016) **Q**: What happen after the first world war?

1017) **Q**: What happen after the second world war?

1018) **Q:** What is ILO standard and legal considerations?

1019) **Q**: What consist of International Labour Standards Framework?

1020) **Q**: What is the first rule in the ILR?

1021) **Q;** What is the second rule in the ILR?

1022) **Q**; What is the third rule in the ILR?

1023) **Q**; What is the fourth rule in the ILR

1024) **Q**: What is the fifth rule in the ILR?

1025) **Q**; What is the sixth rule in the ILR

1026) **Q;** What is the seventh rule in the ILR?

1027) **Q:** How can the activities of ILO be classified?

1028) **Q**; What does these rules depend?

Chapter 28
CORRUPTION (MNEs

1029) **Q:** How will one describe corruption?

1030) **Q**: Defined corruption

1031) **Q:** What is corruption linked?

1032) **Q:** How do one view Corporate integrity?

1033) **Q**: What is the world bank view on corruption?

1034) **Q**: How thus corruption affect governance?

1035) **Q:** What was Lord Falconer view on corruption

1036) **Q:**What effect of corruption?

1037) **Q**; Who are involve in corruption?

1038) **Q:** What is the relationship among corruption, governance, and human rights

1039) **Q:** What is Julio Bacio Terracino view on corruption?

1040) **Q:** How does MNEs (multinational enterprise) involvement in corruption?

1041) **Q:** Summaries International initiatives combat trans-national corruption

1042) **Q:** What other initiative taken to combat corruption?

1043) **Q**; What Role does the European Parliament Play to combat corruption?

Chapter 29
MNEs

1044) **Q:** How does corruption Impact of Multinational Enterprises (MNEs) and Globalisation

1045) **Q:** What powers does MNEs have?

1046) **Q:** How does corruption increase threat of imitate medicines?

1047) **Q**:How is corruption combat in medicine?

1048) **Q**;; What are stipulations against corruption to combat at the national level?

1049) **Q:** Briefly describe The US (United State) Foreign Corrupt Practice Act 1977

1050) **Q:** What has happened since the Actin 1977?

1051) **Q**: How does the FCPA control corruption in organization account?

1052) **Q:** What is UK (United Kingdom) Response to organisational corruption?

1053) **Q:** How is global bribery combated?

1054) **Q**: Which sector is the bribery Act targeted?

1055) **Q**: How does corruption affect the world?

1056) **Q;:** Do all countries and MNEs help to combat corruption?

1057) **Q;**Is it easy to monitor corruption compliance?

1058) **Q**: What has evolved in multinational corporation?

1059) **Q**: What have MNEs influence?

1060) **Q:** What should lawyers consider with regard to MNEs?

1061) **Q**; What can corporate provide?

1062) **Q**: What is the negative side of corporate?

1063) **Q:** can regulatory corporate prevent their negativity?

1064) **Q**: With case evidence, what powers were given to MNEs

1065) **Q:** What are some influence of MNEs on stakeholders and community?

1066) **Q;** Do some of MNEs privileges experience in other countries?

1067) **Q:** Is it fair to blame all MNEs for abusive practice

1068) **Q;** Give some MNEs who contribute to public wellbeing

1069) **Q:** How do MNEs benefit from their good deeds to the public?

1070) **Q**; What can MNEs get away with due to their generosity to the society?

1071) **Q:** Give an example of company who got away despite unethical activities?

1072) **Q;** What does Governance refer in relation to MNEs?

1073) **Q:** How do MNEs spread internationally?

1074) **Q**; Name another gap in corporate governance?

1075) **Q**: What is the consequence of MNEs harshness on some workers?

1076) **Q**: How do the public view on MNEs breach of corporate governance and CSR?

1077) **Q**; What other MNEs abuse their position?

1078) **Q**: How has globalization help MNEs to abuse their power?

1079) **Q:** What evidence that some MNEs are hypocrite?

1080) **Q**: What measures for effectiveness of Monitoring and Enforcement methods?

1081) **Q**:How can enforcement be implemented?.

1082) **Q;** How difficulties to hold MNEs accountable?
1083) **Q:** How can third party be monitored?
1084) **Q**: What has resulted due to lack of universal monitoring of MNEs?
1085) **Q:** How I reflect on MNEs?
1086) **Q**: What is my conclusion on MNEs research?

Research Diary

1087) **Q:** Although argument is blood line of law. How do one carry out research by using diary?
1088) **Q:** What were the sources?
1089) **Q;** Give an example of how you will carry out research to write assignment in law?
1090) **Q:** Give example of you would outline research in a table form?
1091) **Q:** Give conclusion of the research?
1092) **Q**:What is the difference between secondary and primary source research?

Chapter 30

WOMEN

1093) **Q**; How can one argue equality for men and women?
1094) **Q:** What actions might be used as male dominance over women?
1095) **Q:** Are all women the same?
1096) **Q**: Do the law favours women?
1097) **Q:** How do men and women differ

Chapter 31

ABORTION

1098) **Q:** Define abortion

1099) **Q:**What is the difference between foetus and embryo?

1100) **Q:** What is quickening

1101) Q: who made that decision?

1102) **Q:** when was abortion criminalised?

1103) **Q:** What was the punishment for abortion?

1104) Q; Why were women have to undergo penance?

1105) **Q:** What power had the church in people lives?

1106) **Q;** What was the punishment for abortion when the church power deteriorated?

1107) **Q**: When was Lord Ellenborough's Act

1108) **Q:** How was the punishment for abortion under Lord Ellenborough's Act

1109) **Q:** How do one compare the changes in the law?

1110) **Q**: Give summary of Offence against person Act 1837

1111) **Q**: What happened to the quickening

1112) **Q:** When were Offence Against person's Act

1113) **Q**; Why was the Act of 1861?

1114) **Q**; When was the infant life preservation Act
1115) **Q:** What did the infant Act 1929 sought?
1116) **Q:** Why was the abortion Act 1967 introduced?

Chapter 32

FGM (Female Genital Mutilation)

1117) **Q**; What do you think of FGM
1118) **Q:** What does the term FGH means in law?
1119) **Q:** How does it affect the victim?
1120) **Q:** How is it classified by WHO?
1121) **Q:** What is United Kingdom Law on FGM
1122) **Q:** Give some details of the 2003 Law. Section 1
1123) **Q**: Give some details of the 2003 Law. Section 2
1124) **Q**: Give some details of the 2003 Law. Section 3
1125) **Q**: How was it amended in 2015 Act in sec.70
1126) **Q**; what is section 73 of the 2015 Act
1127) **Q**:What is section 72 of the Act
1128) **Q:** When was a woman first convicted in United Kingdom?

Chapter 33

Family Law

1129) **Q**: How will you describe the media in relation to family court
1130) **Q:** When was family proceeding amended

1131) **Q:** Should media be allowed in family court

Chapter 34

SILENCE

1132) **Q:** Why will individual be advised to remain silence when being interview by police?

1133) **Q:** Can remain silence be construed as guilty?

1134) **Q:** In what situation might one choose to be silence at interview?

1135) **Q:** Can individual stop police interview at any time?

1136) **Q:** Can police interview be void and why?

Chapter 35

Assault

1137) **Q:**What happen if government servant, employer, or people in higher position say something during interview that resulted one develop symptoms of neurosis such as reactive depression, anxiety, phobia what can one do?

1138) **Q:** What happen if the symptom developed after a week.

1139) **Q;** Personal injury claim stipulate that it must be claim within three years, is there any way round it.

1140) **Q:** What happen if you have chronic Psychiatric diagnoses.

Chapter 36

Chapter 3

CRIMINAL LAW

Chapter 3.1

ACCOMPLICE AND LIABILITY(accomplice, principal, aid, Abert, procure, actus reus ,mens rea.)

Principle of legal defence and accomplice liability

1) **Q;** what is accomplice; ?

A: To help someone to commit a crime.

2) **Q:** How can accomplice be successful prosecuted?

A; for successful prosecution, the prosecutor has to prove all the elements which include Mens rea and actus rues. Beyond a reasonable doubt rather than on a balance of probability in specific crime.

Example Jane committed the actus reus of theft with appropriate Mens rea.

3) **Q;** Who is principal offender?

A; If there is more than one who committed the crime, the person who actually commits the crime sometimes known as the main man is call principal offender

4) **Q**; what law support accessories?

A; Accessories and Abettors Act 1861 section 8 state that accomplice\assisted are liable.

5) **Q;** What is Actus reus of accomplice

A; There are four namely Aid, Abert, Counsel or procure the commission of the offence.

a. **Q:** What Act can the Aid, Abert Counsel or procure be found?

A: They can be found in the section 8 of accessories and Abettors Act 1861.

6) **Q;** what does Aid and abet mean?

A; to assist in performance of a crime either before or during (not after). Aiding is material assistance providing the goods (such as weapon, tool, cars act), it could also be encouragement.

7) **Q**; what is Counsel?

A; Is given advice or method to commit crime.

8) **Q;** What is procuring?

A; Is to produce by endeavour. One procures a thing by setting out something and to see that it happen or taking the appropriate steps to produce that happening.

9) **Q;** Which law support accomplice liability?

A; The accessories and Abettors Act 1861 regard those who assist the principal offender to commission the offence as equally culpable with the person who actually committed the offence. It is secondary to crime.

Chapter 3.2

MENS REA

10)Q: What is MENS REA**?**

A; This is refer to as guilty mind. Did they intend to do what they actually did? This is essential element of the offence hence in theory if a defence has manse rea, the defendant is fully aware, It can be construed that he\she planned the crime committed.

11)Q: Does it matter if defendant claim insane and why?

A: It does not matter whether he claim insane, diminish responsibility, intoxication, or recklessness This is because it is crime of basic intent.

12)Q ; What is the mens rea of accomplice?

A; The are two elements namely; intention and knowledge

13)Q: Explain mens rea of intention?

A; An intention to aid (proved by a positive act of assistance which is voluntarily done. To intend to provide the assistance and the encouragement or procured the commission of the offence or intentionally spoke the words that advised procured or encouraged the crime. Or in fact gave to the principal offender or had wilfully encouraged.(Megaw L . J)

14)Q; Explain mens rea of knowledge?

A; According to Lord Devlin J. " knowledge of the circumstances"

15)Q; Explain this what Lord Devlin might mean?

A; The accomplice must know about it. In case of Johnson. V. Youden (1950) 1 KB 544,

16)Q; How did Lord Goddard explain knowledge?

A; Lord Goddard CJ stated " The essential matters which constitute that offence--- the defendant did not have to know that a crime had been committed because he may not know that the facts constitute an offence and ignorance of the law is not a defence.

17)Q; What must accomplice do to be convicted?

A; Accomplice must either advice, encourage before the crime occur or must be present at the scene of the crime to encourage or help or assist and at the time.

18)Q; Give an example of just stood and watches?

A; In R.V. Clarkson (1971) 1WL.R 1402 where two people heard a woman being raped; they only went and stood to watch. They were found not guilty of accomplice

19)Q: What about non-accidental presence?

A: In R. v. Coney (1882) 8 QBd 534, it was decided that non-accidental presence at the scene of the crime is NOT conclusive of aiding and abetting (Hawkins J said "It is no criminal offence to stand by, a mere passive spectator of a crime, even of murder" "non-interference to prevent a crime is not itself a crime" or stand for a child to drown.

20) Q: Is it a crime to fail to act?

A: In England and Wales, failing to act is not a crime except in contracture or relative.

21)Q: What is sentence difference between principal and accomplice?

A:The accomplice will get the same sentence as the principal offender example, for a murder; life imprisonment for all.

22)Q: What about the actus reus of both accomplice and principal?

A:The actus reus and Mens rea of the principal offender might be different from the accomplice but it does not matter, the sentence will be the same.

23)Q: Give two cases on accomplice?

A; In R. v. bland (1988) Crim LR 41; a woman living with a drug dealer, aware of what he was up to but said nothing, she never encourage him

Appeal Court Verdict; her conviction was quashed

A; Wilcox v. Jeffery;(1951) 1ALL ER 464; If one purchase a ticket and attend illegal concert or gathering\assemble he\she could be charged as accomplice since it will be seen as aiding, abetting or encourage.

24) Q: How can owner of a car be charged as accomplice?

A; If owner of the car sit in the passenger seat and the car driven dangerously or over speed limit without the owner said nothing, the owner could be charged as accomplice refer to the case Duress. v. Lambourn (1907) !KB.40

25)Q; Give example of duty to Act in accomplice?

A: R. v. Willet (2010)EWCA crim 1620; If one have duty to act or care (in close relation such as brother, mother sister) and fail to intervene at crime scene and not control the principal offender can amount to encouragement of the offence and can lead to accomplice liability.

26)Q: What case that a bar owner charged as accomplice?

A; In Turk. V. Robinson (19700 1 WLR 741; the owner of a bar who said nothing when customers drunk after licence hour was charged as accomplice.

27)Q; What is the actus reus element of accomplice liability?

A: The actus reus for accomplice liability that the defendant must be proved to "aid, abet, counsel or procure" the commission of the principal offender.

28)Q: What difference if accomplice action is before or after the crime?

A: Accomplice could proof evidence of help, encouragement to the principal offender either before or at the time and will be liable

29)Q: What is the accomplice position after the crime?

A: Help and encouragement after the crime does not attract accomplice liability, but may be charge with perverting the course of justice whereby the defendant must have both actus reus and manse rea.

30)Q; How can insanity (lacked mental capacity) be used as defence)?

A; defendant can argue that his psychiatric condition meant he did not know it was wrong to commit a crime. In such case he\she is using insanity as defence

Chapter 3.3

ACTUS REA

31)Q: What is Actus reus (guilty conduct)

A; Is the action or doing the crime (conduct)? Is anything the defendant does other than the state of mind example rape, murder, theft. What they have done, is it capable of being criminal offence?

32)Q: How do you know what the Actus reus of a particular crime is?

A: All criminal offence is defined by case law (common law) or statute which the actus reus are state in.

33)Q: How does one find out the element of crime?

A: One needs to check the definition to know the element of the conduct (actus Reus) expected.

34)Q: How do you know whether certain circumstances have existed?

A: Cases or common law give example of predetermine cases.

35)Q: What does actus reus of criminal damage?

A: It requires that the defendant must damage or destroy property belong to another

36)Q: Give an example of actus reus criminal damage?

A: To establish actus Reus; example the defendant dragged (done something) his key along the car (act), the relevant consequence (car been scratched (damaged), the relevant circumstance exist. The car belongs to somebody else. This brings actus reus complete.

37)Q: What is positive conduct of actus reus?

A: The defendant must have done something such as murder, rape (action)

38)Q: Are there some crimes that only need actus reus to convict?

A: Yes. In most criminal negligence liability.

39)Q: What is the test or judgement for this liability/?

A: The judgement is to compare the defendant "to act below the standard of the reasonable person doing the same Act." Without good reason (lawful excuse).

40)Q: What is the objective standard required for such strict liability?

A: "The standard is an objective, impersonal, fixed in relation to the safety of other users on the Highway. It is in no way related to the degree of proficiency or degree of experience attended by individual drivers.(This quote can be used for careless driving) section 3 of road traffic Act 1988.

Chapter 3.4

DURESS (duress, necessity, circumstance**)**

41)Q; What is Duress?

A; Is a situation where the defendant is forced to commit crime because his power of resistance had been overborne and the threat must be immediate.

42)Q Is duress a defence for murder?.

A;) Duress is not a defence for murder, however duress can be used as defence if the threat of death or serious injury are made which, in effect force a defendant to commit a crime.

43)Q; What crime can duress be used as defence?

A: Duress is a defence for all crime except murder.

44)Q; Give an example of a case on duress.?

A: R. v. Howe (1987) 1AC 417; the House of Lords decided that duress cannot be a defence to murder regardless of circumstances.

45)Q; Can duress be defence for attempted murder?

A; In R. v. Gotts (1992)2 WLR 284, the House of Lords confirm that duress is not available for attempted murder.

46)Q: Can threat be used as duress in defence?

A: Example, He was compelled to act that is to give statement or gave money because of threat to him and family. He would be arguing the defence of duress.

47) Q; What is duress necessity

A; As it is term, it must be necessary to use as defence.

48)Q: What are the elements of duress necessity?

A1 The act is needed to avoid inevitable and irreparable evil.

A2; No more should be done is reasonably necessary for .

A3: The evil inflicted must not disproportionate to the evil avoided.

49)Q: Give a case in duress necessity?

A; Re A (children) (conjoined twins; surgery operation (2000)4 ALL ER 961.

50)Q; What is duress of circumstances.

A; The actus reus or elements of duress of circumstances are similar to duress in that

The harm the defendant is trying to avoid must be death or serious injury.

51)Q: How is the defendant expected to act in duress circumstances? And give case example.

A: The defendant must act reasonably, that is a person of reasonable firmness, showing the characteristics of the defendant would have responded the same.

Example of a case is R.V. Conway (1988) 3 WLR 1238

Chapter 3.5

Driving

52)Q: What used to be the maximum find for careless driving and kill someone?

A; It uses to be £5,000.00 and possible 3-9 points endorsement. On 18th August 2008 the law changed to five years imprisonment for killing someone. If no death then the defendant can get away with fines or\ and endorsement (you must check current).

53)Q: Can this driving offence be increased?

A:Yes. For more serious example for voluntary drink and drive and kill road user, the judge can use section 2A or 3A plus up to 14 years imprisonment.

54)Q: How are motor accident assessed or judged?

A: In assessing motorist who have cause accident and killed, It is the manner of the driving that is important and not what happens as result of that driving, hence killing someone or damage property will might not incur conviction (except proven careless driving)

55)Q; How would you describe a driver who is drunk?.

A; in law the person could be described as reckless (basic intent that no excuse)

Chapter 3.6

INTOXICATION

(Voluntary, involuntary, basic intent, strict intent, negligence)

56)Q; What is intoxication?

A; if a defendant argues that "I was so drunk (voluntary), I did not know what I was doing. I certainly did not intend to cause her any harm and I was past thinking about what I was doing" If the jury believe that then she might have actus reus (doing) but lack of manse rea will result not guilty verdict.

57)Q; How easy to use intoxication as defence?

A: Using intoxication as a defence might be complex example App. Majewski using intoxication which if accepted, the next thing is to consider if it was voluntary or involuntary

58)Q: What is involuntary intoxication or misbehaviour?

A: Is a situation when a defendant drinks non-alcoholic and is spiked with alcohol or drugs which then lead to lack of manse rea.

59)Q: Can involuntary intoxication be used as defence?

A:Yes, It might be used as defence to all type of crime provided the defendant did not have mens rea at the time

60)Q: Does this include specific and basic intent?

A: Yes for all crime, defendant must not have manse rea of intended (specific intent) or foresaw the risk (recklessness).

61)Q; Give example of cases on involuntary intoxication?

A; If during examination in court defendant state that despite involuntary intoxication he still have mens rea for the offence then he/she will be guilty. Example R. v. Kingston (1994)3 ALL ER 353; Lord Mustill said; If a person did not have and not intend that is no mens rea. If however he developed mens rea after the spike of drink and after commits the crime, then he is not guilty. This is because he did not have it during the commission of the crime.

62)Q; Give another example of involuntary intoxication case?

A; In R.v.Hordie (1984) 3ALL ER 848; A man took Valium prescribed by a doctor to calm him, but instead he became aggressive and set fire to property.

Court verdict; He was found not guilty because of the side effect of the drug.

63)Q: What is voluntary intoxication?

A: Voluntary is when the person is aware of taking the drug or alcohol.

64)Q: How can voluntary intoxication be used as defence?

A:To use this as defence, one has to consider if specific intent or basic intention is.

65)Q: What is specific intent voluntary intoxication?

A:This is sometimes term Dutch language which means that the defendant got drunk specifically intended the consequence of his actions which means he\she has manse rea and therefore in most cases guilty of the crime example murder.

66)Q: What is basic intent (voluntary)

A: This is when a crime or offence is committed with some menses rea other than intention.

67)Q: What has the prosecutor have to proof?

A:The prosecutor has to prove that the defendant was reckless, or he foresaw risk of his action and went on to take the risk without justification.

68)Q: Is voluntary intoxication a defence to basic intent crimes?

A: Using that on its own as defence is unlikely to succeed. Example Offence Against person Act section 18,20, 47, 39 (check date) OAPA

69)Q; Give some cases of voluntary intoxication?

A: R. v. Stewart (James) 2009) 1WLR, R. v. Wood 2507 CRIME lr (2009,11,807-809

70)Q; in what situation that voluntary intoxication not defence?

A; Voluntary intoxication is no defence to any crime that can be committed recklessly.

71)Q; what about negligent due to voluntary intoxication?

A; Voluntary intoxication has no relevance to crime that can be committed negligently, or if is one of strict liability.

72)Q what about basic intent crime in relation to voluntary intoxication?.

A: Voluntary intoxication can never be a defence for a crime of basic intent.

73)Q; what case relates to voluntary intoxication?

A; DPP.V. Majewski (1977) 2 WLR 623

74)Q; in what situation might voluntary intoxication be used as defence?

A; voluntary intoxication could only be a defence to crime of specific intent (example murder, section 18 of offence against person Act 1861, s.1 of theft Act 1968) where the defendant is so drunk\drug that he or she did not form the necessary intention for the mens rea of the offence.

75)Q what case relate to this exception in voluntary intoxication as defence?

A; R .v. Kingston (1994) 3 All Err 353This was a case where the defendant drink was spike with drugs resulted him sexually assaulted a young boy.

Court verdict; The House of Lords state that if someone knowing and willing get so drunk or drug that can and control their action deserves no concessions from the law. Lord Denning call the person irresponsible

76)*Q:* In what other way can voluntary intoxication be a defence?.

A; This can be used only if the defendant had no knowledge that he was taking any alcohol or drugs or if he developed side effect to prescribe drugs, the he can use it as defence. However if he misused the drugs such as over dose or drank alcohol when he had been told not to. In such circumstance he\she will be liable to the crime committed as he would be regarded as reckless.

77)Q; what is Dutch courage?

A; this is when someone get drunk or take drugs in other to give him courage to commit crime.

78)Q; Give an example and can the defendant plea insanity?

A; Attorney General for Northern Ireland's. Gallagher (1963) A. C. 349 HL; Defendant plan to kill his wife so he got drunk (alcohol) to get courage. His plea of insanity in the appeal was dismissed. Lord Denning said " The wickedness of his mind before he got drunk was enough to condemn him couple with the act which he intended to intended to do and did do.

It appears that Challenger had already the mens rea (intention) he needed accomplice to help him "Dutch courage"

79)Q; What about drinking in moderation? example If one is drinking alcohol in moderation but unknown that that it was spiked with vodka and get drunk more than he would have.

A; In this situation there will be balance between voluntary and involuntary intoxication if he underestimate the amount then it will be voluntary intoxication and cannot use it as defence R.V. Allen (1988) Crime LR 698

80)Q; Can involuntary intoxication is used as defence?

A; Example when the victim drink\food is spike or injected or any form to get the illicit substance (drugs or alcohol) into the body and become involuntary intoxicated, it can be used as defence for both specific intent and basic intent for all other crime as long as the defendant has no menses rea.

This means that if someone lacks menses rea for specific intent then he might not be guilty of murder s.20 of offence against persons 1861 (Which is crime of specific intent, but the defendant could be convicted of manslaughter

81)Q; what happens if two people were drunk and one kills the other?

A; This could be termed drunken mistake.

Court decision; In the case of R.V. Grady (1987) 3 WLR 321 The court of appeal state that defendant with voluntary intoxication and have mens rea who commit crime cannot rely on intoxication as defence in murder or manslaughter or even sexual offence or Offence against person Act 1861.

.

Chapter 3.7

LIABILITY (Strict Liability, Absolute liability, Lawful excuse)

82)Q; What is Absolute liability;

A: In absolute liability, one may be punished or found guilty even though the act may be, or the conduct may not be voluntary that is he\she did not know about it

83)Q What is strict liability;

A: In statute, strict liability means "rule of law"

In strict liability, the conduct must be voluntary but lack menses rea in relation to each actus reus. Strict liability requires at least one element of Actus reus without proof of blameworthiness in terms of no evidence needed for intention, recklessness or negligence.

84)Q: Give example of strict liability?

A: Example; He drove a motor car on a road or other public places with an excess amount of alcohol in the driver's blood or urine. All these statements are actus reus (no menses rea) He drank and drove voluntary. (A defendant is likely to say," I did not know I was doing that, I did not mean to)

Case law (authority) Sweet & Parsley (1970) Lord Reid.

85)Q; Explain crime of strict liability?.

A; Is when defendant conduct must be voluntary? Is offence where individual can incur criminal liability notwithstanding the fact that he/she was not blameworthy in relation to his/her conduct?

Example sections 1 & 2 of the contempt of court Act 1981 conduct treated as contempt of court as tending to interfere with course of justice.

86)Q: Where do you find strict liability? give example.

A: Strict liability offence is in some statutes and the court or judge will normally remind the jury as such. Example road traffic offence with alcohol or drugs or driving without licence, parking ticket (licence laws (contempt of court act 1981.

87)Q: What is strict liability use for;

A: It is generally used to protect the public and be vigilance plus to prevent unfair outcome.

88)Q; Does strict liability breach European article?

A; Yes it can be argued that strict liability breach article 6 (2) of the European human Right Act.

89)Q; What is crime of absolute liability?.

A: absolute liability is one where the defendant can be punished even though his or her conduct could not be classed as voluntary,

90)Q; What is **lawful excuse?** and give an example.

A: This is dealt with under section 5 (2) a of the criminal damage Act 1971.

In Jaggard .v Dickson (1980) 3 ALL ER 716; Defendant broke to a house that she thought belong to her friend and honestly believe that the friend would have consented, but it turn out to be wrong house because she was drunk (voluntary intoxication). Court verdict; She was found not guilty as lawful excuse;

Chapter 3.8

OMISSION (fail to Act)

91)Q: What happen if someone fails to act?

A: There is no statutory duty of care.

When defendant failed to act and something drastically happen such as death or injury, the law is very clear in this, if you have no duty of care then you will be at risk if anything happens to the victim. Example seeing a stranger on the road side injury call ambulance (although you do not have to) but do not torch him/her

92)Q: What happen if you are a career or exceptional case?.

A: If there is special relationship between the defendant and the victim such as relative, a carer\nurse coast guide, a visitor act and failed to act will render criminal liability if you failed to act (omission). Example R. v. Stone and Dobinson, R. v. Insant, R.v. Ruffel.

93)Q; what other liability for omission to act.

A; If someone assume duty of care, you must not stop until the victim is taken over such as being sent to hospital or the parent come to take care. Other liability include; if you accept payment for the care, contractual obligation, childminder, life guard, motorist nurse

94)Q; what happen in dangerous situation?

A Where someone created dangerous situation, the law imposes a duty of care on the person to take reasonable steps to remove the danger.

USING FORCE

95) What happen if you prevent crime using force? According to criminal Act 1967 section 3, A person can use such "force as is reasonable in the circumstance" to prevent a crime being committed. The argument in most cases is what one regard as reasonable force?

Chapter 3.9

MISTAKE

96)Q What if the defendants claim to be making mistake? Or if the defendant claim of making mistake about the need to prevent crime?

A: It does not matter as long as the defendant uses reasonable force.

97)Q: What about if the defendant was intoxicated when he \she used the force?

A; If the defendants action is due to involuntary intoxication then it does not matter as long as reasonable force is used (section 3 of the criminal law Act 1967)

98) Q; What about if the defendant was involuntary intoxicated?

A; If the intoxication is involuntary, the reasonable force cannot be used as defence according to section three.

99)Q; If "A" say to "B", "kill my friend" but B did not, can A be charged of accomplice.

A : A cannot be charged with accomplice to murder as actus reus did not happen (death)

100) **Q**: What can A be charged?

A: A can be charged with INCHOATE offence that is encouraging or assisting an offence under serious crime Act 2007.

Chapter 3.10

Miscellaneous (rape innocent agent)

101) **Q:** When did husband can rape his wife started?

A: The sexual offence Act 1956 section 1 and section 142 of the criminal Justice and Public Act 1994 example R. v. R (1992) AC.

102) **Q:** Who is an innocent agent?

A: An innocent agent is someone who commits the actus reus of a crime but who is not guilty of the crime because he or she lacks menses rea prior to being asked or because he\she has a specific defence available to him\her.

103) **Q:**What happen to the instigator?

A: The instigator is likely to be charged of the crime as the principal offender rather than as accomplice. This is the cases where adult use children under the age (ten) of being charged an offence.

104) **Q:** What happen if Actus reus had been committed who can be convicted?

A: Once the action\conduct had been committed then any one can be convicted as accomplice. A lack of menses rea or any valid defence on the part of the principal offender does not prevent conviction of the accomplice.

105) **Q:** What is the appropriate charge in sexual offence

A: The appropriate charge is sexual offence would be that of acting as an accomplice having procured the commission of the offence rather than a charge of being a principal offender acting through an innocent agent.

106) **Q:** What about female using a male to commit rape?

A: In that case the principal could not commit rape (female to rape) as principal offender. The charge will be that the person was an accomplice who procured an innocent person to commit actus reus of the offence. What happen if 15-year-old girl persuade a boy of 21 to have sex with her?

The boy has the element of action (actus Reus) and mens rea and therefore will be committed f rape under section 9 of the 2003 sexual offence Act,

107) **Q;** Will the girl be charged?

A; No, because she is the victim and the law protect under 16 years old.

Chapter 3.11

Murder (types, death, homicide, unlawful killing, felony, euthanasia, malice, mercy killing. GBH, provocation**)**

108) Q; How many types of murder?

A; There are two; first and second-degree murder.

109) **Q** What is first degree murder?

A: First degree murder is intentionally killing or killing through an intention to do serious harm or injury with awareness of a serious risk of causing death because of intent known as specific intent.

110) **Q**; what is second degree murder?

A; Second **degree murder** encompass killing through an intention to do serious injury (even without awareness of a serious risk causing death or killing where there is awareness of causing death couple with intention to cause injury fear risk.

111) **Q;** what is Actus reus of murder.

A; causing the death of human being with malice aforethought

112) **Q**; what is mens rea of murder?

A; An intention to kill or an intention to cause grievous bodily harm (it must not be recklessness).

It is important to know that mens rea is entirely subjective test by juries. The juries ask them. Did the defendant intend to kill or cause grievous bodily harm.

113) **Q:** What is legal definition of **death**?

A; Death is irreversible death of the brain stem that control the basic function of the body.

114) **Q :** Name the three main **homicides**?

A; These are a) murder which could be voluntary or involuntary

b) Manslaughter also voluntary or involuntary

c) Infanticide also voluntary or involuntary.

115) **Q;** What is the common element on Homicide?

A; ACTUS Reus; the guilty conduct, how the homicide perform that is "**unlawfully killing** a reasonable person who is being and under the Kings peace, and the death following within a year and one day "coke 3 into 47 (This is to be changed to three years if approve by statue

116) Q: Why was a year and one day rule introduced in1994?

A; The law commission felt "It would be wrong for a person to remain almost indefinitely at risk of prosecution for murder, hence "a year and one day" section 39 of the Corona and Justice Act 1996 propose amended in2009

117) Q; Define **Homicide**?

A; Homicide is causing another person death without justification and is regarded as the most serious criminal offence.

118) Q; What is the main element to replace " **A year and a day"**

A; the injury alleged to have caused the death was sustained more than three years.

119) Q; what is **Felony**?

A; Is a person who has committed serious crime

120) Q; What is voluntary **Euthanasia**?

A; A person who request someone to assist him\her to die.

121) Q; what law does murder comes under?

A; Murder has always been common law not statute.

122) Q; what are the elements of murder?

A; 1) Express malice which is when defendant actually intended to kill his victim.

2) **Implied malice**; where the intention was to cause GBH (grievous bodily harm) to victim but lead to victim death

3) **Constructive malice;** this was abolished in the homicide Act 1957) It used to have two circumstances.

A) Defendant killed victim in the cause of felony.

B) Defendant kill victim in cause of resisting arrest, rescued from legal custody.

123) **Q:** give an example of **mercy killing**?

A; In Ingles (2002) EWCA crim 2637; in the appeal court, A mother injected her son with heron as he was in hospital and seriously ill. Appeal court ruled that mercy killing is unlawful.

124) **Q:** What case support mercy killing?

A; " r (Hickson) v. Ministry of Justice (2012) EwHc 2381 (admin)

125) **Q;** Name some partial defence available for murder or **GBH** (gracious bodily harm)

A: One can use loss of control (this used to be called provocation);The court look at what triggered it.

Insanity

Diminished responsibility; this is only available for murder which if successful can be reduced to voluntary manslaughter

None-insane automation

In feticide

Involuntary intoxication

Chapter 3.12

SUICIDE PACT (Diana Pretty, Mr. Purdy)

126) Q: What law does the suicide Act 1961 under?

A:The suicide Act comes under Coroners and Justice Act 2009.

127) Q: What are the main element of suicide pact?

A:The main element of the suicide Act is a person who aid, abeits, counsels or procures the suicide of another, or an attempt by another to commit suicide shall be liable on conviction on indictment to imprisonment for a term not exceeding fourteen years.

128) Q: What will the defendant be charged

A: The charge will be murder or manslaughter.

If there is suicide pact for person or third party to perform the act of killing unlawful.

129) Q; What is a suicide pact based on?

A; Suicide pacts is based on probability and is defined in section 4(3) of homicide Act 1957 as a common agreement between two or more person having for its object the death of all of them, whether or not each is to take his own life or helped by other, but nothing done by a person who enters into a suicide pact.

130) Q; name case law to support suicide pact?

A:Case; R. v. Hendley, R. v. Crowley (2004) 1WLR 2111CA.

131) Q; What law can the court use to refuse application for suicide pact?

A; In R.v.Mcshane (1977) 66 Cr. App.R.97 at 102. Orr LJ said a Mrs Mott application was refused on section 2(1) of the suicide act 1961.

132) Q: Explain the case of **Diane Pretty** (2001)

A; This is one of the most publicised cases in 2001. Mrs Pretty was terminally ill and requested the DPP (director of public prosecution) to allow her husband to assist her to die but she was refused.

In R. (on application of Pretty).UK (2002) 1AC800, The House of Lords ruled that DPP has no power to grant Mrs Pretty her request.

Mrs. Pretty took the case to Europe in Pretty.v.UK (2002) 35 EHRR1,The European courts confirmed that House of Lords was right to refused Mrs.

Pretty application because member state was entitled to prohibit assisted suicide in order to protect vulnerable people.

133) **Q:** Explain the case of **Mrs Purdy** (2009)

A; Mrs Purdy suffered from severe multiple sclerosis and wished her husband to help her travel to a country where assisted euthanasia was permitted. DPP refused and so she took it to the House of Lords and to the European court. European court agreed that Article 8.1 was engaged, Mrs Purdy argued that the prohibition of suicide Act 1961,Prohibition s.2 (1) amount to interference with her right to respect for her private life under Article 8 (2) that the law should be accessible and foreseeable. The House of Lords unanimously allowed

Chapter 3.13

Manslaughter (voluntary, involuntary, domestic violence, vulnerable adult, self- defence, aggressor, excuse of homicide)

134) **Q:** What is manslaughter?

A; This is unlawful homicide which is not murder. There are two types; voluntary and involuntary.

135) **Q;** What is voluntary manslaughter?

A; This is when a person kills another but due mitigation circumstances such as loss of control ,insanity the person is not convict of murder.

136) Q; What is involuntary manslaughter?

A; This is the case where the victim dies after a while of being injured.

137) Q; What was the sentence for manslaughter

A; The judge has discretion of specific number of years in prison to life in prison.

138) Q; When and what was abolished in the Corona and Justice Act 2009?

A; It abolished defence of provocation and replaced it with loss of control and that took effect in 14\October\ 2010.

139) Q; What is the hierarchy of homicide cases?

A; The prosecution and the defence lawyers would be argue first for murder then it be changed to voluntary manslaughter, and then to involuntary manslaughter.

140) Q; which law protect the vulnerable persons?

A: The domestic violence crime and victim Act 2004. This was amended in 2012.Section 5 lay down the protection for vulnerable child or adult.

141) Q Explain section 5.1 (I) of the domestic violence Act 2004?

A: The victim being a member of the same household includes a lodger or visitor. Section 5.1(C) at the time of death there was significant risk of serious physical harm cause to the victim.

142) **Q;** Explain section 5.d (ii)

A; defendant failed to take such steps as he could reasonably have been expected to take to protect victim from the risk.

Section 5.d (iii) the act occurred in circumstances of that kind that defendant foresaw or ought to have foreseen.

Section 5.(6) Defendant act include a cause of conduct or an omission such as failure to feed, clothe or given medical attention.

143) **Q:** How will you define vulnerable adult?

A: In a case Khan (2009) EWCA crim 2, the appeal court struggled for the definition of vulnerable adult; In this case the victim was lonely, friendless and relied solely on the husband and his family in strange country.

It was decided that children, elderly, disable people are regarded as vulnerable.

144) **Q:** What is **self-defence** in homicide and give an example?

A; Self-defence is where force is used to protect him\her self or his property to prevent crime being committed is excusable subject to judge's decision.

145) **Q;** Use case law to explain self- defence?

A: In a case; Devlin. V. Armstrong (1971) N1.13, Lord McDermott CJ referred to self-defence as a "plea of justification". This was based on condition that the other person (deceased) was the aggressor. As Lord McDermott put it " It is better that the injury be suffer by the aggressor"

146) **Q;** What are the two reasons for self-defence?

A; 1) It is the aggressor (victim) who prime course of the mischief 2 The rule allows defensive action tends to inhabit aggression.

147) **Q;** What rule can be used as "**Excuse of Homicide"?** and state the theory

A; The rule on "the theory of Excuses"(1982) G. William crim.L.R.732,739

148) **Q;** Explain "the theory of Excuses"

A: t state that one can use force to protect himself or his\her property provided 1)The victim or the aggressor is the prime aggressor or the mischief. 2) The rule allows defensive action tends to inhibit aggression or at least to restrain its continuance as a rule forbidding defensive action would tend to promote it.

149) **Q;** Give another case to support "excuse of homicide"

A: The case on this self-defence is Devlin. v. Armstrong (1971)N1.13

Chapter 3.14

ASSIST to prevent or commit crime (trespass, assassin, ignorance, GBH, EU)

150) Q; What is the rule to one who assists against assassin in self-defence?

A; The rule is " no one who assist the self-defence should not be guilty; R.V. Wheeler (1967) W.L.R.1531,at P1533.

151) Q; using case law, explain rule on self-defence?

A:Example; in R.V. Rose (1884)15 Cox 540; the son short his father as his father got his wife throat to kill her. In judging this case the son must honestly believe, and had reasonable grounds for the belief that his mother life was in imminent peril that the son action in shooting the father was absolutely necessary for preservation of the mother's life.

152) Q; What happen if someone helps to fight and\or cause injury to another?

A; In a case R.V. Duffy (1967) 1Q.B.63. Duffy sister and someone Akbar were fighting, Akbar was on top of her. Duffy hit Akbar with a bottle as he could not get him off his sister.

Court verdict: Both Duffy and her sister were convicted of GBH because the sister life was not in danger.

153) Q: Give an example of landlord tenant in self-defence?

A; In a case R. V. Hussey (1924) 18 Cri.App.R.160;Land lord and his friends went to the tenant house which was rented, arm with hammer, spanner, poker and chisel. The tenant barricade himself inside, Landlord made a hole in the tenant door, tenant short through the door and wounded one of the landlord friends

Court Verdict; The tenant was found "not guilty" because the landlord did not give enough notice, and moreover , it is only the court to issue warrant for the tenant to move out.

154) Q; What law did the landlord breach?

A; As the landlord has no warrant to threaten the tenant, he breached article 6 of the European Convention Act 1998. The landlord also breached the trespasses law and hence the tenant has the right of self-defence.

155) Q; What does the criminal law say about the self-defence ?

A; The criminal law Act 1967, section 3 state that "A person may use such force as is reasonable in the circumstance in the prevention of crime---"

156) Q; is ignorance a defence?

A; It is important to know that ignorance in law is no defence, if a defendant has mens rea and he thinks reasonable people may not agree with his delusion then he has insight.

157) Q: what happen if the person have no insight in the criminal action? Give example

A: This must be psychotic mental illness such as schizophrenia, manic depressive or psychopath., where there is lack of insight. Example could be Peter Sutcliffe was not legally insane because he had actus reus and mens rea in killing women R.v. Johnson.

Chapter 3.15

INSANITY (special verdict, non-insane automatism**)**

158) Q; Can one use insanity as defence?

A; Insanity is a defence in both specific and basic intent. This was established when in the 19th century McNaughton was found not guilty for murder due to insanity.

159) Q; What does the defendant have to prove for insanity?

A; The defendant has to proof on balance of probability by evidence.

160) **Q:** If accused is found guilty what powers under the criminal procedure (insanity and unfitness to plead) Act 1991 the judge can to order?

A; The judge has discretion to sentence the defendant to psychiatric hospital, guardianship, supervision treatment order or absolute discharge.

161) **Q;** What is **special verdict**?

A; This is when the defendant is found guilty by reason of insanity?

162) **Q:** What is the disease of the mind? (NOT the Brain)

A; The mind controls the mental faculties of reason memory and understanding. R.V. Kemp (1957) IQB.399.It is important to bear in mind that the condition of the brain is irrelevant. Lord Devlin put it The main thing is "defect of reason".

163) **Q;** what is **Non-insane automatism?**

A; The person has defect of reason due to a disease of the mind, he\she does not know the nature and the quality of his act or that he\she did not know what he is doing is wrong and not conscious of the action.

They could plea insanity if the offence happens when they are in that state.

164) **Q;** Name some diseases of the mind under none-insane automatism?

A: Epilepsy (R. v. Sullivan) (1984) AC156

Diabetes (R.v.Hennessy) (1989) 2 ALL ER9

Sleepwalking (R.v. Burgess) (1991)2 QB 92

165) **Q**: Describe non- insane automatism.

A: As this is often referred to as automatism. It involves unconscious conduct caused by some external factor (such as blow to the head to cause concussion) where there is no claim of insanity. A person is not criminally liable for acts carried out in a state of non- insane automatism since his conduct is all-together involuntary. Is the act done by muscle without control of the mind such as spasm, reflex action, convulsion or act of person not conscious of what he was doing which is known as involuntary act as the dower cannot remember

166) **Q:**Give case example of non-insane automatism?

A: Example case is Hill. v. Baxter (1958) 1QB 277 9 this involved dangerous driving, but he could not remember doing so.

167) **Q;** Can one claim non-insane automatism after the act?

A; Loss of memory after the act is not a defence. It is important to remember that when symptoms start such as diabetes, the person has to mitigate to prevent getting into serious problem. This could be where the symptoms are gradual like diabetes, the person has to eat or take insulin. If he failed to take such precaution then he\she cannot rely on non-insane defence as it could be regarded as being recklessness

Chapter 3.16

DIMINISHED RESPONSIBILITY:

168) **Q:** Explain Diminish responsibility

A; This can be found in section 52 (1) of Coroners and Justice Act 2009 and also section 2(1) of the Homicide Act 1957

169) **Q** Explain the Corona and Justice Act 2009?.

A; The Act state that a person is not to be convicted of murder if suffering from

1) abnormality of mental functioning

2) as result of recognised medical condition (explanation of the defendant act and omission)

3) Substantially impaired the defendant ability to rational judgement, and/or excess self-control which provides an explanation for his act or omission in doing or being party to the killing.

It can be used to defend a murder (specific intent)

A case; R.v. Byrne (1960) 2QB 390

170) Q; How could this be argued with someone with concussion?

A; Defendant could argue that the concussion was medical condition that impaired her mental function. The prosecution will argue that the defendant has the ability to understand the nature of his/her conduct, form rational judgement and to exercise self-control and that the impairment has to be substantially impaired.

171) Q; What happens if the defendant was drunk?.

A; If the defendant claims diminished responsibility because of intoxication, a medical expert has to establish that the alcohol had substantially impaired her ability. R.V. Dietschman (2003) 1 ALL ER 897.

Chapter 3.17

SOME CRIMINAL TERMINOLOGY(civil matter, summary, either way, Indictable, truly criminal, outlandish, exonerate, weakness, protagonist, intervene event, But for,)

172) Q; what are the two main elements in criminal case?

A; The two essential ingredients\elements to establish that defendant is guilty are: Actus reus and mens rea

173) Q; How is criminal action viewed?

A; Criminal action is seen as a case the state and hence express as R (Regina\queen).v. Defendant.

174) Q; What is a civil matter?

A; This is a matter\dispute between individuals, rather than the state.

175) Q; Name some criminal punishments?

A; There are wide range of punishments the court have to impose on guilty people include; imprison, rehabilitation, pay back through community service, deprivation of liability, protection of the public, example of vulnerable people like the young, elderly, disable. Punishment has limits as per the offence.

176) Q: What is the first thing that a lawyer to do in a case?

A; The lawyer has to double check the definition of the offence to find out the elements needed to defend the defendant.

177) Q; What do the type of offence prescribe by parliament?

A By statue or Act of parliament

178) Q: What precaution must the judge consider in common law?

A: Common law; Some by the court through case law and refer to as precedent.

In any case the court must see that all the elements of particular offence have been satisfied.

179) Q; Which court does criminal cases start?

A; Criminal cases start at magistrate court whose power is much lower than crown court.

180) **Q;** How are criminal offences classified?

A; They are classified as 1) summary 2)"either way" 3) Indictable

Summary offence is trial in magistrate court

Indictment cases are triad in crown court only such as murder, robbery, rape.

Either way cases could be tried in magistrates court or crown court depending on the seriousness example theft, assault.

181) **Q;** What is **truly** criminal?

A; These are those that cause physical and mental harm to the claimant.

182) **Q;** What is quasi- criminal?.

A; Lord Reid define quasi criminal as those " Which are not criminal in any sense but are act which in the public interest are prohibited under a penalty."

183) **Q:** Give an example of **quasi-criminal**?

A: Example of this is driving without a valid vehicle tax disc or failing to submit company account in time. In such cases it is against the law, but the public do not care as the police are there to enforce them.

184) **Q;** What is Outlandish?. And what test can be used?.

A; something which is strange, odd or bizarre.

The test of "But For" if used alone may be unfair to the defendant as it makes him responsible, no matter what outlandish things happen to their victim after they are attacked and before they die.

185) **Q;** What is Protagonis**t**?.

A; The leading character or the principal offender. The court is not keen to let the original protagonist off except in the most extreme cases.

186) **Q;** what is Exonerate?.

A; To acquit, clear a defendant for criminal offence

187) **Q:** Give example of **Exonerate**

A: Example; if "A" attack "B" and B taken to hospital but B was misdiagnose and wrong medication given and B dies, if it is established that the original injuries inflicted by A was partly to blame, then A would be found guilty.

188) **Q:** Explain Weakness/Vulnerability?

A; If someone frightens someone who have a heart attack and died, then the person be found guilty.

189) Q; Give example of outlandish?

A; There are some intervene event which might be unconnected such as natural disaster. Example; A attack B and B twisted her ankle as result while B was waiting in the A&E in the hospital, then a gun man short most of the people including B.

Court verdict; The court decided that A did not cause the death because the intervening event is completely unconnected. In this scenario, if the test "**BUT FOR**" is used the A would be not guilty because B went to the A&E due to An assault.

190) **Q;** What is Intervening event?.

A; Is incident that happen to result a person condition getting worse or even die.

191) **Q;** Give example of intervening event?

A:Example; A If A punch B to the ground, then C accidentally dropped a glass that break and wounded B.

Verdict; A will be found guilty because C did not have mens rea, C actus reus was accidental so A will be charged with GBH since A put B on the ground.

192) **Q:** What is needed to establish guilty in intervening event?

A; If causation cannot be established then the actus reus of the offence is not complete hence defendant must be acquitted. that is defendant action has to be established.

193) **Q;** What is the "**But For**" test

A; The but for test is used to decide causation; example A push B and B breaks his leg. An ambulance that was taken B to hospital involved in accident and B died. Who caused the death? Verdict; But for A not push B, B would not have been in the ambulance hence A is guilty
of murder

Chapter 3.18

BURDEN OF PROVE (civil liberty, evidential burden, rule of law, appropriate**)**

194) Q; who has to proof what;

A: The prosecution has to prove the burden of prove that the defendant is guilty of the offence because the law says "Person is presumed innocent until proven guilty"

195) Q; Give an example of case on burden of prove is on the prosecution?

A; Viscount Sankey who was the Lord Chancellor said, " Throughout the web of the English criminal law, one golden thread is always seen, that is the duty of the prosecution to prove the prisoner guilt" This was supported by champion of English justice; In Rumpole of the Bailey.

196) Q; How must the burden be proven?

A; The standard of proof prosecution must be absolute sure of a defendant guilty beyond a reasonable doubt.

197) Q: Why the standard of is prove so high?

A; This is because the defendant civil liberty, reputation at stake and must prevent miscarriage of justice. All the elements of charge have to be proved.

198) Q; What is evidential burden?

A; After the prosecution finished his or her evidence witnesses then the defendant have "evidential burden" to challenge.

199) Q; On what can the defendant use to challenge?

A; Defendant can prove his innocence outright or use some of the defences instrument such as insanity, diminished responsibility, provocation, duress act.

200) Q: What is the "**rule of law**"

A; No one can be found guilty or no criminal liability or innocent unless the rule of law is satisfied

There are two fundamental rules of law. First, it must be conduct specifically prescribed by law. Second, a proper and fair trial according to the procedure of the law

201) Q; Where do one find the offence law?

A; These are created by statute (parliament) and common law (courts through case law)

202) Q; Can defendant give any reason for offence?

A; Reason or why someone does criminal act, or something is not relevant. What is considered is the defendants mens rea

203) **Q**; What do you understand by **appropriate** in law?

A; This is suitable, right, to the point.

In criminal case, the procedure also has to be followed as they have to prove that there is evidence against the defendant that is why prosecution call their witness first. "Wilmington versus DPP (Director of public prosecution)

204) **Q;** give example of appropriate?

A: In section 1 of the theft Act 1968 it state "A person is guilty of theft if they dishonesty appropriate property belong to another with the indentation of permanently depriving that other of it.

Chapter 3.19

DIRECT AND INDIRECT INTENT

205) **Q;** What is Direct intent?

A; If one set out to do some damage (actus Reus) or kill, and one actually inflict the damage means that the person wanted to do it (mens rea). The person aim, purpose, goal desire, intention has been satisfied\achieved therefore a direct intent.

206) **Q;** what is Indirect or Oblique intent?

A; If someone wanted to set fire to destroy content of a house, but as the content destroy so are the occupies died.

207) Q; In what circumstances can one be found guilty in indirect intent?

A; a defendant can be found guilty if consequence was virtually certain to occur and being reckless. That the defendant foresaw the consequence as virtually certain to occur. As long as these two are have been satisfied then the defendant be found guilty as charged by indirect intent.

208) Q; What is **incapacitation**;

A; this a is a punishment that the court can impose on defendant. Is to deprive of, disable, out of action. A person committed crime, the court will punish him by ensure incapacitate of the offender liberty, rehabilitation, community work. It serves as deterrent to committee another crime and to protect the public.

Chapter 3.20

DISHONESTY (theft, subjective, objective Ghosh test), oblique intent, incapacitation)

209) Q; How is dishonesty defined?

A; The theft Act 1968 did not define dishonesty hence no actus reus or mens rea.

210) Q; How do one judge dishonesty?

A If the person action and he\she aware that the act is dishonest. The theft Act 1968 and Ghosh test can be used to judge dishonesty.

211) Q; how can one use theft Act to understand dishonesty?

A; section 2 (1) of the theft Act 1968 provide three subsection or situation test which one is applicable means the defendant is not dishonest (that is he is honest)

212) Q: What are these situations in the theft Act?

A: All three situations are **subjective test** that is asked you if the defendant believed that one of these situations outlined existed.

A) TA (theft Act0 1968 s.2 (1) a There was in law the right to deprive the person.

(if he think the person does not have legal right but have moral entitlement then section 2 (1)a does not apply)

B) TA (theft act0 1968 S.2 (1) b That the person has consented.

C) TA (theft Act) 1968 s2 (1) c That the other could not have been found by taking reasonable steps.

213) Q; what can **Ghosh** test be applied?

A; Ghosh test can be applied to all crimes that has dishonest in mens rea.

214) Q; what are the procedure to use Ghosh test?

A: The case R.V. Ghosh (1982) QB 1053. It is use in situation where section 2(1) of the theft Act does not apply.

215) Q: What two important questions a judge direct the July to as themselves to for honesty?

A: There are two questions that the jury must ask themselves to deduce honesty

First one is **objective test;** The jury is to ask themselves whether what was done was dishonest according to the ordinary standard of reasonable and honest people. If the answer is yes then they must ask

Subjective question/test;

216) Q: Give an example of subjective question/test?

A:The jury must ask themselves whether defendant realised that reasonable and honest people would regard what defendant did as dishonest. If the answer is yes then defendant is dishonest. If the answer is no then he is not dishonest.

Chapter 3.21

INFANTICIDE.

217) Q; what is infanticide?

A; The infanticide Act 1938.s.1 where a woman causes the death of her child who is under twelve months old.

218) Q; What diagnoses or circumstance to lead to infanticide?

A; There must be circumstances such as loss of control, insanity, diminish responsibility, however if these circumstances are not the case, a murder charge. Example Kai- white wind (2005) EWCA Crime 1092, the court of appeal ruled that there was no consideration for mitigation circumstance such as insanity. This resulted the reviewed of the infanticide law to consider circumstances.

219) Q: Give another example of infanticide?

A; Gore (2007) EWCA Crime 2789; A child was delivered at home unattended, few hours later the child was found in dune of sand near Gore house. Pathology reveal that child died from neonatal anoxia due to blocked air way. Gore pleaded guilty, CCRC refer the case back to appeal court due to circumstance of insanity diminished responsibility.

220) Q; What is the amended infanticide act of 1938 s. 36

A: The infanticide Act 1938 comes under The Coroners and Justice Act 2009 and it was section 1 and s. 2 amended

Chapter 3.22

LOSS Of CONTROL (recklessness, foresaw, transfer malice)

221) **Q:** What offence can loss of control are used?

A: Loss of control can only be used as partial defence for murder and not to any other crime.

222) **Q;** What is the test to establish loss of control?

A; There are two test 1) subjective test; was defendant provoked by things said or done outlandish to trigger. Objective test: Would the thing said or done make a reasonable person lose his self – controls

223) **Q;** What are elements of loss of control?

A; There are three elements to use self-control as partial defence for murder which must be satisfied Defendant act or/and omission in doing or a party to kill.

224) **Q;** What might trigger loss of control?

A; The loss of control has qualifying trigger (outlandish). A person of defendant sex and age, with normal degree of tolerance and self-restraint and in the circumstance of defendant might react.

225) **Q;** What is Recklessness?

A; There had been case laws to establish the criminal meaning of recklessness.

In case of T. v. Cunningham which is traditional test and is subjective requires that recklessness require proof that the defendant foresaw the risk and went on to take.

This was supported by R.V. Stevenson (schizophrenic who lit fire to haystack. That risk must be unreasonable to a normal reasonable person.

226) **Q**; What was the House of law verdict on these cases.

A: In a case MPC .v. Caldwell) this was objective test, the house of lords ruled out the above and introduced a second of two point.

A: Defendant foresaw a risk of damage or destruction and went on to take that risk Or

B; He failed to give it a thought to that risk of damage or destruction occurring.

This judgement resulted some confusion because not everyone is capable of foresee as reasonable person example Schizophrenic (Mr. Stephenson)

227) **Q;** What did the House of Lords decision on Caldwell case?.

A: The House of Lords overruled Caldwell in another case R.V. G (2003) by Lord Bingham

228) **Q;** What happened in R. v. Cunningham case?.

A; maliciously was replaced by recklessness that is the defendant involved foreseeing a risk and going on to take it without justification. This is final meaning and is subjective test.. No objective test needed.

229) **Q:** What is transferred Malice?

A; If someone have actus reus and manse rea to kill "A" if he kill unintended "B", then he is still guilty of murder. This is because the actus reus is to kill a human being and therefore satisfy both actus reus and manse rea (Human being) the authority case is R.V. Latimer).

230) **Q:** Give another example of transfer malice?

A: Transferred malice is general mens rea (not specific) example If one want to cause damage to one an person, his mens rea "malice" could be transferred to any unintended victim and he 'she will be responsible for the person damage.

This doctrine applies to any offence against people, animals properties.

231) **Q;** What is the exception to transferred malice?

A; There are two exception to the doctrine

1; If the nature of the transfer is not the same as what one aim, it then not guilty example If one throw a stone at human but it hit somebody's window then not guilty or to attempt GBH but cause criminal damage. The defendant might be guilty of another charge.

2; Defendant aim for assault not criminal damage which defendant did not have actus reus and manse rea.

232) **Q;** What is the manse rea of transferred malice?.

A; In court the Jury are to consider subjective view in making decision,

233) **Q** What is subjective test

A; that is to judge the defendant by what a reasonable person would have done or foresee. Or judge the defendant by what the state of mind. The jury are to judge if the defendant think what ordinary people think of his action. In other words the jury decide whether the defendant intend or foresee that result by reference to all the evidence as appear proper in the circumstances

234) **Q**; How do Jury be sure using subjective test.

A ; For someone to be guilty, the manse rea and actus reus must CONCIDE. There must be some sequence event.

Using the test "But for" must be established before criminal liability can be established example R.V. Le Brun and Thobo-meli.

235) **Q;** Name the section of Offence against person's act 1861?

A; Section 47, 18, 20.

236) **Q;** What is section 18 of offence against person?

A; To cause grievous bodily harm to "any person" that includes the claimant.

237) **Q;** What is section 20?

A; Is to cause GBH to any person but exclude the defendant.

Chapter 3.23

CRIMINAL ATTEMPT (inchoate crime, substantive offence)

238) **Q**; What law relate to criminal attempt?

A; The criminal attempt Act, 2) the criminal Act as amended by criminal attempts Acts 1981

239) **Q;** What does Inchoate offence mean (inchoate crime)

A ; any crime which is in its preliminary, undeveloped or just begun.

240) **Q:** What are the three main offence under attempt?

A; Attempt or inchoate started as common law but is now statute. The three main offence under this are a)attempt, b) conspiracy c) incitement

241) **Q;** What is substantive offence?

A; These are offence is intended to bring about even though the aim not achieve.

242) **Q;** What is the principal feature of Inchoate crime?

A; These crimes are deemed committed even though the substantive offence is not completed, and no harm done or result.

243) **Q**; What is the definition of attempt under criminal Attempt s.1 (1),2,3,4, 1981.

A; Section 1 of the Act state that if a person with intent to commit an offence (mens-rea), the person does the act which is more than merely preparatory to the commission of the offence (Actus Reus).He/she is guilty of attempting to commit the offence.

244) **Q;** Which court can section 1 (1) be triad

A; It is indictment offence and can be triad in crown court.

245) **Q;** Give an example of complete attempt.?

A: R . v . Mohan (1976) QB.1. “A” drove his car at a police man (intend to kill him).

Verdict; A was convicted of careless driving to cause GBH to police man.

246) **Q;** Give a case that support actus reus of attempt.?

A: R . v . Jones (1990) 3 All Er 886. Jones was convicted of attempted murder of boyfriend “F” of former girlfriend. “F” manages to get the gun from Jones.

Appeal Court; The court allow the appeal as the last stage was not commission (the finger on the trigger but not fired).

247) **Q;** Give another case to support attempt.?

A : R .v. Geddes (1996) Crim LR 894; The defendant entered and run away from school toilet when he saw a teacher, but left his rucksack containing a knife, rope and tape)

Court verdict; Appeal court allow appeal as he has not done more than preparatory for attempted false imprisonment.

248) **Q;** Give an example of manse rea of attempted (intend to commit the offence)

A;; R .v. Whybrow (1951) 35 Cr App R 141. The defendant wire up a soap dish to the electricity supply with intention to electrocute his wife

In R .v. Millard (1987) Crime LR 393. Defendant was convicted of intent to cause criminal damage (reckless) to properties.

249) **Q;** Give an example of **attempted offence.**

A; If “A” wants to steal “B” wallet but he stole C wallet by mistake.

Law; “B” was the target so “B” can sue “A”A for attempted theft and sue “A” for theft (theft Act 1967).

250) Q:What must prosecutor has to show in attempt offence?

A: To prosecute in this case, one has to show Actus reus that defendant took some steps to commission the theft but did not succeed. The mens rea is already established. These principles have questions by establishing Actus reus and mens rea

Chapter 3.24

ATTEMPT IMPOSSIBLE

251) Q; what law covers attempt impossible?

A: Criminal attempt Act 1981 section 1(2) and 1(3). A person may be guilty of attempting to commit an offence to which this section applies even though the facts are such the commission of the offence is impossible (Actus Reus)

252) Q; what does the criminal Attempt act 1981 section 1 (3a) state.

A; This state that in any case where apart from this section, a person intention (manse rea) would not be regarded as having amounted to an intent to commit an offence.

253) **Q**; What is section 1 (b).?

A; If the facts of the case had been as he believe them to be his intention will be so regarded, then for the purpose of section (1), he/she will be regarded as having had an intent to commit that offence.

254) **Q**; Give an example of attempt impossible?.

A: "A" is pickpocket expert, he put his hands in "B" pocket to steal the purse, but the pocket is empty. Verdict; In this case attempted theft was impossible but he had intention and commission (Actus) the fact that pocket was empty is irrelevant.

255) **Q;** Give another example of attempt impossible.

A; in a case R.shivpuri (1987) AC1; Shivpuri was caring a package of lawful harmless legal package, but he thought it was illegal drug such as cannabis or heroin.

Court Verdict: He was found guilty and the House of Lords dismissed his appeal because of his intent which made him guilty of attempting to know concern in dealing with illegal substance.

256) **Q;** what law covers attempt which cannot be attempted.

A; Criminal Law Act 1977 section 1

Chapter 3.25

CONSPIRACY (justification, recklessly, aiding, abetting, procuring)

257) **Q;** what statute law on attempt which cannot be attempted.

A; Section (4) of the criminal Attempt applies to any offence which, a) if it were completed would be friable in England and Wales as indictable offence other than (does not have to be completed).

b) Also Conspiracy (At common law or under section 1 of the criminal law Act 1977 or any other incitement

C) Aiding abetting, counselling procuring or suborning the commission of an offence.

d) Offence under section 4(1) assisting offenders or S.5 (1) which is accepting or agreeing to accept consideration for disclosing information about arrest able offence of the criminal law Act 1967.

258) **Q;** what is justification?

A; in criminal law, what defendant thought is justify is not issue. The court wants relevant concern by using a test "Would a reasonable honest person have considered there was any merit in taking that risk" (Coroner and Justice Act 2009 section 1).

One decision before trial is to decide the justification of the defendant Actus Reus.

259) **Q;** what is recklessly.

A; in criminal law recklessness involve foreseeing a risk and going on with what is one doing without justification and to take that risk. Or ought to have foreseen the risk.

260) **Q**; what is unlawful/strict liability.

A; is a crime "without a defence"

261) **Q**; How do you define maliciously.

A; in criminal law it could mean intentionally or recklessly. It could also be defined as "----the word maliciously does import upon the defendant---- an awareness t5hat his or her Act may have the consequence of causing some physical harm to some other person----"This was a case R.Mowatt by Lord Diplock.

Chapter 3.26

THEFT

262) **Q**; what is theft.

A; Section 1 (1) of the theft Act 1968 state that;

A person is guilty of theft if he/she 1) dishonestly 2) appropriate 3) property 4) belonging to another with the intention of 5) permanently depriving the other of it and thief and stealing shall be construed accordingly.

263) **Q;** what is Actus reus of theft?

A; Appropriate, property belonging to another without consent.

264) **Q**; what is manse rea of theft?

A; Dishonesty and intention to permanently deprive the other.

265) **Q**; what must be concise in prosecuting someone for theft?

A: The entire five elements must be present at one time before somebody can be regarded or charged with theft. For criminal liability, the Actus reus and mens rea must be concise.

266) **Q**; what is the definition of "appropriate"?

A; A dictionary definition is to take somebody ideals or something belonging to somebody for your own use, especially illegally or without permission.

267) **Q**; How does the law define Appropriate?

A; Appropriate as any assumption by a person of the rights of an owner and this include where he has come by property (innocently or not) without stealing it, any later assumption of a right to it by keeping or dealing with it as owner.

268) **Q;** what is property?

A: Tangible property include; money, real property, personal property, things in action.

There are intangible property as per section 4 (1) of 1968 Act

269) **Q;** Summarise Theft Act 1968?

A; Appropriation (s 3) TA 1968 R.v. Gomez, R .v. Hinks –Property –s.4 ---Belonging to another ---S.5 TA (exceptions—if clearly not applicable--- Dishonesty---S. 2 ---exceptions if clearly not applicable--- R .v. Ghosh – if clearly not available--- Dishonesty-----Intention to permanently deprive ---s.6 TA.

Chapter 3.27

"MAKING OFF WITHOUT PAYING"

270) **Q;** what law covers making off without paying?

A; the theft act 1978 section 3(1)

271) **Q;** Explain with reference to Actus Reus, making off **without paying**?

A; this is theft whereby one might go to a shop pick up item a goes off without paying.

The Actus reus include 1) Goods must be supplied or service done, 2) the defendant must make off from the spot where payment is required. 3) Without paying as required or expected.

272) **Q**; What is payment on the spot in "making off without payment"

A; Section 3 (2) of the theft Act 1978 defines "payment on the sport as including payment at the time of collecting goods on which work has been done or in respect of which service has been provided.

273) **Q;** what is mens rea of making off without payment?

A; This include 1) dishonesty as define in the theft act 1968 and also in a case R .v. Ghosh. 2) Knowledge that payment on the spot was required or expected. 3) Intention to avoid payment permanently

274) **Q:** Name some Act that came into force in 1861?

A) Offence against person's Act 1861

B) Accessory and Abettors Act 1861

C) Malicious damage Act 1861

It is interesting to know that American civil war between Federal union .v. Southern states was 1861 to 1865

Chapter 3.28

BATTERY

275) **Q;** what is the Actus reus of battery?

A; the defendant has inflicted unlawful personal violence on the victim.

276) **Q;** what is the mens rea of battery?

A: The defendant intended to inflict the unlawful personal violence or was reckless as to such infliction.

Chapter 3.29

ROBBERY

277) **Q;** Explain robbery?

A; Robbery comes under section 8 of the theft Act 1968. It is regarded as aggravated theft as it combine theft and violence where defendant use force or threat and cause the another to fear immediately before or in order to steal.

Since robbery is more serious of theft, one must consider all the five element of theft Act 1968 section (2) 1 a, b, c. which cover Actus reus and mens rea. Therefore to convert someone of theft the prosecution must proof theft.

It is also worth knowing that using force or threat could cover thief to robbery.

278) **Q;** When is no robbery?

A: If there is no theft then no robbery. Therefore all five elements of theft must occur (Actus reus and mens rea).

If however one of the elements is missing the defendant could still be charged of attempted robbery or common assault.

279) **Q;** what is Actus reus of robbery?

A; a) that the defendant stole (i.e. committed offence of theft as define in s.2 (1 a,b,c of the theft Act 1968. And

b) Either that the defendant used force on any person or put or sought to put any person in fear of being then and there (immediately) subjected to force

c) That the force or threat was immediately before or at the time of the theft.

d) That the force or threat of force was used in order to steal

280) **Q**; Name two cases of robbery?

A; R.v. Dawson (1976) 64 Cr APP R 170.

R.v.Clouden (1987) Crim LR 56

Chapter 3.30

BURGLARY/GBH

281) **Q;** which law covers burglary?

A; Burglary involve aggravated property offence and is under section 9(1) a and 9 (b) and also section 9 (2) of the theft Act 1968.

282) **Q;** define section 1 (a) of the theft Act 1968.

A; Burglary is committed when one a) enter b) any building or part of building as C) trespasser d) **intending** to commit one of the offences listed in

Section 9 (2) include theft, inflicting of grievous bodily harm or criminal damage.

283) **Q;** Explain conditional intent?

A; this could be express as “once inside “I will steal” or threat the person “I will break his/her leg”

The House of Lords say that conditional intent to steal or GBH or criminal damage was sufficient to be convicted.

284) **Q;** Define section 9 1 (b).

A; Burglary is committed when one a) enter b) any building or part of a building d) as trespasser (without consent) and e) commit theft or inflict GBH (grievous bodily harm or **attempt** (extra element) to steal or to inflict grievous bodily harm.

In this section the extra element is intent.

285) **Q;** What is the deference between (.1(a) and 9 (2) of the theft Act 1968

A; a) In 9 (1) b, the additional element is that once inside the building he/she **attempted** to steal. There may not be criminal damage.

b) In section 1. (a) it state the intention to steal theft act 1968 s.3, GBH Offence against person Act 1861 of Criminal damage 1971l

286) **Q:**Explain inflicting GBH in both Section 9 1 am and section 9.1 b of the theft Act 1968?

A; a) in section 9.1 (a0 is only intention to inflict GBH enough.

b) In section 1 (b) there must be a **prove** of causing GBH

287) **Q;** What defence can be used in Burglary?

A; All defence or partial defence are available for burglary example;

To use defence under Theft Act 1968 section 2 (1) a, the defendant must honestly believe that he/she has legal right to the property

b) Can use self-defence for inflicting grievous bodily harm when he was inside (using this might result not guilty verdict.) The criminal law Act 1967 s.3 provide element of self-defence.

c) Defendant could plea that it was accident in inflicting GBH

d) Other defence include 1) lawful excuse 2) insane) none insane automatism, diminished responsibility.

288) **Q;** what is the Actus reus of Burglary?

A; under section 9 1(a) of the Theft Act 1968 the element are a) Enter b) building (or part of the building) c) as trespasser. If this element cannot be established then there is no burglary committed.

289) **Q;** what is the Mens rea of Burglary?

A; Intention to commit to commit one of the offences such as theft, inflicting GBH

290) **Q;** what does the court say about consent to burglary?

A; in a case R.V. Collins (1973)1QB 100 the court of appeal confirm that a person would be trespassing if;

b)The one in fact enter without consent and b) At the time of that entry, he or she knew he was entering without consent or was at least recklessness as to whether or not he had permission to enter.

Chapter 3.31

ARSON

291) **Q;** Define Arson?

A; Arson is intentional or reckless destruction or damaging of property by fire without "lawful excuse"

292) **Q:** What is Arson under the law?

A; under section 3 of the criminal Damage act 1971, Arson is destruction on damaging property by fire shall be charged of arson. The defendant will be triad on indictment and be liable to imprisonment for life.

293) **Q**; why is Arson trial as indictment?

A; although arson is not indictment of criminal damage, it could still be trial under indictment because the punishment could be for life imprisonment whilst other criminal damage is punishment is up to ten years in prison example the case R.v. Cooper and Cooper (1991) crim.L. R. 524

Chapter 3.32

SELF-DEFENCE

294) **Q;** When can a defendant use self-defence as defence?

A; In section 76 of the criminal and immigration Act 2008 and a statutory defence under s.3 (1) of the criminal law Act 1967 of reasonable use of force in preventing crime.

A defence recognise that a person may use such force as is reasonable in the circumstance as honestly believes them to be in the defence of oneself or another

295) **Q;** what is the condition in using reasonable force.

A; a) the force used in the circumstance must be assesses objectively.

b) Force will not be “reasonable” where it is proportionate unless in a householder.

296) **Q;** What about if the defendant has made a mistake?

A; However if the defendant has made a mistake about the circumstance, the reasonableness of the force will be assessed on the basis of the facts as he honestly believe them to be. This is supported by a case R. v. William (Gladstone) (1984) 78 Cr App R 276.

Chapter 3.33

CONSENT

297) **Q;** in offence against person Act 1861, when can consent be used?

A; the House of Lords agreed that consent must only be used as defence to sections 47, 20, 18 of offence against person Act 1861. If the activity was in the public interest such as games (football, boxing, rugby act).

The Lords ruled out sado-masochism as it involves violence and sex.

298) **Q;** When can consent be varied?

A; The House of Lords state that for consent to be varied, the identity of the person (opponent) and the nature and quality of the act which the consent is based.

Chapter 3.34
COWARD as defence

299) **Q;** when can one use weak willed or coward as defence?

A: In a case of r. V. Graham (1982)74 Cr APP R . 235, the House of Lords stated two elements which must be satisfied. 1) The defendant must take part in the crime because of the threat, but also the court must consider reasonable test that is 2) Reasonable person of reasonable firmness sharing the same characteristics of the defendant would have responded in the same way by caring out the crime.

Chapter 3.35
CRIMINAL GANGS

300) **Q**; what happen if a person belonging to criminal gangs commit a crime?

A; The House of Lords (Lord Lane CJ stated; “where a person has voluntarily and with knowledge of its nature joined a criminal organisation or gang which he knew might bring pressure on him to commit an offence and was active member when he/she was put under such pressure, the one cannot avail oneself of the defence of duress"

The cases to support this are R.V. Sharp (1987) 1 QB 853 and R.v. Hasan (2005) 2 AC 467

301) **Q;** what does the law say about smacking children?

A; The covers reasonable chastisement on children state that a mild smacking that physical punishment causes visible bruising, grazes, scratches, minor swelling or cuts are unlawful and conviction carries five years in prison.

Chapter 3.36

SEXUAL OFFENCE. Assault, rape, consent intoxication, presumption)

302) **Q;** what was the date of sexual offences Act?

A; the first one was 1956

Second one was 1997 which was implement in 2001

Third one was 2003 (20/11/2003) and came into effect on 01/05/2004.

303) **Q:** What section of the sexual offence covers rape?

A; section one the 2003 Act.

304) **Q;** what section covers assault by penetration?

A; section 2

305) Q; what section covers sexual assault?

A; Section 3

306) Q; what section covers where children are victim?

A; Section 5 to 7 and section 13.

307) Q; what did the old law said about husband and wife?

A; The old law said, on marriage, a woman was consenting to sexual intercourse with the husband whenever he wanted.

This was the House of Lords decision in a case of R.v. R (1991) 4 All ER 481.

308) Q; When and what section can law on rape and was extended to men and women.

A; Criminal Justice and Public order Act 1994 stated that victim of rape could be men or women., this considers those who have underwent surgery to change their sex can commit S.1 or s.2 of the 2003 Act.

309) Q: What is the element of rape?

A; There are two definitions in the Actus reus of rape

a) The penile penetration by a person (defendant) of a vagina, anus or mouth of another (victim)

2) Who (the victim) at the time does not consent to the penetration and the defendant must be at least ten years old.

310) **Q;** Can a woman rape? If not then how can he be charged?

A; No but can be charged as accomplice (if she suggest or restrains the victim).

311) **Q:** What is penetration in the Act 2003?

A; Penetration is continues act according to sexual offence Act 2003 s. 79 (2).

312) **Q;** at what stage is consent?

A: If a woman or man gives consent at the beginning, but if during the penetration or at any time during the Act, the woman said “NO” or “stop” and if the defendant continue a second after that and do not withdraw then it became rape.

Example case is R.v.Kaitamaki (1985) AC 147.

313) **Q;** Define consent as in SOA 2003 s.74.

A; A person consent if he or she agrees by choice and have capacity to make that choice.

314) **Q;** what happen if the defendant put pressure or deceive the victim?

A; In a case R.v.Jheeta (Havinder Sing) 2007 EWCA Crim. 1699. The court of appeal stated that the complainant choice for consent was not free.

315) **Q;** what are it and how many elements in mens rea for rape?

A; There are positive and negative element

The positive is the defendant must be intentionally and deliberately penetrate the victim vagina, anus or mouth (mens rea)

The negative mens rea is there is lack or absence of reasonable belief in consent.

Example case; R.V. Cunning and R.v. G.

316) **Q;** Define sexual assault by penetration?

A: Under section 2 of sexual offence Act 2003, sexual assault replaces indecent assault.

Definition is by Actus reus and mens rea

317) **Q;** what is Actus reus of sexual assault?

A; this is element that a defendant "A" penetrate the vagina or anus of "B" (victim" with any part of "A" body or anything else. That the penetration is sexual, that "B" does not consent to the penetration (i.e. using finger, toes. tongue or vibrator)

318) **Q:** What is the mens rea of sexual assault;

A; This element is "A" intentionally (deliberately) penetrate of "B" vagina or anus "2) lack of reasonable belief by the defendant "A" that victim "B" consented.

Section 2 offence can be committed by man or woman as penetration can be with any part of the body or anything.

319) **Q;** What is the definition of sexual assault under section 3 of the sexual offence Act
2003?

A; This is less offence which involve touching which is sexual; example "A" intentionally torches another person "B" and that the torching is sexual, that "B" does not consent to the torching, and "A" does not reasonable belief that "B" consent.

320) **Q**; Define sexual as in sex offence Act 2003?

A; Under this section, sexual is define as any penetration, torching or any other activity, if a reasonable person consider it sexual because of the nature and circumstances or because of its nature, circumstance, purpose or motive. This is objective.

321) **Q;** Define **purpose**

A; Purpose is important to decide whether or not the torching is sexual.

322) **Q;** Define torching under section 78 (8)

A: Torching is define inclusively by section 78 (8) as torching with any part of the body, or with anything else, or through anything in particular touching that amount to penetration such as using object or through their clothes.

RAPE

323) **Q;** what is Actus reus of rape? (assault by penetration)

A; A penile penetration by the defendant of the vagina, anus or mouth of another person with a part of the defendant body or anything

b) That the penetration is sexual

c) That the victim does not consent to the penetration.

324) **Q;** what is the mens rea of rape? (assault by penetration)

A; Intentional (deliberate) penetration of victim vagina, anus or mouth (this is
Positive element) b) and absence of reasonable belief victim consent (this is negative element)

325) **Q:** What statute define attempted rape

A: The sexual offence Act 2003 did not cover attempted rape so the criminal attempt Act 1981 section 1 (4)

326) **Q;** What is the Actus reus of **attempted rape**

A; A defendant does an act more than merely preparation to commission penetration without victim consent.

327) **Q;** What is manse rea of attempted rape

A; Defendant intent to penetrate without consent.

328) **Q:** What is the leading case in attempted rape?

A; R.V. Khan (1990) 2ALLER783. The mental element is distinction between "act" (penetration) and their circumstance (lack of consent on the part of the victim)

329) **Q;** what is the definition of consent under the sexual offence Act?

A; A person consents if he or she agrees by choice, and has the freedom and capacity to make that choice.

330) **Q;** what did the High court advice where the torching is not by nature "sexual" to consider?

A; The high court advice jury to ask two questions;

a) Would the Jury as 12 reasonable people consider that touching could be sexual?

b) Whether the jury as 12 reasonable people and in all circumstances of the case, would consider that the purpose of touching had in fact been sexual?

331) **Q**: What is the difference between defendant and victim of sexual offence in intoxication?

A; In a case R.v. Heard (2007)3WLR 475, the court of appeal decided under section 3 of 2003 Act defence as result of intoxication is " basic intent" which means that defendant cannot use intoxication to deny mens rea (guilty mind).

332) **Q:** Which section is specific intent?

A: Section 3 of the sexual offence Act 2003 is a crime of specific intent and it required proof of intentional touching, but sexual touching is not a crime of specific intent.

The similarity between section 1, 2, 3, of the sexual offence Act 2003; the manse rea are the same that is intention to torch and lack of consent.

Chapter 3.37

PRESUMPTION

333) **Q**; what is presumption?

A; Section 76 (2) (a,b) Set out two irrebutable presumption conclusive of rape or sexual activity, that lack of consent may be presume and that the defendant did not believe that the complainant consented to the relevant sex act

Section 75 (2) a, b, c, d, e, f, set out six circumstances which are a rebuttable presumption arises.

334) **Q:** What does 76 (2a) state? Of the sexual offence Act

A; "the defendant intentionally deceived the complainant as to the nature and purpose of the relevant "act" (intercourse)

335) Q: What does 76.s 2b of the sexual offence Act?

A; Section 2b state that "The defendant intentionally induced the complainant to consent to the relevant act (sex) by impersonate a person know personally to the complaint. Example a man disguises himself as the victim boyfriend or identical twins deceive the victim The consent given is void, rebuttable evidential presumptions about consent

336) Q: What does section 75 say about consent?

A; Section 75 (1) state that if the has or did the act (sex) b) that the circumstances specified in s. 75 (2) existed and defendant aware they existed. It will be presume that the complainant did not consent unless sufficient evidence to rebut otherwise.

337) Q: What are the circumstances in section 75 to support evidence presumption?

A; There are six presumptions

1) Any person was, at the time of relevant act or immediately BEFORE it began; using violence against the complainant to or causing the complainant to fear that immediate violence would be used against another person.

2) Any person was at the time of the relevant act or immediately BEFORE it began causing the complainant to fear that violence would be used against another person

3) The complainant was, and the defendant was not, unlawful detained at the time of the relevant act (kidnap)

4) The complainant was asleep or otherwise unconscious at the time of the relevant act.

5) Because of the complainant physical condition/disability, the complainant would not have been able at the time of the relevant act to communicate to the defendant whether the complainant consented.

6) Any person had administered to or caused to be taken by the complainant, without the complainant consent a substance which, having regard to when it was administered or taken was capable of causing or enabling the complainant to be stupefied or overpowered at the time of the relevant act.

338) **Q;** what happens in intoxication in sexual assault?

A; Victim intoxication means that they may lack the capacity to consent to relevant sexual offence.

339) **Q;** Can defendant rely on intoxication for sexual offence?

A; in voluntary intoxication, the defendant will not be able to rely own intoxication in relation to a mistaken belief in a victim's consent.

Chapter 3.38
CHILDREN UNDER 13 IN SEXUAL OFFENCE

340) **Q;** what is the differing between section 1-3 and 5-7 of the sexual offence Act 2003.

A; Section 5-7 plus s.13 dealt with sexual activity for children as victim.

There is strict liability as to age and consent for victim under 13 which means neither consent of the victim or the defendant's belief in consent is relevant issues.

341) **Q;** what are mens rea for children under section 5-7 for children under 13 years of age?

A; The **mens rea** for section 5 & 6 is intentional penetration and for section 7 is for sexual touching.

342) **Q;** what are the Actus reus for children under 13 (s.5-7)?

A; For section 5 and 6 are sexual penetration of victim's vagina, anus or mouth where victim is under 13.

Actus reus under section 7 is sexual touching.

343) Q; Explain section 9 of the sexual offence Act 2003?

A; Section 9 (1) state a person age 18 or over commits an offence if he intentionally touches another person, b) and the toughing is sexual. C) and if the victim is under 16 and does not reasonable belief that victim is 16 or over or victim is under 13. Defendant is guilty as charged.

344) Q; What does section 9 (2) of the sexual offence Act 2003 say?

A; It is an offence if touching involve penetration of the victim's anus or vagina with a part of the defendant body or anything else. Or

Penetration of the victim's mouth with the defendant penis.

Penetration of the victim anus or vagina with a part of defendant's body

Penetration of victim mouth with defendant penis.

345) Q; Who can commit offence under section 9?

A: This section can only be committed by defendant who is 18 or over and victim is either under 13 or under 16 (without consent).the maximum sentence is 14 years.

346) Q; What about defendant who is 18 or under?

A; Section 13 of the sexual offence Act 2003 is replica of section 9 (over 18) but the sentence is 5 years or under.

347) Q: Can a child of 12 be guilty of sexual offence?

A; Yes a child of 12 in a case of Rivet (2009)2 WLR 1088.

348) Q: What was the rule of thumb?

A: This abolished law state that a man could beat his with if she misbehaves and that on marriage the woman consent to obey the man's wishes.

Chapter 3.39

FRAUD

349) Q; What is the Fraud Act?

A; The fraud Act 2007 is CONDUCT crime and no need to prove that any result ensure. Dishonesty played major part in assessing fraud. DPP V. Ray.

350) Q; When does fraud occurs?

A; Fraud occurred as soon as the false representation is made. There is no need for any consequences as long as the defendant has the requisite manse rea.

351) Q; In the 2006 Act what replaces by fraud?

A; In the Act Fraud replace deception

352) Q: What did the law commission comment?

A: This is section 2 of the fraud Act 2006 in which the law commission emphasis on simple clear law would be fairer for both the legal team and the defendant.

353) **Q;** What happened to the common law?

A; The government did not abolish the common law on fraud which is more flexible to use as it include conspiracy/collaboration.

354) **Q;** What is the important of Fraud Act 2006?

A; According to the Act 2006 the main points is not misled but "simple to the defendant dishonestly making a false representation with intention of making a gain for himself or another or causing loss to another.

355) **Q;** What happen if the gain or loss is temporary?

A; It is immaterial if the gain or loss is temporary. immediately it's made fraud occurs.

356) **Q;** What was repealed after the 2007 fraud Act?

A: Deception offences in sections 15, 15A, 16 and 20 (2) of the theft Act 1978. There are more specific which the Act covers (please research).

357) **Q**; What is the meaning of false representation?

A; Representation is fact or law including representation as to the state of mind of the defendant such as intention, opinion, implied. This can be express in words or communicate by conduct, written or spoken or website.

358) **Q;** What is **Actus reus** of fraud by representation?

A; Sections 2 (1) and (2) of 2007 fraud Act state that the Actus reus is making representation (conduct) and that the representation is false (circumstance) s. 2 (2).

359) **Q;** What is the **mens rea** of fraud by misrepresentation?

A; The mens rea include;

a) Be honest

b) Intend by making the representation to make a gain for one self or cause loss to another or to expose another to risk of loss.

c) Know that the representation is, or might be untrue or misleading. (s.2 (2). Intention to gain or make loss.

360) **Q;** Does the defendant mens rea only needed?

A; No It include second participant and the accomplice.

There is a link in the mens rea example being dishonest, intend to make a gain for oneself and/or another and to cause loss to the victim.

361) **Q;** Summarise the element of fraud by false representation?

A; using key; Actus Reus=AR, mens rea=M, D =defendant

1) AR—D made false representation (s2 (2a), s.2 (3) s.2 (4), s2 (5) of the fraud Act 2006

2) MR; D know the representation was or might be untrue or misleading) s.2 (2) b

3) MR; D intend to make gain for him/herself or cause loss to another.

4) MR-Was D dishonest (s.2 (1) a and R.v.Ghsh

5) Then D is guilty of fraud irrespective of loss or reliance on representation.

362) Q; How are the law deals with cheque and credit cards?

A; a) If cheque is used and the donor know that there is no money in the account then it is fraud.

b) If cheque is used and supported by cheque guarantee card that is also fraud.

c) If one use credit card, knowing there is no money or over spends, that is fraud

Example case is MPC.v.Chartes (1977) AC 177.

363) Q; What about using the pin of credit card to withdraw?

A; Using one pin to withdraw or self-service, when bank has inform you not to use, is regarded as false representation section 2.5 of the fraud Act 2007.

364) **Q:** How is property covered in fraud?

A: The fraud Act 2006 and the Human right Act Article 1 protocol 1, property means money, things in action and other intangible property.

365) **Q;** How does being silence relate to fraud?

A; If one sells property or offers service and been aware that there is fault but said nothing, it is fraud. If however the person did not know that there is fault and sell the item and as long as the purchaser did not ask, then it is not lie and not implied misrepresentation.

366) **Q;** Give an example of the right to be silent?

A; Rice.v.Connolly (1966) 2 QB 414

Chapter 3.40

Police (Pace, silence, Act)

367) **Q;** What happened in PACE (police and criminal evidence) section 34 (to remain silent)

A; This allows the court to draw adverse conclusion. example Murray.v.U.K (1996) 22EHRR 29

368) **Q;** What does the European Article on silence?

A: Article 6 (2) delete Pace s. 34 in that "It is presumption of innocence not to incriminate himself in criminal procedure and therefore, it is the prosecution to proof beyond reasonable doubt and not for the accuse to proof his innocence

369) **Q;** What can lead police to abuse their power?

A; The wording in section 24 a (2) state "---May act on reasonable suspicion.

370) **Q:** What can give rise to police being challenged?

A; Most police powers are discretionary

371) **Q;** Give an example of defendant being given access to solicitor?

A; example case is Ireland. V. UK (1978) 2 E H RR. The evidence would be void.

372) **Q;** What happens to escape unlawful arrest

A; example of a case is Kenlin.v.Gardner (1967) 2 QB 510, the defendant can claim compensation under s. 89

373) **Q;** Give an example of unacceptable police statement?

A: It is not acceptable for police to say that " ---It is necessary---in cause of duty" example R.v. Waterfield (1964) 1 QB 164.

374) **Q;** What police order control Marching?

A; POA (police Order Act) 1986 section 12 imposes control on March while it took place

Also police have common law powers to prevent a breach of the peace

375) **Q:** What European article can police rely on protesters?

A; Police can rely on limitation in Article 10 (2) and article 11(2) to justify restriction on protesters, provided police complied by the principle of proportionality.

This is because Article 10 (right to freedom of expression and article 11 (freedom of peaceful assembly) are qualified and therefore can be restricted as long as prescribed by law, legitimate and necessary in democratic society.

376) **Q;** What else does Article 10 (20 and 11(2) give to police.

A; Police as public authority and independence execution have obligation to maintain public peace. Section 6 of Human right Act.

Example case is R (Daly's. Secretary of state for the Home department

377) **Q;** What does Police Order Act 1986 section 14?

A; This gives police power to impose condition if police have reasonable believe that there might be serious public disorder PACE (police and criminal evidence) include power to arrest and search

Chapter3.41

(criminal liabilities)

Scenario

378) **Q;** Name three cases of criminal liability by omission?

A; **R v Instan** (1893)1 QB 450

R .v Stone and Dobinson (1877) 1 QB 354 (1977) 1 QB 354 (1977) 2 ALL ER 341

R.v. Ruff ell (2003) EWCA Crim 122

379) **Q:** Summarise ; **R v Instan** (1893)1 QB 450

A: R.v. INSTAN (1893)

A: The defendant lived with her 73-year-old aunt who was healthy until 12 days prior to her death when she developed gangrene. She was incapacitated and unable to summon outside help. The defendant was the only one aware of his condition but failed to provide her aunt with food or seek medical assistance's aunt died and the defendant was convicted of her manslaughter with her appeal dismissed.

380) **Q;** What was the verdict in the above case (R.v. Instan (1893)

A; Defendant was found guilty. The negligent of the defendant failed to provide the aunt with food, nor seek medical assistant for her cost the aunt her death .

381)Q; What was the reason of the court decision on R.V**. Instan** (1893)

A; Defendant was convicted of manslaughter, His appeal was dismissed by Lord Coleridge, CJ Defendant means read (intention to cause harm with consequence of death. Actus rues were the failure to discharge her legal duty to the aunt.

382) **Q:** Why was the judge in favour of moral obligation?

A: The judge placed a lot of emphasis on moral obligation to close blood relative, that is legal duty in common law to show duty of care as paramount especially to vulnerable relative who is part of the house hold. Judge said "---legal duty is founded on moral obligation—the defendant was accommodated and fed with the deceased money".

Deceased relied totally on the defendant for right of life. The defendant failure to implement common law duty accelerated the aunt death. Whilst there was no precedent case directly, Lord Coleridge CJ said "---It would be slur upon and discredit to the administration of justice in this country if there were any doubt as to the legal principle, or as to the present case being within it".

383) Q: What was the court of appeal findings?

A: The court of appeal (Coleridge LJ) find a clear common law duty on the defendant to impact to the deceased such that was necessary to sustain life and that the defendant did not disc arched at duty at least accelerating death of the deceased, if it did not obligation to the defendant from which arise a legal duty towards her which one wilfully and deliberately left under performs (accelerating death).The court of appeal accordingly rejected the Appeal

384) Describe similar case:

A: Similar opposite case was judgement by Erie C.J in R v. Charlotte Smith (1865) 10 Cox 82 (where a master was not convicted of homicide for his failure to give his servant sufficient food and lodging).Erie continued "The law is undisputed that, if a person having the care or custody of another who is helpless, neglect to supply him with the necessaries of life and there by causes or accelerate his death, it is criminal offence. But the law is clear, that if a person having the exercise of free will chooses to stay in a service where bad food and lodging is provided, the death is thereby caused the master is not criminal liable

385) Q: Summarise R .v. Stone and Dobinson

A: "S" who was 67 partially deaf nearly blind and of low intelligence lived with D (43) described as "ineffectual" and in "adequate" also living with them was S 'S subnormal son. In 1972 "F", S's younger anorexic sister came to live with them. She stayed in her room most of the time, albeit she was known to creep down to the kitchen to cook when S and D went out. S and D tried to find "F" 'S doctor but she would not assist. By jury D and a neighbour washed "F" when she was bedridden and double incontinent...The "D"'s due to their limitations were unable to use the phone and the neighbour was unable to get a local doctor to visit F No one was informed of F condition despite frequent visit from social worker to see S's son. F died in August having needed urgent medical attention for days if not week's .S and was charged and convicted of manslaughter.

386) Q: What was the court verdict?

A: The court found 1) the D undertook the care of an infirmed person unable to care for herself.2) that D was grossly negligence with regard to that duty of care 3) By reasoning of the negligence3 "V" died i.e. the negligence caused V's death.

A:The court found further that D'S did make effort to care as such the Jury were entitled to find that duty had been assumed by the V's and once helplessly infirm D's under duty to summon held or care for V themselves. So having under taken the duty of care as in (1) above for a blood relative staying in their house they were liable for their negligence for failing to adequately perform that duty.

387) Q; Summarise R.v. Ruff ell (2003) EWCA Crim 122

A; D failed to render assistance to V who has passed out after taking drugs at D's house. Having seen V was unconscious "D" made some effort to revive him and telephoned his mum lying that he was sick due to too much alcohol and that he was sitting on the doorstep of his house. V'S mum asked D to take him in doors and cover him with a blanketed agreed, but did nothing and died from hyperthermia and opiate intoxication.

388) Q: What was the Appeal court decision (r. v. Ruffell) (2003) EWCA crim. 122.

V became ill in "D" house so "D" d had duty of care owes to V even though he was not a blood relative and not a lodger. The court felt that the fact that V was in D house and D assume responsibilities Total duty of care for "V". D lied to V mother which resulted the mother not given appropriate advice such as to call the ambulance since drugs (mixture of cocaine and heroin) was more serious that of alcohol intoxication.

Brett. J. in R. v. Nicholls (1875)13 Cox 75 "If a grown person chooses to undertake the charge of a human creature helpless either from infancy, simplicity, lunacy or other infirmity, he is bound to execute that charge without (at all event) wicked negligence.

389) **Q:** Summarise the case of **R. stone and Dobinson** (1977) IQ .B.354 (summary)

A; "S" was 67 years old partial deaf and mental retarded, lived with 43-year-old "D" (inadequate to deal with situation) who was effectively also carer for "S" mentally subnormal son. In 1972, they accepted S younger sister "F" who was suffering from eating disorder (anorexia nervosa) who was known not to care for herself including cooking for herself.

In 1975 "F" refused to tell S & D the name of his doctor. "F" condition deteriorated became bedridden and double incontinent (of urine and faeces) and could not fens herself. One day D was helped by the neighbour to wash F. but defendant did not know how to use the phone (he is retarded) and the neighbour could not get the local doctor to visit S &D did not even alerting the social worker who did come to see "S" son."F" died in August and post mortem revealed lack of medical attention.

390) Q: What is the decision and why on the case of **R. stone and Dobinson** (1977) IQ .B.354 (summary)

A; S and D were convicted of manslaughter and appealed dismissed.

The main reason that "F" came to S and D was to be given physical care (or summons for medical assistance) such as feeding "S" and "D" saw gradual deterioration of her health but defendant . Both had no menses rea, but their acts rues were not total to save him. The court felt that they should have make pro-active effort for care including call for help emergency service such as ambulance or social services when condition got worse. The court appreciated the partial care but was not total.

Geoffrey Lane L.J cited three mains reasons to dismissed the appeal; that the defendant accepted the responsibility to care for the infirm person,2) their grossly negligence to discharge care duty led to the death of blood relative of S who was one of the houses holds. 3)" That by reason of such negligence "F" died.

COMMENT ;the jury appeared not to take into consideration of defendant mental retarded and couldn't even care for themselves.

391) Q; Summaries for all the three cases and the effect of R.v.Insan (1893) 1qb

For r. v. stone and Robinson (1977)1qb 354 (1977) 2 ALLER 341 and R.v.Ruffell (2003 ewca crime 122.explain how you consider they developed the law from R.v.Instan (1893) 1qb 450.

A; All three come under law of omission.

R.v. Instan, Lord Coleridge CJ made this case a precedent or common law when he said "There is no case directly in point; but it would be a slur upon a discredit to the administration of Justice in this country if there were any doubt as to the legal principles, or as to the present case being within it “and stated that “----every legal duty is founded on moral obligation”

He introduce obligation direct proportion to legal duty enforce by common law especially the helpless or infirm expect duty of care (from a note included a relative living with you in the same house hold)

In R.V. Stone and Dobinson, Geoffrey Lane L.J was specific that a **blood relation** or a **lodge**r who is part of the house hold and who become infirm or helpless expect total duty of care from the able person which include arrange for external service to step in.

R.V. Ruffell, This duty of care went further to include a visitor to a host who became ill, that partial duty of care not accepted be regarded and can be convicted of manslaughter. The HRA 1998 article 2 and 3 come to play in support of the common law started in R. Insan.

These three cases are example of how common law elements are created and the expanded. All the deceased were adult vulnerable, helpless. The defendant was awarded of the consequence of the circumstances and foresaw or ought to have foreseen the consequences. All three cases breached section 5 of domestic, violence, crime and victim act 2004 as amended in 2012.

All defendants are aware of significant risk by their unlawful act.

(Distinguishable from Instan as "D" did nothing in that case exercise their duty but were just fatally useless at so doing.)

Instan was duty of care to helpless infirm relative who died of neglect,(Duty from the start) extended in S and D where still a blood relative to one D same care is provided by D (hampered by their own lack of mental and physical faculties) but partly so as the V still dies due to inadequate fulfilment of the duty of the duty of care to provide adequate care(the required stranded of care appears not to diminished even where they Would be carers are of low intelligence and cannot really look after themselves) (duty acquired and relative)

Ruffell extend the obligation to a visitor, a non –blood relative who became amiably helpless again whilst some steps were taken by D to care the inadequacy by the steps taken still resist in the death of V and connection of D. Thus once the duty is undertaken as D can't simply wash his hands of it (duty acquired by limited assistance and acknowledgement of V's helplessness).

Chapter 3.42

GANG

392) Q : summarise this scenario on gang?

A; Jake is being initiated as a member of a gang called the Boston Boyz. Gang culture is extremely wide spread in the area where he lives. There have been some shootings and beatings of rival gang members by the Boston Boyz in the last couple of weeks in which Jakes has not been involved.

Jakes initiation task involves a street fight with another new recruit, Kyle. Jake and Kyle are both keen to prove that they are good fighters. Jake brings with him a flick knife just in case he uses to use it. He conceals the flick knife in the pocket of his jeans.

During the fight, Kyle and Jake exchange numerous punches and both suffer some bruising. Kylie seems to be winning. Believing, he might lose, Jake pulls out the flick knife and tries to slash Kyle on the arm and causes a cut about an inch long which requires stitches.

After the fight, Jake is told he will have to one final initiation task involving a shooting. Jake is unsure about this and tells Latif, the gang leader, that he does not want to be involved. Latif tells him he is either in the gang or not and gives Jakes a hand gun and shows him how to use it. Latif the shouts out "There they are shoot them "indicating a car full of rival gang members. Jake deliberately aims the gun slightly to the right of the car, closes his eyes and fires a shoot. The gun jerks violently in his hand as he pulls the trigger and one bullet goes through the open car window lodging in the **arm** of a rival gang member who **survives** the shooting but only after undergoing a lengthy operation.

393) **Q:** Discuss the criminal liability of Jake only. When doing so you are **NOT** required to consider any **attempted** offences. You are **NOT** required to consider any liability of **Kyle** or **Latif.**

A; The liabilities of Jake include; 1) Joining unlawful\illegal gang of violence conducts (Boston Boyz) 2) possession of dangerous weapon (Knife with intent) to cause\inflict harm. 3) Charge with unlawfully and maliciously wounded Kyle with a knife under section 20 of OAPA (offence against person Act 1861) 4) Possession of and using gun without licence with intent to cause grievous bodily harm. 5) Unlawful and malicious wounded a person under section 18 of OAPA 1861.

394) Q: How did the court view Jake with flicker knife?

A: With regard to the flicker knife, he had menses rea to Kyle, as intention to causing or inflicting grievous bodily harm. Actus reus transfer malice to striking the arm instead of the intended. This cut both the upper and lower skin, bled and needed stitches. Section 20 of the 1861 of OAPA, Jake foresaw the risk of some physical harm or must be he intend or foresee either wounding or grievous bodily harm.

395) Q : How is Jake likely to plea?

A; Jake is likely to plea self-defence or preventing Kyle o commit crime, but he is likely to be convicted since the culture of the Boston Boyz is inflict violence\wound.

396) Q: What will be Jake argument?

A: He made it clear that he did not want to use the gun. And without waiting for Jake to consider his option. He was forced to take the gun and shown how to use. He still could have choose to use but then Latif shouted, “There they are shoot them” (this is hit of the moment It was not his intention to cause grievous bodily harm ,that was the reason he recklessly deliberately aimed the gun slightly to the right of the car

397) Q: What will be the charge

A; Jake would be charged with section 18 of OAPA (Offence against person Act)1861.

398) Q ; What will be likely defence for Jake?

A; He is likely to plea duress as he could not resist overborne due to threat. When Latif said to him "Either in the gang or not"

Argue **duress** necessity to avoid inevitable and irreparably necessary for the purpose or the evil inflicted was not disproportionate to the evil avoided. (Very important that he was being initiated and he might withdraw).On the other hand he could plea that he was weak \coward when he was told by Latif that "Either with us or not" and he feared being shot. This argument will fail as in R.V. Graham (1982) 74 Cr App R 235 appendix-R.V Howe (1987) 1 AC 417 for see or ought to fore see consequence of joining violent organisation.

399) Q; Why was his plea on necessity failed

A: His plea on the ground of necessity or on circumstances failed the house Lords said defendant foresee or ought to foresee the risk of being subject to any compulsion by threat of violence from them and he or she be threaten at a time when he or she is voluntary associated with them. Example R.V. Sharp (1987)! QB 853 (gang of armed robbers appendix-or R.V Hassan (2005)2 AC 467 (terrorist) appendix or R.V. Hudson and Taylor and Abdul- Hassan.

400) Q; What sentence Jake likely to get?

A; Sentence up to 5 years; example R.V. Mowatt (1968) 1 QB 421 at 426 (2) appendix--- 2) R.V. Birmingham (2002) EWCA crime 2608 Appendix------- 3) R.V .Chan-Fook (1994) 1W.L.R. 689 CA-appendix----4) DPP.V. Smith (1961) AC 290, Moriarty.V. Brooks (1834) 6 C and P 684

401) Q: Give similar case and the reason of the court decision?

A; In R.v. Sharp court of appeal; Lord Lane CJ stated that "where a person has voluntarily, and with knowledge of its nature, joined a criminal organisation or gang which he knew might bring pressure on him to commit an offence and was active member when he was put under such pressure, he can not avail himself of the defence of duress.

The court of appeal ruled that a defendant who joined with his free will a renowned criminal organisation whose culture is violent conduct cannot rely on duress when the violence is turned on him. Lord Lane said "-if a person can avoid the effects of due by escaping from the threat without damage to himself he must do so".

402) Q: Give similar case and the reason of the court decision?

A; In R.v. Sharp court of appeal; Lord Lane CJ stated that "where a person has voluntarily, and with knowledge of its nature, joined a criminal organisation or gang which he knew might bring pressure on him to commit an offence and was active member when he was put under such pressure, he can not avail himself of the defence of duress.

The court of appeal ruled that a defendant who joined with his free will a renowned criminal organisation whose culture is violent conduct cannot rely on duress when the violence is turned on him. Lord Lane said "-if a person can avoid the effects of due by escaping from the threat without damage to himself he must do so".

403) Q; Why was the appeal court not sympathetic with Jake predicament?

A: One may expect the appeal court to consider the predicament and have sympathy on such case like Jake, but **Lord Bingham** said "I cannot consistently with principle---- has no opportunity to avoid complying with threat-----"Jake could argue that a reasonable of the same sex, characteristics of Jake and possible consequence of refusal would probable felt compelled to act as he did. Or use Ghosh test for honesty.

404) Q; What did criminal law review think of Lord Bingham decision?

A: Professor David Romero in criminal law review in 2006 (Crim.L.R.2006,feb,142-146)stated "Lord Bingham approach is too strict, surely a defendant who fears, genuinely and reasonably, that he will be cut up tomorrow unless she perjures herself today ought to be allowed a defence of duress".

It may be debatable if Jakes would be charged of section 18 which said cause or in "section 20 it state inflict" Lord Steyn in R.v. Burstow (1007) 4 ALL ER 228 cause is wider than inflict are not synonymous he said.

Chapter: 4

PSYCHIATRY

405) **Q;** How is psychiatry injury classified?

A: Psychiatry injury is classified as pure economic loss unless the claimant can satisfy two conditions, or two features are fulfilled

406) **Q;** Explain the two conditions?

A; 1)Suffered medically recognised condition such as personality disorder, miscarriage, PTSD, pathological grief, depression, anxiety, neurotic symptoms, or PTSD.

2) Sudden occurrence (not gradual) this means that it must be initiated by sudden shock Example sudden appreciation by sight\sounds, hearing or event or mollifying event which violently agitate the mind. These leads to mental anguish, distress, upset, anxiety depression.

407) **Q;** what happen when these two are established:

A: CLAIM; after the medical diagnosed and suddenness is established, the claimant can pursue claim under tort negligence. Claimant must establish negligence of duty of care and the breach of that duty needs to be established, leading to consequential loss\damage which is NOT being too remote.

408) Q: How does the law classified psychiatry injury?

A; There are primary and secondary victim and the court give more care to primary victim.

409) Q; what condition one has to satisfy before claim of psychiatric injury without physical injury.

A: That the claimant must be at the scene of incident or went there immediately aftermath. Must have close relation with the victim, develops recognise psychiatric illness

410) Q What was the reason of rule on psychiatric claim

A; 1)To avoid floodgate.

2)Differentiate genuine from bogus claim

3) To prevent Nervous disposition people who could make unwarranted claim.

4)Defendant will not be able to assess their potential liabilities especially cases of road traffic accident.

411) Q: Name some cases relate to psychiatric injury?

A; Alcock v. Chief constable of south Yorkshire

W. V. Essex County council

Page v. Smith

Mc Louglin v. O Brien (1982)

412) Q; Summarise the case in McLaughlin v. O'Brian (1982)

A; Mrs. McLaughlin received a phone call to come to hospital, where on arrival she found one of her children dead, another badly injury, the husband and the third child injury and distressed. She suffered shock, depressed and personality change.

413) Q: What was the court's decision and why?

A: The **High court** held that the injury was not foreseeable and hence no compensation.

414) Q: What was the appeal court decision?

A; The **court of appeal** stated that there should be no recovery on the grounds of public policy i.e. that it would open the "flood gates" of claim.

415) Q: What was the house of lords decision?

A) **House of Lords** rejected the appeal court and found a duty of care existed but imposed guild lines; proximity to the accident. Claimant relationship to the injured person and degree of seriousness of the accident.

416) Q; Summarise the case in Alcock v. Chief Constable of south Yorkshire (1992)

A; Case; this was a tragedy at Hillsborough football grounds where a large number of Liverpool supporters were killed in overcrowded part of the grounds. Claimant suffers shock, psychiatry, anxiety and some saw these on the television.

417) Q; what was the court's decision?

A; Court; Defendant (police) were successfully sued for negligence by claimant directly affected (primary victims) and some secondary victims who saw on the television were mentally affected;

418) Q: What condition for The House of Lords allowed the claim.

A; there were with three conditions.

1) The event witnessed must be single traumatic event.

The claimant must have witnessed, the event through his \her own unaided senses (this exclude TV viewers)

If the incident was not witnessed, the claimant must have come onto the scene in the immediate aftermath.

Decision by the House of Lords is still partially based on policy to avoid "floodgate claim"

419) Q; Summarise the case in Page v. Smith (1996) Ac 155

A; Case; this was about car crash .the claimant was driving with care when suddenly without warning;

defendant driving opposite direction turned into his path and collided. Both cars were damage but none of the passengers physically hurt...Claimant never recovered from mental diagnosed.

420) **Q**: What did the court do in this case?

A; Court; the House of Lords stated two victim, Primary and secondary.

Primary victim; is someone who was actually involved in the accident i.e. was in the actual area of danger. And reasonable believe that he was in danger.

Secondary victim; who is not at the scene but satisfy the three conditions

421) **Q;** An what did the judge said about actual bodily harm in these cases Hobhouse. L.J in R.V .Chan-Fook (1994)1W.L.R.689 CA?

A; This was a case of nervous condition. Hobhouse L.J. state" what is meant by actual bodily harm"? It does not have to be permanent. It does not have to be serious. It is some harm which interferes with the comfort of the individual, for the time being, describe as any hurt or injury calculated to interfere with the health and comfort of the victim.

422) **Q:** Can symptoms of nervous system be regarded as a psychiatric assault?

A; An assault that causes a hysterical or nervous condition is capable of being an assault causing actual bodily harm. Hobhouse stated that “harm” is a synonym of injury” and “actual” indicate that the injury should not be so trivial as to be wholly insignificance. Section 47 of OAPA 1861 i.e. assault that cause the victim some injury.

423) **Q;** What was the court decision and why?

A: Chan- Fook was convicted of assault occasioning actual bodily harm.

424) **Q;** What did LYNSKEY .J. said about actual bodily harm in R. V. Miller (1954)2 Q.B 282)

A; LYNSKEY .J. (in R. V. Miller (1954)2 Q.B 282) state “ The body of the victim include all part of his body ,including his organs, his nervous system and his brain (not just his skin, fresh and bones) Bodily injury therefore may include injury to any of those parts of his body responsible for his mental and other facilities

425) **Q;** What did Lord Wilberforce said about the body and mind in McLaughlin .O’Brian (1983) 1 AC 410,418?

A; Lord Wilberforce in McLaughlin .O'Brian (1983) 1 AC 410,418 said

"Whatever is unknown about the mine-body relationship? Could the area of ignorance seem to expand with that knowledge) It is no accepted by medical science that recognisable and severe physical damage to the human body and system may be caused by the impact, through the senses on the mind. There may thus be produced what is as identifiable an illness as that may be caused by direct physical impact." Actually bodily harm is capable of include psychiatric injury. But it does not include mere emotions such as fear or distress nor panic nor does it include, such state of mind that are not they evidence of some identifiable clinical condition.

426) **Q;** What case did the court dealt with distress and grief?

A: Attia. V. British gas plc (1988) Q.B 304 and Alcock.v.chief constable of south Yorkshire police (1992) 1 AC 310.

The court of appeal attempted to drawn between on one hand –the emotions of distress and grief and on the other hand some psychiatric illness such as anxiety neurosis or reactive depression. " actual bodily harm" is capable of including psychiatric injury. Considering whether or not a psychiatric injury has been caused is something which is more than a strong emotion such as extreme fear or panic, can amount to actual bodily harm. Where there is evidence that the assault has caused psychiatric injury, the injury should be directed that, that injury is capable of amounting to actual bodily harm. (This expression includes the mental state of the victim following the assault.

427) Q; Comment on case In R.v.Robert,56 Cr App. R.95?

A; In R.v.Robert,56 Cr App. R.95 to include offence of aggravated assault comprises section 47 and simple assault causing the victim to apprehend immediate and unlawful violence example Fagan .v. Metropolitan police commissioner (196901QB.439, where the victim relied on psychiatric injury and defence had not admitted, evidence witness should be called by prosecution claim " ASSAULT OCCASIONED PSYCHIATRIC INJURY". House of Lords in Ireland and Barstow (1998) AC 147 required proof of a psychiatric condition supported by expert evidence.

428) Q; Comment on case In Morris (1998)1 Cr.App.R.386.?

A; In Morris (1998)1 Cr.App.R.386.it was held that General fractioned report stating that victim suffered anxiety, fear, tearfulness, sleeplessness and physical tenseness was held to be insufficient to actual bodily harm.

429) Q; What happened when both Savage and Parmenter?

A; In R.V. SAVAGE and R.v. Parmenter both were convicted of assault. Savage appeal was reduced to s.47 from s.20 of OAPA 1861.Parmenter convicted on s. 20 but quashed on appeal (both were dealt with in the House of Lords at the same time"

430) Q; What did Lord Acker said about assault occasioning actual bodily harm?

A; Lord Ackner state the mental element of particular kind of assault "an assault occasioning actual bodily harm "which are descriptive of the word "assault" for psychiatric.

NB; Savage threw bottle of glass with bear which caused injury to the victim. Parmenter wounded her body by breaking bones.

Chapter 5

VICARIOUS LIABILITY

431) Q: What is the definition of Vicarious liability?

A: vicarious liability is impose on one person for torts or crime committed by another although the former is not personally at fault.

432) **Q:** When will the employer be vicarious liable?

A; The employer is only liable for employee acts that are committed in the cause of employment. If employee is not liable neither is the employer (Murkowski v. Guys and Saint Thomas NHS Trust (200&0 1 AC 224.

433) **Q:** What three elements that make employers liable?

A; The three fundamental elements that employers is held vicariously liable for their employee acting within the course of their employment are; must be an employee, has committed tort and this occurred in the course of their employment.

434) **Q;** What is the general rule to make employer liable?

A; The general rule is If the employee action is authorised by the employer or within the contract terms, and if employees were careless or made mistakes or failed to act or omission when they have contractual duty of care, these will be deemed as the employee acting in the course of employment, due to legal special relationship between employer and employee.

435) Q; What about if the employee act is not authorised by the employer?

A; However If the act is unauthorised but closely connected with authorise act which a reasonable\ court consider it fair and just, employer would be vicarious liable. The maxim “Qui facit per alium facit perse” (he who does anything by another does it by himself) in order words, the employee represent the employer in act that the employer would have done himself.

436) Q; What did the courts view on vicarious liability on manner and scope? And give example.

The court decides the nature relationship between the employer and the employee and to weigh the employee act of carry out “course of employment” If the employers instruction relate to the manner, any breach leaves the employee inside his employment hence vicarious liable, but if it relate to the scope, any breach takes the employee outside his employment and not vicarious liable.

Example an employee was employed as a bus conductor, but he drove a bus and caused accident injured pedestrian, the court ruled that he acted outside the scope of his employment. Igbal v. London transport executive (1973)16 KIR this if fair, but sometimes it has been difficult to prove scope.

437) Q: what is Lord Phillip view on vicarious liability?

A; Policy dictates judgement; Lord Phillip said the policy on vicarious liability for tortuous wrong is borne by defendant with the means to compensate the victim (various claimant v. Catholic child welfare society (2012) 3 WLR 1319.

438) Q: What test did the House of Lords introduce in relation to employees?

A: The House of Lords introduced pragmatic test of "acting within the course of employment". "How the employee act must be closely connected to their emolument". This is between the employee and their action (Lister and others), and to decide how employee action is closely connected with the course of employment that would be fair and just to hold employer liable.

439) Q ; Give reasons for the court's decision?

A; The court reasons for imposing vicarious liability on employers, that morally, the employer to take more care of the employee to prevent injury or damage. Since the employers make profit they must bear the cost of employee who makes it possible.

Secondly practically; employers have finance, they can take insurance against liability and can pass the cost of liability to the custom. "A person who employs others to advance his own economic interest should in fairness be placed under a corresponding liability for losses incurred in the course of the enterprise" By Fleming (law of Torts (9th edition) p 410s

440) Q: What are the three reasons for vicarious fairness?

A; Three reasons of vicarious fairness ;employer control employee, employers benefit from employers work and must therefore take responsibilities at their action, the employer made the choice in employee their representative (London Butter-worth)(1967).Tort view that the employer employs and introduces risk (employee) into the business and therefore has to pay.

441) Q; Why must employee take full responsibility of employee action?

A; a) Employers must take full responsibility of their employee action because the misconduct could be minimise or avoided if they follow the rules and regulation as laid down by statute\common law They must vet prospective employee; obtain CRB for criminal records strict reference, must invest in continue staff trainee include health and stay and the aspect that relate to the employment, appraisals implement disciplinary action.

b) " Those who set in motion and profit from the activities of their employees should compensate those who are injured by such activities even when perform negligently "Viasyatems (Tyneside)Ltd v. Thermal Transfer (Northern) Ltd (2006) QB 510 at 529.This implies that it is the employers fault in their selection of employee.

c) Employer is solvent and have insurance cover (Vicarious liability and the master's indemnity (1957) 20 MLR 220. Also the employer can recover the cost of liability by increase cost of products, insurance, company liability. They can claim indemnity from the employee under civil liability (contribution) Act 1978. (Lister v. Romford Ice & cold storage co Ltd (1957) AC 55

442) Q; Why is it unfair to impose vicarious liability on employer?

A; Employee can do act negligently\carelessly or in his own manner, which is forbidden but as far as he is doing it closely relate to what he has been instructed, the employer is still vicarious liable for any damage cause. (Rise v. Plenty. Lord Denning commented on prohibition act "It depends very much on the purpose for which it is done. If it was done for his employers business, it is usually done in the course of his employment even though it is prohibiting Act". The rule that the servant must be engaged on his masters business and "not on frolic of his own" (Joel v. Morrison (1834) 6 C & p 501. This is the degree of departure from the task that the master has set the servant. Is abuse. Harvey O'Dell Ltd (1958)2QB 78

443) Q; Give example of vicarious liability?

A; Some unfair court judgement in favour of employee;

a) an employee delivering petrol caused explosion when he carelessly threw match on the floor. (Century Insurance Co Ltd v. Northern Ireland road and transport board.
b) b) An employee assaulted boys in care home he was working, the court decided that the crime was closely connected with his employment hence vicarious liability. (Lister and others v.Hesley Hall Ltd (2001).

c) In some cases employers can be liable for independent contractors act. (Mataria v. National provincial Bank Ltd)

444) Q; What is the author (my) view on vicarious liability?

A: From the cases highlighted, statute and common laws favour the employee. The servant can ignore the master's express instruction, leaving the employer liable but on balance of probability, employers gain from this relationship and deserve to be vicarious liable

445) Q: What is the reason why hospital liable for doctors/employee negligence?

A; 1) **vicarious** liability is impose on one person for torts or crime committed by another although the former is not personally at fault.

2) The employer is liable for employee acts because the negligence was committed in the cause of employment (Murkowski v. Guys and Saint Thomas NHS Trust (200&0 1 AC 224.

3) The three fundamental elements that employers is held vicariously liable for their employee acting within the course of their employment are satisfied these include; must be an employee, has committed tort and this occurred in the course of their employment.

4) The general rule is If the employee action is authorised by the employer or within the contract terms, and if employees were careless or made mistakes or failed to act or omission when they have contractual duty of care, these will be deemed as the employee acting in the course of employment, due to legal special relationship between employer and employee.

446) **Q;** What about if the employees act is not authorised by the employer?

A; However If the act is unauthorised but closely connected with authorise act which a reasonable\ court consider it fair and just, employer would be vicarious liable. The maxim “Qui facit per alium facit perse” (he who does anything by another does it by himself) in order words, the employee represent the employer in act that the employer would have done himself.

447) **Q;** what did the courts view on vicarious liability on manner and scope? And give example.

A; The court decides the nature relationship between the employer and the employee and to weigh the employee act of carry out “course of employment” If the employers instruction relate to the manner, any breach leaves the employee inside his employment hence vicarious liable, but if it relate to the scope, any breach takes the employee outside his employment and not vicarious liable.

Example an employee was employed as a bus conductor, but he drove a bus and course accident injured pedestrian, the court ruled that he acted outside the scope of his employment. Igbal v. London transport executive (1973)16 KIR this if fair, but sometimes it has been difficult to prove scope.

448) **Q**: what is Lord Phillip view on vicarious liability?

A; Policy dictates judgement; Lord Phillip said the policy on vicarious liability for tortuous wrong is borne by defendant with the means to compensate the victim (various claimant v. Catholic child welfare society (2012) 3 WLR 1319.

The House of Lords introduced pragmatic test of “acting within the course of employment”. “How the employee act must be closely connected to their emolument”. This is between the employee and their action (Lister and others), and to decide how employee action is closely connected with the course of employment that would be fair and just to hold employer liable.

449) **Q;** Give reasons for the court's decision?

A; The court reasons for imposing vicarious liability on employers, that morally, the employer to take more care of the employee to prevent injury or damage. Since the employers make profit they must bear the cost of employee who makes it possible.

Secondly practically; employers have finance, they can take insurance against liability and can pass the cost of liability to the custom. "A person who employs others to advance his own economic interest should in fairness be placed under a corresponding liability for losses incurred in the course of the enterprise" By Fleming (law of Torts (9th edition) p 410s

Chapter 6

TORT and Vicarious liability

450) **Q:** What is the purpose of tort?

A:The purpose of tort is to compensate. No punishment in tort

451) **Q:**What must claimant satisfy?

A; The claimant has to show the elements DOC; Duty of care which could be established by or novel case laws or statute

BOC; Breach of duty of care, this can be compare to reasonable person in the same situation.

CIL; Causation in law where there must be damage to the claimant and this damage could also be caused by another person in a form of contributory negligence.

RIL= Remoteness in law that is foreseeable of the injury.

Failure to show these means there is no liabilities in tort negligence. When these are established, the next thing is to investigate possible defence and any contribution negligence by the claimant.

452) Q; Name other types of harm that comes under tort negligence?

A; There is other type of harm that comes under tort

1) Nuisance the claimant enjoyment of his land had been interferes with.

2) Product liability (this is no- negligent liability) but the consequential damage is tort.

3) Tort of defamation.

4) Trespass of land

5) Trespass of person

6) Occupies liabilities

453) Q: Name the types of defamation?

A: There are 2 type of defamation 1) liable (this is permanent form) example newspaper article 2) slander is not permanent form and often spoken words

454) Q: Are there overlaps in tort and crime

A; There are some harm which can be claimed both as tort and criminal example assault, Batley. Criminal damage of property.

455) Q; Give an example of where tort and contract law can be used together?

A: Example CPA 1989 can be used on contract law for product defect (sue the retailer) whilst tort be used for consequential damage.

Sue in contract is better as one can proof easier and get more compensation than tort.

Scenario on tort

One year ago Edward was driving his car carefully along the road when he saw a car driven excessively fast by Morgan coming towards him on a wrong side of the road. Edward was unable to avoid collision. Edward was trapped in his car and was cut free by the fire service attending the scene.

As a result of the initial collision, Edward suffered two broken legs a chest injury. The effect of the chest injury were more severe than normal because Edward already suffered from illness affecting the lungs, also in cutting Edward free, the rescue workers accidentally cause painful abrasion to his arms because of the confine space that they were working in.

Whilst in the hospital, Edward developed a secondary infection and was given injection of antibiotics by Kiahna, a junior doctor. Unfortunately Kiahna neglected to check Edward medical notes prior to the administrating the injection and did not see that Edward was allergic to this particular antibiotic. As the result of this Allergic reaction, Edward went into coma. Edward did regain consciousness from the coma, but he suffered a permanent brain injury as result.

456) Q: Advise Edward as to his potential claim in facts explaining the issues which have arisen on the facts.

A: In this scenario, I have set the answers similar to how lawyers might organise after the interview or for my law students, one way of presenting assignment or examination .In some cases I have quote the law or cases to support the claim

457) **Q:** What will be Edward claim under?

A; All Edward claim will be tort negligence which is defined as defendant foresaw harm\damage but carelessly went on to take the risk without justification. This is civil liability (claim) Act 1978. Page v. Smith.

458) **Q:**What will Edward be advised to do and why?

A: Edward will be advised to sue the hospital for all the damage (thin skull) for vicarious liability because the hospital has limitless insurance cover. This is where employer is vicariously liable for the action of employee even though the employer has done nothing wrong. It would then be possible to sue

Kiahna personally. Limpus v. London General Omnibus (1862)1 H& C 542. Also to sue Morgan, if he has no insurance, the motor insurance bureau will pay within their limit. Edward cannot sue the fire services (Minors) .Bedfordshire county courts council (1995) AC 633.

459) Q: Summarise in table form the potential claim.

A;

<table>
<tr><th colspan="4">THE FOLLOWING POTENTIAL CLAIMS ARISE</th></tr>
<tr><td>CLAIMANT</td><td>DEFENDANT</td><td>LOSS SUFFERED</td><td>RELEVANT TORT</td></tr>
<tr><td>Edward</td><td>Morgan</td><td>Physical Personal injury and property damage</td><td>Negligence</td></tr>
<tr><td>Edward</td><td>Hospital and Kiahna</td><td>Physical Personal injury. And psychiatric injury</td><td>Negligence</td></tr>
<tr><td>Morgan</td><td>Hospital\Kiahna</td><td>Contributing joint liability.</td><td rowspan="2">Contribution between joint tortfeasors.</td></tr>
<tr><td>Hospital \Kiahna</td><td>Morgan</td><td>Contributing joint liability.</td></tr>
</table>

KEY: DOC=Duty of care, **BOC**=Breach of care, **CIF**=causation in fact, **RIL**=Remoteness in law, **GD**= General defence.

460) Q; Give brief account of Duty of care?

A; in law of negligence, it is very important to establish if **duty of care** exist in the circumstances. (If this cannot be established there is no claim under negligence but in other form of tort could be used) remember there is no duty of care in omission example if you see a person injured on the road side or a child being drown in river and you do not have any form of connection with the person, you will be at risk if you help if anything goes wrong such as worsen the injury or the victim accuse you. Moral plays little in law. The rule is that you must protect yourself first, help others if only you have legal duty to do so and even that if you feel your own life will be at risk then reconsider your option.

There are established or statute duty of care such as fiduciary duties; doctor and his patient, teachers and student, bank manager and customer road users. Act. Were in doubt, test can be used to established duty of care exist.

461) Q; Name two cases to support duty of care?

A; First test=Donohue. v. Edward son (1932) AC 562 (owe duty of care)

Second test; **Caparo** industries Plc. V. Dickinson (1990)2 AC 605 involve foreseeable, proximity and fair, just for the court to impose duty of care. (Duty of care)

462) Q: What can Edward claim from the fire service for the injury he sustained?

A; Edward v. Fire service

Public authorities include fire service, Public authorities such as the police, ambulance, coastland, fire service do not owe duty of care to Edward as individual, their duty of care is to the public, and as such there is no claim against them. Have no duty of care in tort the court decision to exempt public authorities are mainly policy related and not to put constraint and restraint on them in pursue of their job in fear of being sued. Hall.v. Chief Constable of West Yorkshire (1989) AC 53 (police negligence cannot be liable as they only have duty to the public and not to individuals)

The abrasion caused by the fire service was in a cause of saving Edward life and did not affect his recovery or prognoses.

Edward has the knowledge of established agreement of risk of the fire service that were called to rescue him because his life was in immediate danger. In Baker v.TE Hopkins (1959)1 WLR 966-the law state that emergencies team must not be criticised when they act to save life in dramatic manner.

There is no breach, no fault, no causes, is too remote CIF and does not need defence. Defence. There had been very rear occasions when public authority had been liable; Swinny.v. Chief Constable of Northumbria (No1) 1997 QB 464.

463) **Q:** What can Edward cliam from Morgan with reference to duty of care,

A; Duty of care

Morgan owes Claimant legal established duty of care, as road user (Nettle ship v. Weston) His conduct fell below the standard of reasonable competent driver. In breached of RTA 1978 and his action failed the two tests of duty of care is :(Donohue) (Caparo). Donohue .v. Edward son (1932) AC 562 Lord Atkins said "You must take reasonable care to avoid act or omission that you foresee would be likely to injury your neighbour. He foresaw the danger, but he was careless on the road and cause harm to Edward whose proximity is close.(Caparo industries test).Lord Wilberforce in case (1978)AC 728 at 751 said "Careless on his part may likely to cause damage to the later, in which case a prima facia duty of care arises".

464) Q: : What can Edward claim from Morgan with reference breach duty of care?

A: Breach duty of care

Road users is establish duty of care public access, driving too fast on the wrong side of the road causing physical injury and damage properties breached duty of care owe to other road users (Nettle v. Weston). He failed the two tests, question of law; he ought to have known of breaking the law and "Res Ipsa loquitur" the fact of the case. Standard of care expected from reasonable motorist is high to avoid risk of accident to other road users. (Blythe\ Nettleship). . Accident is a strict liability caused by the defendant civil evidence Act 1968 section 11.

465) Q: What can Edward claim from Morgan with reference to causation.

A: Causation in fact

"But for" (test), Morgan careless driving Edward would not have suffered multiple injury of two broken legs, chest injury, coma, unconsciousness, permanent brain damage, pain and suffering, damage to his properties (car and clothes), are link to the causation in fact hence prima facie satisfied (Performance cars v. Abraham).

Morgan's conduct might not be the only cause of Steve damage (brain damage) but is enough to infer that he made a material contribution. (Pennington Casting Ltd. Wardlaw). There is no intervening act. A considering the fact of the case reasonable person will have no doubt that the claimant damage was the defendant's faults. (Objective test).

466) **Q:** What can Edward claim from Morgan with reference to remoteness

A: Remoteness in law; here one need to established how remote the injury would have occurred as result of the defendant action.

Morgan accidents that cause Edward physical injury is foreseeable type of harm and is not too remote. Morgan might argue that the existing chest\ lungs contributed to worsen of Morgan condition. The original injury is foreseeable. The established rule that defendants has to take their victim as they find him, ("egg shell rule" Smith v. Leech Brain). As such Morgan was responsible for the original injuries and the later coma and permanent brain damage, Edward can claim full amount without reduction, unless Morgan can raise defence.

467) Q; what defence can Morgan raise?

A; Base on the facts, there is no general defence applicable and no Contributory negligent. (Law of contributory negligent Act 1945.

There is not enough information about Morgan to determine any defence such as age, mental and physical condition, drink and drive, diminished responsibility or insanity. His offence is strict liability and irrefutable presumption.

468) Q; Explore the possible claim by Edward from the hospital and the doctor?

A: one has to follow the sequence of duty of care, breach the duty, causation in fact, remoteness

Duty of care

469) Q: Was there duty of care for Edward?

A: There is established duty of care between doctor and patient is very close, she foresaw the injury, higher or specific standard is expected from her, and therefore is fair, just for the court to impose duty of care on the hospital. (Caparo industries Plc. V. Dickinson (1990)2 AC 605. "The law takes no cognizance of careless in abstract it concern itself with careless only where there is duty of care and failure in that duty was has caused damage". Lord McMillan case (1932) Ac 562 at 618

470) **Q;** Was the duty breached?

A: Her behaviour would be regarded as breach duty of care. The court and society expect the defendant conduct to be measured against "reasonable person standard "which she breached (objectively test). " Objective and impersonal" per Lord Mcmillard (Glasgow group Muir (1943) AC 448. Kiahna breached her professional (General medical) and her employer's code of practice which include fiduciary duties as much higher standard expected from her. Kiahna failed Bolam test Bolam. Frien hospital management committee (1959)2 ALL ER 118" (doctor to show degree of skill as "reasonable doctor"). Even though she is a junior doctor, she is qualified and expect special standard as of any other doctor (Wisher's. Essex area Health Authority.

471) **Q:** What must the claimant proof with regard to Causation in the fact of the case?

A: Claimant must prove on balance of probability (Wisher).Using the Factual Causation Test.

"But for" given the unchecked antibiotics Edward would not have suffered allergic reaction to antibiotics become coma and subsequently permanent brain damage. Barnet v Chelsea and Kensington hospital management committee (1969) it could be argued that her conduct was not the only cause of Edward injury of Coma and brain damage, but it is enough that she made contribution to risk of harm. (McGhee.v.NationalCoal Board)

472) **Q:** How was remoteness of the injuries?

A: Subjectively the defendant the extent of injuries attributed to them is not too remote. Lord Denning said "it is not what the person think but what he\she says and does" Kiahna's fault is irrefutable. The allergic cause immediate shock leading to recognised psychiatric symptoms (brain damage).and this is claimable.

473) **Q:** How would you summarise the claim?

A: Remote in law by considering the whole case

It is established that doctor and patient relationship and the cause of the injury is **not** too remote. The statement of fact shows that causation of claimant damage is satisfied. (Causation test) Kiahna is liable for all the loses which flows from her conduct whether or not that injury was foreseeable by her both culpability and compensation. Polemis and Furness Withy and Co Ltd (1921)3 KB 560.The injury is Reasonably foreseeable which a reasonable person would have foreseen. Or "If a reasonable person cannot foresee the damage, it cannot be recovered". (Rule of remoteness) Wagon's. Mould (no 1) (1961) AC 388

Antibiotics allergic reaction was expected but not the severe damage to result brain damage (Bradford v. Robinson rentals Ltd (1967. There may be the issue of claimant existing chest problem, but this can be rebutted by "egg shell skull" rule. Smith v. Leech Briar and Co (1962)2 QB the injury was foreseeable.

474) Q: Are there any defence?

A; There is no general defence applicable in this case base on the fact.

Morgan \hospital\Kiahna v. hospital\Kiahna\Morgan. This case lean itself to contributing joint liability. Medico- legal expert independence report might be needed for the two defendants to apportion claim that is responsible for the injury such as the brain damage, degree of the chest \lungs injury and prognoses.

475) Q: What conclusion will you reach in this case?

A; There is not enough information to reach fair conclusion, to employ defence, such as contributory negligent (seat belt) or Morgan reason of conduct (diminished responsibility act.)This is civil liability (c) Act 1978 and is joint liability. Edward will be advice to sue the hospital “thin skull) rule. The claim will include physical, psychological, mental impairment; medical, nursing care and social care, loss of earning, potential future earnings, adaptation of his properties including car for disabilities, for the rest of his life. I will deal with these types of claim late in the book.

Chapter 7

PURE ECONOMIC LOSS

476) **Q;** Define pure economic loss?

A; Pure economic loss is due to the fault of the defendant but **not** consequential on damage property, personal injury, damage coursed by defective chattels or property, negligence statements to third party property causing claimant to suffer. The claimant cannot recover the loss; even if it can be proved that the defendant carelessness caused the damage. This is because there is no duty of care between the parties.

477) **Q:** Define negligence in relation to pure economic loss?

A; Definition of Negligence in relation to pure economic loss is Breach of duty of care owe to the claimant by taken unjustifiable risk to cause loss. If the claimant suffers physical injury or damage to his property, or misrepresentation, misstatement, it could be claim under tort negligent. Economic loss on statement\negligence did not arise until 1964 when judgement in the House of Lords on Hedley Byrne (negligent of the bank staff) resulted in pure economic loss.

478) Q; What are the rules when considering pure economic loss?

A; RULES; these are common laws which have developed through case laws and apply by the court.

A) GENERAL RULE; where a defendant suffers damage which is class as pure economic loss, the loss is **not** revocable.

B) COMPLEX STRUCTURE THEORY RULE EXEPTION;_Where one have a large item made up of smaller components, example computer; if one of the components is defective means the whole items affected and the item can be classified as damage property._Lord Bridge however said this theory cannot be attributed to building defect or collapse.

C) "WAGON MOUND" remoteness of change and foreseeable rule

 Overseas Tank ship UK. V. Morts Duck and Engineering Co Ltd (1961). In this case it was regarded as too remote and not foreseeable which is not fair because after few days when the oil caught fire, the expert who gave permission felt it was too remote. They should have been made liable as they failed to clean up.

D) The claimant must pass tort negligence test and all the three elements; duty of care, duty is breached, and the consequence causes the loss\damage, causation in fact and is **not** too remote.

E) There are **established** rules on duty of care such as relationship between doctors and patients, solicitors and their client or road user. Hedley Bryne & co Ltd v. Heller & partners Ltd (1964) AC 465.The principal of this case confirmed a duty of ca was owed for a negligent statement if a "special relationship" could be established.

479) Q; Name a test in considering duty of care?

A; Novice duty of care test can be established by the proximity of the parties and foresee ability (Caparo).

Four **tests** arose in the Caparo industries (1990) the House of Lords criteria to establish what statement is NOT Pure economic Loss and when the defendant owes duty of care; The Lordship said that the adviser must know; the purpose of which the advice was required by claimant or his agent, that the advice will be communicated to the advisee (or specifically member of the ascertainable class, that the advisee was likely to act on the advice without independent inquiry, or ought reasonably to know that the claimant was relying on their skill and judgement, or ought to have known that the claimant was relying on their skill and judgement. and Reliance; the advice was acted on by the advisee to his detriment.

480) Q; Define psychiatry injury in relation to pure economic loss given case laws in support?

A; Psychiatry injury is classified as pure economic loss unless the claimant can satisfy two conditions;1) Suffered medically recognised condition such as personality disorder, miscarriage, PTSD, pathological grief, depression, anxiety, neurotic symptoms.2)SUDDEN OCCURRENCE (not gradual) this means that it must be initiated by sudden SHOCK. On balance of probability these rules are fair as in psychiatry it would be difficult to differentiate genuine from bogus claim, and to prevent Nervous disposition people who could make unwarranted claim. Some leading cases are; Adcock v. Chief constable of south Yorkshire, W. V. Essex County council, Page v. Smith, Mc Louglin v. O Brien (1982).

481) Q; What is reasons rules on pure economic loss in relation to Psychiatry injury ?

A; Reasons for rules include; Pure economic loss is common law which started in 1964.The main reason is policy\political decision as the judges feel negligence base on pure economic loss will open the flood gate for indefinite, defendant liabilities will be endless-boundless to an in determine number, not to undermine contract law (protecting business) which regulate economic loss. Claim of pure economic loss are limitless, Claimant may not even know the defendant and vice versa (example Journalist), Prevent defendant to assess the multitude of the claim; prevent the insurance and the big company being liquidated. (In close relation one might be able to claim pure economic loss).Imagine if there are no rules on pure economic loss, how many claim example weather forecasters who do not get it right all the time.

482) **Q**; Give reasons why pure economic loss is not recoverable in tort of negligence?

A; The reason pure economic loss is irrevocable under tort law is "no one owes duty by omission to the world" with few exceptions (contractual, relative). This means that defendant will not be liable for where there is no physical injury or property damage or if the loss is caused by actions (Weller v.Foot and Mouth). However if he\she attempts or gives assistance to individual which is then term as "assumption of duty of care and the consequence of the defendant will be NOT pure financial loss.

483) **Q**; Explain consequential economic loss, give case law in support?

A; Consequential economic loss is inflicting personal injury or damage to property and is claimable on tort negligence. In such claim the statement of fact will determine which part of the claim is pure economic and which part is tort claim, or damage based on third party (personal injury or damage to third party property is pure economic loss. It is crucial to differentiate pure economic loss from consequential on physical damage (Spartan Steel and Allys Ltd v. Martin and Co (contractors) Ltd (197301QB 27 this is where electricity board cable was damage causing no electricity to the claimant business of melting. He was only allowed to claim damage to the furnace content (property) and the profit he would have got from the loss. However he was not allowed to recover the loss of time that the electricity was out of function.

484) **Q;** Explain pure economic loss by in relation to property?

A; Economic loss caused solely by acquiring a defective item is regard as pure economic loss because there is no duty of care owe to the customer or the claimant (Murphy v. Brentwood District Council).Lord Bridge said that no duty of care arising from purchasing defective goods. In this case the claimant cannot claim under tort, but could claim under contract law. However if the defective item caused physical injury to the claimant and damage to his property the claimant can sue the manufacture as they owe duty of (Murphy) to recover.

485) Q; Give example of fairness in implementing pure economic loss?

A; Cattle market was closed to prevent virus which the defendant negligently action allowed to escape. This was regarded as pure economic loss as none of his property was damage and no physical injury occurred this is fair for public health. Weller & Co v. Foot and Mouth (1966) 1Qb 569

Pure economic loss cause by journalist have advantage and disadvantages, It highlight issues which could help the court to update common law and the law reform to consider changes in the society. Also make the Public aware of individual behaviour or danger within society especially criminal acts, delinquencies, suspect social unrest; they protect society or make society. Example advertising (Caparo industries) (Donoghue v. Stevens) Professional negligence Spring v. Guardian assurance.

486) Q: Who does the rules protect?

A: The rules also protect the public from the professional and public authorities such as economic loss caused by statement or professional services to a specific individual and if damage occurred, then it is revocable under tort because the adviser has assume responsibilities or duty of care as it will not be pure economic loss. (White .v Jones).Welton v. North Cornwall District Council (1997)1WLR 570 An environmental officer who made a claimant to work which was not require was held to owe duty of care and the claimant was not pure economic loss. Is an example of protecting the public from abuse of power by authorities? ROSS V. COUNTERS (1980);A solicitor drawn up a will negligently so the beneficial did not receive the money in the Will, court decided that there was a duty of care since the solicitor ought to have had the plaintiff in mind when he gave the advice. Yianni v. Edwin Evans & son (1982) A valuar (Evans) reported falsely and negligently that the house which he valued was sound, was made liable, this prevent fraudulent

487) Q: What has been the advantages?

A: The advantage had been for business and politician, example prior to budget some of the details might be leaked to the newspaper which make the people aware and start panic buying such as cigarettes alcohol, petrol, alcohol, even people rush to complete purchase of land\houses in order to save money on land register fees or possible VAT increase. The media sometimes get it wrong as their information is not certain in subject or object matter; these are pure economic loss which is irrevocable

488) Q: What did Lord Atkins warned about duty of care?

A; Lord Atkins warned about established duty of care and foresees ability said "You must take reasonable care that your act or omission does not cause damage to your neighbour "He further went on about Proximity that your neighbour is the one who your action affect. Donoghue v. Stevenson (1932)

489) Q; What are the restriction or unfairness in pure economic loss?

A; restrictions\unfairness rules are_supported by controversial judgements among the Law lords regarding pure economic loss and in some cases the House of Lords had retracted earlier judgement. Example Ann's v. Merton LBC (1978) AC 728 allow damage to property which was originally built. This case went against traditional rule that, property damage describe the situation where someone's existing property is damaged.

490) **Q:** What did the court decided in Murphy case?

A: In Murphy, The court decided that the builder was not liable for damage that because the fire as this was irrecoverable economic loss but only liable for the loss of the possessions in the building. This decision caused outcry among the Law Lords who then overrule the decision of (Ann) in the case decision of Murphy. Similarly Murphy also overrules another case (Junior Books Veitch (1983) Ac 520 where claimant was originally allowed to claim against subcontractor under tort. This case undermines Contract law. Lord Schliemann LJ described the decision as odd. In Duncan Wallace (2000) 116 LQR 530 he said The court of Appeal obviously felt some embarrassment in explaining and justifying this particular consequence of the Murphy speeches as well as resulting judicial characterisation of what was in reality catastrophic; physical fire damage as legally irrevocable "pure economic loss". In D & F estates Ltd v. Church Comer for England (1989) A 177; Lord

Bridge and Lord Oliver express difficulties in reconcile the decision in the case of Ann.

491) Q: What did Lord Lloyd said I Aswan case?

A: In case Aswan Engineering v. Lupine (1987) 1WLR .Lord Lloyd LJ indicated that he would consider the loss of the Lupine as property damage and therefore claimable under Tort, Whilst Nicholls LJ took the view that it would be economic loss. This differing opinion is not isolated of establishing duty of care between property damage and pure economic loss. Lord Reid in Hedley Bryne said" I would think that the law must treat negligent words different from negligent acts. These highlight the recent expansion of the duty of care into other areas such as services which has blurred distinction between statement and acts. There is still difference in law between claim for negligent statement and acts.

492) Q: How has policy or politics plays part in decision\judgement?

A: Policy\politics has played major part in the judgement in favour of public authorities which are not fair in fact the. House of Lord has agreed to this, but some Lords do not actually concord to the policy. In a case of Candler .v Crane Christmas and Co (1951) 2 KB 164 Lord Denning express dissenting view that the accountant owe care to the third parties similar to the circumstance to the Hedley Byrne case.

493) Q: What do you think of the inconsistent in some judgement?

A; There had been inconsistent judgement which Lord Lawton in case of Spartan Steel said, “The difference which undoubtedly exists between what damage can be recovered in one type of case and what in another cannot be reconciled on any logical basis----such differences has reason because of the policy of law”. Example in S.1 of the defective premises Act 1972 did impose duty on builders and other undertaking work in the provision of dwellings the obligation’ policy decision. Lord Wilberforce expresses the common law to take reasonable care “nothing more and nothing less.

Lord Denning in Spartan “I think the question of recovering economic loss is one of policy---whenever the courts draw a line to mark out the bounds of duty.” “In order to limit the responsibility of the defendant”.

Supreme Court in Canada Winnipeg condominium corporation No 36 v. Bird construction co (199501SCR 85 la foster said “In cases involving the recoverability of economic loss in tort, it is preferable for the court to weigh the relevant POLICY issues openly”

494) **Q**: What do you think of terminology used in the judgement?

A:Terminology has been used to confuse the issue more, example in (Ann v. Merton) there was new introduction of "relationship of proximity or neighbourhood" was used in place of "special relationship which replaced the knowledge test.

495) **Q;** Do you ting the law is fair on economic law policy?

A: It is unlikely to entirely agree with the law on pure financial loss not revocable. IT appear to protect some professionals such as accountants\auditors, journalist .These bodies makes a lot of money from their negligence, thousands of people relied on the audited fiduciary duties in the account (Caparo) and lost their money, the defendant income increased as company share increased and newspaper sale increased, the court is meant to protect the public where is the justice. The rules favour public authorities because they only owe duty of care to the public and not to the individual.

496) **Q:** What did the law say about the emergencies team?

A: The law state that emergencies team must not be criticised when they act to save life in dramatic manner.

Haynes v. Harwood (1945) 1 KB 146 In Baker vote Hopkins (1959)1 WLR 966- hence the public cannot claim for their negligence. Another case was Chaudhry v. Prabhakar (198) 1wLR 29, a friend who made a recommendation in social set up to buy a second-hand car was found to owe duty of care because (special relationship) as the court stated that he regard himself as specialist and therefore liable to the damage. It shows that one need to be very careful what and where and when conversation takes place as the court can construe it to be liable.

497) Q; What do you think must be done in relation to the rules?.

A: There must be strict rules for misstatement by journalist and auditors as public rely on them for their judiciary duties. Why policies take precedence? Why protection of the public authorities, large company? Why small companies and sole traders are not protected by policy? The media appears to be in control of the country\people. Media trial, change of regulation or even change of government but on balance of probability the rules are fair but needs expansion to protect the public.

498) Q: Do you entirely agree with the law on pure financial loss not revocable?

A; IT appear to protect some professionals such as accountants\auditors, journalist These bodies makes a lot of money from their negligence, thousands of people relied on the audited fiduciary duties in the account (Caper) and lost their money, the defendant income increased as company share increased and newspaper sale increased, the court is meant to protect the public where is the justice

499) **Q;** who does the pure economic law favours?

A; The rules favour public authorities because they only owe duty of care to the public and not to the individual. The law state that emergencies team must not be criticised when they act to save life in dramatic manner. Haynes v. Harwood (1945) 1 KB 146 In Baker vote Hopkins (1959)1 WLR 966- hence the public cannot claim for their negligence. Another case was Chaudhry v. Prabhakar (198) 1wLR 29,

500) **Q:** Give an example in relation to pure economic?

A; friend who made a recommendation in social set up to buy a second-hand car was found to owe duty of care because (special relationship) as the court stated that he regard himself as specialist and therefore liable to the damage. It shows that one need to be very careful what and where and when conversation takes place as the court can construe it to be liable.

501) Q: What do you think the law should be?

A; There must be strict rules for misstatement by journalist and auditors as public rely on them for their judiciary duties. Why policies take precedence? Why protection of the public authorities, large company? Why small companies and sole traders are not protected by policy? The media appears to be in control of the country\people. Media trial, change of regulation or even change of government but on balance of probability the rules are fair but needs expansion to protect the public.

Chapter 8

PROPERTY LAW (exclusive, estoppels, lease, licence, deeds, overriding, equitable registration of property, easement, TOLATA, estate, tenancy, unities possession, title, interest time. Etc).

502) Q: What is Easement?

A; Is permission granted to use somebody's land? According to the House of Lords, one tenant can have Exclusive possession at rent to freeholder (Street v. Mount ford).However, the Lordship also stated that rennet is not essential in consideration (Ashburn Install v. Arnold) and s.205 (1) (xxvii) LPA 1925 to have absolute possession.

503) Q: What is Licence?

A; Is permission to do something you would not normally be allowed to do, but it is not confined to authorisation given by the state. Licence had been described as "a chameleonic device which performs different kinds of functions (short to long term (Gray & Gray), Land law, 7th edition, OUP 539. Licence does not create proprietary in landsite merely permission that prevent someone being regarded as trespasser. Hardwick v Johnson (1978) 2 ALL ER 35, a woman living in a house with a child, the husband left her. Court of appeal ruled that she had licence to occupy the property.

504) Q; What is Express licence?

A; This is for public access such as shops cinema pub act. Licence and construction travel. Is usually given orally or by invitation._Implied licence allows anyone to walk to the door if there is no gate of the house without express permission to knock at the door for permission to enter9 if there is no notice at the front of the door forbids such person. However the land lord can refuse permission and the person has to leave Robson v. Hallett (1967) 3 WLR 28. Lord Diplock LJ said a licence can be withdrawn but the person needs to be given reasonable time to leave the premises by appropriate route. BARE Licences; is permission granted without consideration i.e. only to do specific thing and nothing else this can be withdrawn. Licence granted is not transferrable. Licence couple with an interest- this could be used to create legal interest s. (2) (a) LPA 1925. Contractual licence

505) Q; Explain Easement in relation to electric cable?

A :For right be capable of an easement in accordance with Ellenborough Park, all the essential characteristics must exist: The right accommodate the dominant tenement and together with servient tenement are not owned and occupied by the same person\people the right to lie in grant. Easement could be created expressly or by implied. It can be of strict necessity (if there is no other means to access the road. It could be common intention. Provided that the easement is continues, and the use is apparent from careful inspection of the land, that its use is reasonable enjoyable of the property and was being used as "quasi easement" at the time of the sale of part. This will be implied, and the only formality needed is transfer been properly created. Express legal easement must be registered on the title of the land affected as appear in the list of registrable dispositions in 527 LRA 2002.

506) **Q**: Distinguishes licences and lease?

A; A person may have a lease (term of years absolute) granted by the freeholder. Leaseholder may grant another lease to somebody else called sublease or underleser and so on. Licences do not have any of these characteristics.

507) **Q;** Distinguished licence from easement?

A; Easement consists of servient tenement that carries the burden by granting the dominant tenement who benefit from this grant. Such arrangement create an interest in land, hence may be expressly created in writing (s. 53 (10 LPA 1925 or legal easement by deed s.52 (1) LPA 1925.Licence does not have these formalities and in most cases a temporary permission (permission for a boy to pick up a ball from neighbour garden).Easement give rise to formal exclusive possession, it is usually a legal interest but may also be equitable. Licence does not have any of these characteristics. (I.e. no legal or equitable interest)

508) **Q;** What is the factors used by the judges ?

A; to make decision may be unfair for landlord and tenant abuse the system. Legist ration put more stringent rule on lease\tenancy example; Act 1977 for residential landlord and tenant Act 1954 for business (part 11) gives tenants more rights which make it more difficult for landlord to regain possession. Neither Act gives possession to licence see. This is the reason why some landlord attempt to find other means to describe agreement as licence such as hotel, bed and breakfast, offering cleaning the person's room, offer lunch or do their laundry.

509) **Q**; What are The "exclusive" possession factors?

A; Have course disagreement among some judges. Example Lord Temple man said tenancy is "grant of exclusive possession for a term at rent" Street v. Mountford (1985) AC 809.This is because the tenant have the right to exclude others from using the subject matter (rooms).In Antoniodes v. Villies (1990) 1 AC 417, it was confirmed that a person have exclusive possession for a period at a rent and has tenant and not licensee. However, the court of Appeal in Ashburn Anstalt v. Arnold (1090) Ch 1 stated that it is not essential to pay rent to be entitled to have exclusive possession. If a person pays capital it is fair for him to have exclusive possession for the agreed period. (Street v. Mountford)

The wording of agreement is very important, example "allocation of the rooms is subject to alteration "this means that none of the tenant have exclusive possession" A G Securities v. Vaughan (1990) 1 AC 417. Equity estoppels could be used to create a binding tenancy and be bound by it if the freeholder refused to grant it.

510) Q: Explain Exclusive possession?

A; Exclusive possession distinguishes leases not merely from licences but also from easement" Landlords use means such as offer laundry, breakfast, cleaning services or Land lord has key in an attempt to prevent "exclusive possession".

511) Q; Explain exclusive possession of easement as per the house of Lords?

A; Easement is permission granted to use somebody's land. According to the House of Lords, one tenant can have Exclusive possession at rent to freeholder (Street v. Mountford).However, the Lordship also stated that rennet is not essential in consideration (Ashburn Anstalt v. Arnold) and s.205 (1) (xxvii) LPA 1925 to have absolute possession.

512) Q: what is exclusive possession?

A: Exclusive possession; A fixed term tenancy where commencing, duration and ending date are restricted access by the landlord is void (Lace v. Chantler (1944) 1 All ER 305.Any uncertainty and restraint on the landlord defeat the rule of certainty and render lease void (Prudential assurance (House of Lords) A person is granted lease but he is entitle to easement which could be express or implied, whilst licence is only temporary permission which can be revoked at any time. Hence a lease holder can exclusively possess easement and licence.

513) Q; Explain licence given case laws support?

A; Licence_ is permission to do something you would not normally be allowed to do, but it is not confined to authorisation given by the state. Licence had been described as "a chameleonic device which performs different kinds of functions (short to long term (Gray & Gray), Land law, 7th edition, OUP 539. Licence does not create proprietary in landsite merely permission that prevent someone being regarded as trespasser. Factors; Hardwick v Johnson (1978) 2 ALL ER 35, a woman living in a house with a child, the husband left her. Court of appeal ruled that she had licence to occupy the property.

514) Q; What is express licence?

A: Express licence is usually given orally or by invitation. Implied licence allows anyone to walk to the door if there is no gate of the house without express permission to knock at the door for permission to enter if there is no notice at the front of the door forbids such person. However the land lord can refuse permission and the person has to leave Robson v. Hallett (1967) 3 WLR 28. Lord Diplock LJ said a licence can be withdrawn but the person needs to be given reasonable time to leave the premises by appropriate route.

515) Q: What is Bare licence ?

A; BARE Licences; is permission granted without consideration i.e. only to do specific thing and nothing else this can be withdrawn. Licence granted is not transferrable.

516) Q: What is licence couple with interest?

A; Licence couple with an interest- this could be used to create legal interest s. (2) (a) LPA 1925

Contractual licence- this is for public access such as shops cinema pub act. Licence and construction travel.

517) Q: Distinguished licence from easement?

A; Easement consists of servient tenement that carries the burden by granting the dominant tenement who benefit from this grant. Such arrangement create an interest in land, hence may be expressly created in writing (s. 53 (10 LPA 1925 or legal easement by deed s.52 (1) LPA 1925.Licence does not have these formalities and in most cases a temporary permission (permission for a boy to pick up a ball from neighbour garden).

518) Q: What is the function of Easement?

A: Easement give rise to formal exclusive possession, it is usually a legal interest but may also be equitable.

Licence does not have any of these characteristics. (I.e. no legal or equitable interest)

519) Q; What must be satisfied for right of easement terms?

A; For right be capable of an easement in accordance with Ellen borough Park, all the essential characteristics of an easement must exist. The right accommodate the dominant tenement and together with servient tenement are not owned and occupied by the same person\people the right to lie in grant. Easement could be created expressly or by implied. It can be of strict necessity (if there is no other means to access the road. It could be common intention. Provided that the easement is continues, and the use is apparent from careful inspection of the land, that its use is reasonable enjoyable of the property and was being used as “quasi easement” at the time of the sale of part. This will be implied, and the only formality needed is transfer been properly created. Express legal easement must be registered on the title of the land affected as appear in the list of registrable dispositions in 527 LRA 2002.

520) Q: Distinguished licences and lease and give the factors to be considered

A; A lease or tenancy; A person may have a term of years absolute granted by the freeholder owner of the land. Tenant or lease may grant another lease called sublease or underleser\ subtenant. The sub lesser \underleser and sub\under lessee all hold lease reversion. Licences do not have any of the characteristics.

521) Q: Distinguished licences and lease and give the factor in relation to tenancy?

A:Legislation put more stringent rule on lease\tenancy example; Act 1977 for residential landlord and tenant Act 1954 for business (part 11) gives tenants more rights which make it more difficult for landlord to regain possession. Neither Act gives possession to licence see. This is the reason why some landlord attempt to find other means to describe agreement as licence such as hotel, bed and breakfast, offering cleaning the person's room, offer lunch or do their laundry.

522) Q: Distinguished licences and lease and give the factor in relation to exclusive possession?

A: The factors use by the courts for "exclusive" exclusive possession has course disagreement among some judges. Example Lord Templeman said tenancy is "grant of exclusive possession for a term at rent" Street v. Mountford (1985) AC 809.This is because the tenant have the right to exclude others from using the subject matter (rooms).

523) **Q** Use another case law to explain exclusion?

A: In Antoniodes v. Villies (1990) 1 AC 417, it was confirmed that a person have exclusive possession for a period at a rent and has tenant and not licensee. However, the court of Appeal in Ashburn Anstalt v. Arnold (1090) Ch 1 stated that it is not essential to pay rent to be entitled to have exclusive possession.

524) **Q;** Distinguished licences and lease and give the factor in relation to agreement?

A; The wording of agreement is very important ,example a house of multiple occupation of about 5, each tenant have their own room but the agreement state that "allocation of the rooms is subject to alteration "this means that none of the tenant have exclusive possession" and therefore licensee A G Securities v. Vaughan (1990) 1 AC 417.

525) **Q:** Give a case law of how words might be interpreted?

A: In case of Gilliam v. Breiden Bach (1982) RTR 323, Mr. Gilham withdrew the police officer licence by saying "Fuck off you planks". Reasonable people might interpret this as leave my premises, but the court however interpreted it as abuse rather than to leave. It appears that some judgement by the court is influence by policy and to protect vulnerable person or public authorities.

526) **Q:** Distinguished licences and lease and give the factor in relation to period of tenancy

A: If a tenant pays say £5000 capital to occupy a property for a period say two years and does not pay any rent during the period means that he has "exclusive possession" for that period based on the test laid down by the House of Lords in (Street v. Mountford), the freeholder cannot gain possession until after the period.

527) **Q:** Distinguished licences and lease and give the factor in relation to avoid granting exclusive tenancy?

A: Another attempt for landlord to avoid granting exclusive tenancy is for them to have a key to the occupier's room. But in a case Aston v. Murphy it does not itself prevent "exclusive possession". However a landlord with a key may restrict the person not to use the room within agreed period (say 12- 2 pm) so that the landlord will do the cleaning\ laundry service, but such arrangement gives the occupier a contractual right (Markou v. Slaves).If it is allege that the Landlord breaks the rule\agreement (Howyler v. Ruddy (1996) 28 HLR 550.

528) Q: How can the landlord be successful

A: The landlord will be successful if he can proof that during the restricted period (12- 2) he unrestricted access the occupier will be regarded as having licence. On the other hand the court might look at the case with scepticism and grant tenancy.

529) Q: Give a controversial case in licence?

A; a controversial decision in a case of Westminster City Council v. Clarke (1992) 2 AC 288, is where the person is in a temporary accommodation with a clause in the agreement that that he could be moved to other room, the court stated that he has licence to stay rather than tenancy. Burton v. (LQHT) landlord and Quadrant Housing Trust (1998) QB 834.This gives more power to tenants to abuse the system.

530) Q: Is estoppels unfair?

A; Someone with no title can create and be bound by it on the basis of "estoppels" (this can arise if the freehold refuses to grant tenancy despite the person ling in the premises for some time) the right of land lords is taken away by equity decision.

531) **Q;** Is the law fair on landlord?

A; Statute gives more right to tenants, leaseholders and lice

It can be argued that where rent is not being charged, the occupier be exclusive for a period and indication that no intention to create a legal relationship and this arrangement is then term as term licence which can be revoked at any time by the freeholder especially if he want to sell the property.

LEASE and LICENS

532) **Q;** Explain Legal and equitable leases

1) **A:**Lease is recognised in statue as ESTATE in land and is valuable assert.
2) To have a lease means that the tenant can sell the lease and give it as gift.
3) The lease can be pass to his hires if he dies doing the lease period.
4) Creation of new lease is the Grant of lease
5) LEASOR is the landlord (the one who grant the lease),LEASEE or the tenant is the one the lease is granted.

6) Lease have the right to occupy the property to the term agree which is called a demise or term of year or leases.
7) SUBLEASE is if the tenant grant lease to another person before the original lease run out.
8) HEAD LEASE is the original agreement and the sublease person (or the SUB TENANT)
9) SUBLEASE agreement is the lease between the landlord and the tenant.
10) ASSIGMENT is when a tenant sell his lease,(selling the estate in land) to sublease.
11) The seller of the lease is called assignor
12) The buyer of the lease is called assignee
13) The person (sub leaser) who buys the lease from the tenant become the tenant themselves.

533) **Q;** Briefly explain licence

A: Is permission to use land.it could be a contractual when the person occupied the land or b)BARE licence when payment is made when required.

A licence have no interest in Land which means that a landlord can terminate the licence and the occupier has to move out (even if there is contractual arrangement between them)

534) **Q;** Explain legal a; creation of lease?

A; DEEDS because lease has legal estate in land, it must be created by deeds.(which contain written document of all the agree terms such as rent and length of the term. And executed by both parties as a deed. Sign in the presence of witness who have to write his name and address on the deeds. If there is no deeds or payroll or equitable lease then it will be licenced to occupy the property.

535) **Q:** Explain if landlord sell the property the rule needs to be followed?

A: rule for registered titles or legal Lease for more than 7 years need to be registered in the land registered Act 2002 s. 27 to bind on the buyer.

If is less than 7 years the leas will have overriding statues it means is binding on the buyer.

However if it is equitable lease, this is not given overriding statues. Equitable lease must be protected by notice in the land register.

If the tenant fail to register the lease (legal\equitable), could still be protected if he was in occupancy at the time. (overriding interest.

536) **Q:** What is the rule on registration of property?

A: if is not registered, it will not bind the buyer and the new landlord can ask the buyer to move out of the property

537) Q: Explain the characteristics for the creation of lease?

A; There are three areas to take into consideration in creating lease

1)Exclusive possession for a term and at a rent for a definite term.

2)The lease must be granted for definite term.(from outset both parties knows the date lease start and date it would end).

3) Payment of rent (is an indication that the payment of rent that the parties intend to create land\tenant relationship) NB Payment of rent has been overrule by the house of Lords.

538) Q What are the main types of lease?

A; There are few types example periodic, fixed, legal, etc.

539) Q; Explain fixed term lease as per agreement

A: (Between a week to 999 years**)** which means the tenant have to vacate the property when the term expires, and the landlord cannot ask the tenant until the term expires.(unleased there is agreement to terminate the lease earlier by given notice say 4 weeks) or vice versa not paying rent or breach the term of the lease.

540) **Q:** What right to forfeit the lease?

A; Whereby the landlord can end the lease if the tenant breach the terms of the lease such as not paying rent or bad tenant.

541) **Q;** What is Periodic lease?

A; This means agreement to pay the rent on periodic basis which could be weekly, monthly or yearly. This lease is the lease is granted for indefinite term. Because the tenancy is automatically renewed at the end of each period. (Notice by the tenant or the landlord must be given at the beginning of each period weekly, monthly quarterly.

542) **Q:** What is exception to the rule?

A: Exception to this rule is that periodic of yearly can give minimum of 6 months' notice.

Exception Minimum of 4 weeks' notice needed to terminate weekly residential property

543) **Q:** What is Payroll lease?

A; Payroll lease is when short lease is given without deeds; could be verbally;

The characteristics of Payroll lease is that **A)** the lease must not exceed 3 years **b)** the tenant right to occupy the property must come to existence as soon as is agreed **c)**Lease must be granted for the best rent which can be reasonable obtained) the tenant must not have paid lump sum instead of the rent.

544) **Q**; Explain not legal lease?

A: Not legal lease ;this is if the agreement is not grated by DEEDS or Payroll lease and therefore cannot be enforceable (unless is equitable lease)

545) **Q;** What is equitable lease ?

A; Is not legal but if there is written agreement between all the parties the court will enforce it.

546) **Q;** Name four characteristics according to Ellenborough Park (1956) CH 131 for easement to exist?

A; For an easement to exist, It must satisfy the following four essential characteristics (Ellenborough Park (1956) ch 131.

1) There must be dominant (who benefit) and servient (carries the burden) tenement.
2) The right must accommodate the dominant tenement.
3) The dominant and servient tenement must not be owned and occupied by the same person.

4) The right must lie in grant that is there must be a capable grantor and grantee and the right must be capable of forming the subject matter of a grant.

547) Q; What are the rules for easement to exist?

A; where necessary implied rules method on easement may be used to support argument which include;

1) Easement as necessity.
2) Easement implied due to common intention of the buyer and the seller at the time of sale.
3) Easement created under the rule of Wheelor v. Burrows (1879) 12 Ch D 31. (Continues, apparent, necessary for reason of enjoyment of land, being used as quasi easement by the seller for the benefit of the land being sold at the time of sale of part).
4) Easement created under section 62 LPA 1925.

5) An easement is capable of being legal as it is equivalent to a fee simple absolute under s.1 (2) LPA 1925.
6) An express legal easement requires a deed (s.52 (1) LPA 1925.An express legal easement requires a deed s.52(1) LPA 1925 in accordance with s. 1

LP (MP) A 1989 and registrations if it appears in the list of registrations in s.27 LRA 2002.

Scenario on joint ownership

In January 2010, five friends, Anne, Belinda, Carol, Diana and Ellen, decided to set up a business offering residential summer camps for children. Ellen did not wish to be involved in the day to day running of the business but wanted to contribute to the venture as an investment. That year they bought a house for the business for 3500, 000.Each person contributed £100,000.The property was transferred to them as joint "beneficial joint tenant".

In June 2010, Diana obtained a better job offer and asked Belinda if she would buy her out. Belinda agreed but, before anything was in writing, Diana was killed in a car accident. She left all of her property to Ellen.

In February 2011, Carol was struggling financially and mortgages her share to her friend, Rob. That year however, the camp was a success and Caro was able to repay Rob. In September.

In March 2012, Belinda decided to go travelling. She wrote to all of the others saying, "I want my share in the house to be bought out immediately". She sent the letters by special delivery to the home address of the other three. Carol and Ellen signed for their letters, but Annes boyfriend signed for her letter on Anne's behalf and then he forgot to give the letter to Anne. Belinda died bungee jumping the following month. In her Will, Belinda left her property to Anne.

In June 2016, all of the surviving friends met and agreed to sell the house, take their shares and go their separate ways. However just after this meeting, Anne had a heart attack and died. Anne's will leave all of her property to Carol.

In December 2016, Carol found a purchaser for the property, Fred, and is proposing to sell it to him. Ellen has come to asked you for advice.

Explain;

a) How the legal and the equitable interests in the property have devolved; and
b) Whether Ellen can prevent Carol from selling the property.

548) Q: What was created when the five friends purchased the property in January 2010?

A: When the five friends purchased the property, a trust of land was created (trust of land and appointment of trustee) TOLATA 1996 s. 6(1) with the legal estate held by Anne, Belinda, Carol and Diana as joint tenants on trust for themselves and Ellen as joint of the beneficial (equitable) interest.

549) **Q:** How can legal estate be held

A: Legal estate can only be held as a joint tenancy (s.1 (6) LPA 1925 by the first four named s. (34) (1) trustee Act 1925.who are of age "suri Juris" and under an implied or express trust of land. It is not possible to create legal estate in tenancy in common. When the purchase was formally completed, legal estate transferred under s. 52 LPA 1925 on a deed, and registered under s. 27 LRA 2002,the transferee therefore vested in the legal estate in the first four named purchaser.

550) **Q;** How can equitable interest be held?

A: The equitable interest may be held may be held by the co- owners as joint tenants or tenancy in commons. 34 (4) LPA 1925.

551) **Q;** How can tenant in common be supported?

A: Tenant in common is also supported by their equal contribution (as opposed to unequal contribution in joint tenant. Payne v web (1874) LR 19 E9 26 Also permit the friends can dispose some or all of her equitable interest \share during her life time or death to any one they choose.

552) Q: What factors to be considered in equitable interest?

A: Factors to consider are the four unities; possession, interest, title and times which appear met from the facts so the equitable interest can be held either as joint tenant or tenant in common. They serve the joint tenancy in equity interest when they declared "Unity of possession to use the property as business partners (Re; Fullers contract (1933) ch 652. Goodman v. Gallant (1986) Fam 106. In support of express declaration they made, Pattern LJ said "The effect of exciting the declaration of trust was to make equitable tenant in common regardless of what the parties may have subjectively intended and to stop from denying the title"

553) Q What happen when Dianna died in June 2010

A: When Diana died, she was entitle to the legal estate as a joint tenant and as there was nothing in writing and no exchange of contract, the right of survivorship therefore applies so that any gift of the property in his will was ineffective. The result was that the legal estate became vested in Anne, Belinda<Carol as joint tenants on trust for the four surviving co-owners. However prior to Diana death, she put on express notice and was agreed by Belinda to buy her out, this sever the equitable

interest. Diana equitable interest falls into her estate and passes under the terms of her will which in this case her equitable interest will be transferred to Ellen assuming that the will is properly executed under s. 9 of the Will Act 1837 (signed by two witnesses excluding Ellen the beneficial in Diana presence who also signed it.

Notice must be placed in the deed (proprietorship) of death and date to indicate that she is no more holders of the legal estates. 52 LPA 1925.Ellen increased in the equitable interest must also be entered\recorded in the deed as majority value as share can be transferred freely in tenancy in common s.53 (1) (b) LPA1925.

554) **Q:** What happen to Carol mortgage to Rob in February 2011?

A: Carol mortgage her share to Rob in the property resulted to severance by alienation. At that date there were three joint tenants holding legal estate and four tenants of equitable interest. Rob receives Carol equitable share as a tenant in common, but Carol continued to hold her original one quarter legal estate share as joint tenant. On the property charge deed, the transaction must be recorded as Rob being mortgagee and carol the mortgagor would be granted equitable estate interest transfers in the property and his money will be held on tenancy in common. s. 53 (1) (b) LPA 1925.Rob.in which deed is required.

555) Q: what happened to the equitable interest when Carol repaid the loan in September 2011

A: When Carol repays the loan to Rob, she gets back her equitable share interest and continues to hold it as a tenant in common. Notice must be placed in the deed to confirm that Rob has no more interest.

556) Q: How important is Belinda letter served on March 2012

A: Belinda letter "I want my share in the house to be bought out immediately" severed the joint tenancy by notice under s. 36 (2) LPA 1925. It shows the correct intention immediately and not in future (Harris v. Goddard).To does this; it needs the consent of all the survivor parties. It is requirement to have notice to be sent to other equitable interest (beneficiaries) and does not need to be signed (Re Draper's).Belinda served the notice correctly as she posted them by special delivery post in line with s.196 (196) (4)LPA 1925.Such notice is deemed served if it is not returned by post office as undelivered. This presumes applies even if it proves that the notice never actually arrived at the destination. (88 Berkeley road NW9 (1971) Ch 648.

557) **Q:** Will the notice varied?

A; In this case s.196 (3) 1925 is confirmed as the notice arrived at their destination. The fact that Anne's boyfriend forgot to give signed letter to other parties with equitable interest is irrelevant. When Belinda died the legal estate vested in Carol and Anne by survivorship (joint tenant) she left her equitable interest to Ann in her Will so her Anne will inherit Belinda one quarter share as tenant in common.

558) **Q:** Who hold the legal estate after June 2016

A; The legal estate was vest in Anne and Carol holding the legal estate in joint tenant for themselves and equitable interest for them and Ellen. On Anne's death her equitable interest passed to Carol as per Anne's Will. Prior to the death of Anne, It was unanimously\mutually agreed to sell the property

559) **Q**: What is the end result of this saga

A: The end result was that Carol holds the legal estate on trust for herself and Ellen in Equity. Carol was the majority equitable interest shareholder, no one to manage the business when she retires, and the court is likely to rule for her to sell the property.

560) **Q**: Can Ellen stop Carol selling

A: Ellen cannot stop Carol from selling the property because Carol holds the legal estate under implied trust of land and a sole survivor registered proprietor with no restrictions initially. Being the only trustee of the land, Carol is invested with absolute owner under s. 6 Trust of Land and appointment of trustee Act 1996.This means she can sell the trust land at any time she decides. However, since they are both beneficiaries with possession, Carol is a duty bound to consult herself and Ellen before exercising her powers to sell. S. 11 (TOLATA) 1996.

561) **Q:** What would have been placed on the deeds and why?

A: A restriction would have been placed in the deeds register warning any prospective purchaser to overreach, as there would be notice that Ellen only has investment and equitable interest. Where there is no restriction, in the property ownership registrar, a purchaser is entitled to assume that Carol is the sole legal and beneficial owner and deals with her as such. If Ellen refused to sell, either can apply to the court under section 14 of the Act 1996.carol application would be for the property to be sold. The court will consider the factors in s. 15 of the Act (TOLATA) 1996 which will include the initial purpose of the trust. Carol can argue that she is the only survivor to run the business and that she wanted to retire and there is no one to manage it. Moreover, she is the majority equitable share holder and her wishes prevail. Furthermore, before Anne died the entire survivor with legal estate (Anne and Carol) and equitable interest (Anne, Carol and Ellen) unanimously\mutually agreed to sell the property. Ellen cannot rebut this argument and the court is likely to grant the sale of the property. The proceeds would be shared between Carol and Ellen after tax in proportion to their equitable shares

Scenario

In 2009, Satvir, the owner of Lyon Hall, a large Victorian house in extensive grounds granted Thomas, a craftsman, a five-year legal lease of a workshop at the bottom of the garden. Shortly after, Satvir gave Thomas oral permission to run an electric cable from Lyons Hall to supply the workshop with electricity. In 2014, Thomas's lease expired, and Stair sold the freehold of the workshop to Thomas, whilst retaining the rest of the

Lyons Hall. The transfer made no mention of the right to run the electricity cable from Lyons Hall to the workshop, but did give Thomas an express right to use the driveway of Lyon Hall to access the main road.

In 2015, Satvir sold Lyon Hall to Alison and, last month, Thomas sold the workshop to Tony.

Alison is planning to demolish Lyon Hall and build flats in its place. She has told Tony that he will no longer be able to use the electricity cable or the driveway. Tony is upset about Alison plans.

Renate owner of the Victoria house next door to Lyon Hall is also unhappy with Alison's plans as it is likely that, when the flats are built, they will block the light to the Victorian conservatory on the side of Reena's house.

Advice Alison, explaining the relevant legal issues, whether;

> She can remove the electricity cable supplying the workshop;
> She can prevent Tony from using her driveway;
> Reena can prevent her from building the flats.

562) Q; What must property have for easement to exit?

A: For an easement to exist, it must have four essential characteristics (Ellenborough Park (1956) ch 131. 1)

There must be dominant (who benefit) and servient (carries the burden) tenement 2) The right must accommodate the dominant tenement. 3) The dominant and servient tenement must not be owned and occupied by the same person.4)The right must lie in grant that is there must be a capable grantor and grantee and the right must be capable of forming the subject matter of a grant.

Where necessary implied rules on easement may be used to support argument which include; 1) Easement as necessity.2) Easement implied due to common intention of the buyer and the seller at the time of sale.3) Easement created under the rule of Wheelor v. Burrows (1879) 12 Ch D 31. (Continues, apparent, necessary for reason of enjoyment of land, being used as quasi easement by the seller for the benefit of the land being sold at the time of sale of part).4)Easement created under section 62 LPA 1925.

563) Q; Give implications of using Electricity cable.

A; The first three essential characteristics are present. Considering the fact of the case and comment made by Lord Denning in Wong v Beaumont property trust Ltd (1965) 1 QB 173.It seems that considering all four methods of implied easement of necessity is the most likely option or common intention)

1) When Thomas began to use the electricity in 2009, he did so with Satvir (then the legal freeholder of Lyon Hall oral permission to run the cable. He had a mere licence for the part of the land (workshop) for the whole of five years lease. However, satvir conveyed the freehold to Thomas and although the conveyance did not contain express grant of electricity easement as sale of part of land. It is possible for easement to be implied or intended easement.
2) If the rule of Wheeldonv burrows or s. 62 LPA 1925 applies Thomas use of electricity had been quasi-easement and this has been both continues and apparent (ward v. Kirkland) (1967) Ch 194. Ungoed Thomas J said "The feature must be one that has a degree of permanence" Thomas has used the electricity since the duration of the five-year lease and continued when he became the legal estate owner, the servient tenement, until he transferred the freehold to Tony and is necessary for the reasonable enjoyment of the workshop.
3) Tony will acquire an implied easement under the rule of Wheeldon v Burrows. Implied easement may applies under s. 62 LPA 1925 which is designed to

ensure that everything on the land or enjoy with it is passed to the buyer.

4) The fact that Thomas bought the freehold when the five-year licence run out means that the wording of s.62 enable Thomas who had a mere licence to use the electricity to acquire easement or convert Thomas licence into easement At the time of the conveyance, Thomas was the dominant tenement and Satvir was the owner of the servient.
5) There was generally diversity of occupation which satisfied the operation of s.62.
6) Alison can attempt to sue former landlord Satvri (sale of reversion) of Thomas sue Satvir (privity of landlord) or Tony sue Thomas who assign freehold.
7) Alison might argue that the deed did not mention about the electricity to the workshop. However during the pre-contract inquiry, Alison did not enquire about the workshop so she might not be able to take free of the easement s.52 LPA1925.
8) Tony has the benefit of a valid easement created by **s.62** LPA 1925 upon the sale of part.
9) Alison will be bound by the easement when she purchased the freehold. Inspection of the deed would show that the workshop was part of the land which should have alerted her to make more inquires.

564) Q; Give an implications of Drive way?

A; 11) Tony purchased the freehold workshop with an express grant of easements he has an interest as fee simple absolute in possession and easement made by deed hence complies with s. 52 (1) LPA 1925.

12) The title of the (workshop) was registered as per s.27 LRA 2002.This section state that a disposition of a registered estate include express grant of an easement **(s.27 (2)(**d) must be completed against the workshop which it was assume was done. However, if it was not done, then it would not be legal easement and Alison would take free from it **(s.29 LRA 2002)** as Sch 3 LRA 2002 does not protect an expressly created legal easement that has not be registered. Tom can claim implied **easement of necessity** which arose on the sale of part (which has continued from his predecessor) It does not have to be an overriding interest It would have been obvious to Tony on reasonable careful inspection of the land and he knew about it.

13)Thomas who sold the workshop to Tony can prove that he had exercise the right in the year prior to the sale to Tony.

14)**Section 62** LPA 1925 will applies as explain under electricity above. Conveyance convey to Tony include all "easement, rights, advantages appertain to the land enjoy **(Wright v. McAdam)**,Tony will continued to have easement of the driveway

565) **Q;** Give example of Building flats?

A; Reena cannot stop Alison from building the flats, but she could present submission to the local authority (planning) which might force Alison to redesign the plans to avoid restriction of light to her Victoria conservatory. There is a safeguard in the planning system that gives people who might be affected by development an opportunity to raise objection.

16)It may be possible for Reena to have right of light in relation to interference with light to conservatory. There is no express right and no sale of part which could give rise to an implied grant.

Since the Victoria house was built more than 40 years and if Reena can prove that the Victoria conservatory was built over twenty years which will then give her the possibility for her to claim a right of prescription as long as Reena can claim uninterrupted user for twenty years without any written consent, her claim to a right of light will be deemed absolute and indefeasible

566) **Q:** How will Reena be advised

A: However, Reena would be advice that, she may have an easement of light, she will only be entitled to "sufficient light according to the ordinary notion of mankind" for the benefit use of her conservatory (Collis v. Home and Colonial stores Ltd (1904) AC 179. This might have reduced the amount of light that he had been used to.

567) Q: Described prescription Act 1832?

Section 2 of the prescription Act 1832 prevents a common law claim to an easement by prescription being defeated where the easement has been enjoyed without interruption for full period of 20 years.

Reena may be advice to wait for a year after becoming aware of the plan to restrict her light so that her claim for right of light may not be ignored for the purpose of the prescription Act 1832, but she must be careful not to miss the dead line for objection to the plan.

Chapter 9

CO-OWNERSHIP (Property law) (joint tenancy, tenancy in common, express, declaration, legal estate, Co ownership)

568) Q: What is co-ownership?

A: Co-ownership is when property is held by more than one person and have interest in the same land.(free or lease hold together.

It can arise by expressly(legal owners for them all) by the parties or implied(the property is held by one owner in trust for owners or may have shares in the property)) due to circumstances. The rest have equitable interest of the land. It is implied trust.

569) Q: Explain co-ownership in relation to trust?

1) **A;** All co-ownership is held in trust of land (TOLATA 1996).
2) The 1996 Act TOLATA sets out the power of the trustee; absolute power; to sell, mortgage act.
3) The trustee must consult with the beneficiary owners. Consider the majority share owner.
4) Court can decide when there is dispute.
5) In joint tenant, the survivor get the whole capital but in tenant in common (hold the property in

undivided shares) the equitable interest passes to their chosen beneficiaries.

6) Only four people can hold the legal title in co-ownership as joint tenant. The only way that another can be legal owner (if one of the four dies) is by being appointed by the court.
7) If there is no document to confirm whether the parties hold the property in joint tenant or tenant in common, then there must be a TEST

570)Q: What are the four tests to establish co-ownership?

A; The 4 unities are possession, interest, time and title but only essential for tenancy in common is "possession"

If all test failed to produce how the property to be held, then it would be deemed to be held **in joint tenancy**

571)Q; What is express declaration in co- ownership?

A ; a)Express declaration in the parties of how the land to be held .this will be the document.(will say that that they have agree to hold the property in either joint tenancy of tenant in common)once this is present then it is conclusive. The other 2 test are no longer necessary. In support of express declaration they made, Pattern LJ said "The effect of exciting the declaration of trust was to make equitable tenant in common regardless of what the parties may have subjectively intended and to stop from denying the title"

b) any words of severance in the transfer to the co-owners example equal share indicate that they hold the property in equal and separate shares in the property.

c) Does equity presume tenancy in common. This is if the property was bought on behave of business, or the buyers contributed different amount of money towards the purchase.(how the property was finance)

d)Time; means they acquire their interest in the property at the same time when the sale was completed.

572) Q: What does title mean?

A; TITLE means they acquire their interest under the same document.

573) Q; What does interest mean?

A; INTEREST; means the interest must be the same nature and interest example share the same freehold or leasehold.

574) Q; What does possession mean?

A:POSSESSION; equally entitle to use and occupied the whole property and not able to exclude each other.

If all 4 unities are present then it may be held on joint tenancy.

If only one survivor and the property is sold, the survivor get everything (capital) if it is held in joint tenant. If it is held in tenancy in common, the other heir of the trust will give their shares.

575) Q: Explain Co-ownership?

A;)Legal estate can only be held as a joint tenancy (s.1 (6) LPA 1925 by the first four named s. (34) (1) trustee Act 1925.who are of age "suri Juris" and under an implied or express trust of land. It is not possible to create legal estate in tenancy in common.

1) When the purchase was formally completed, legal estate transferred under s. 52 LPA 1925 on a deed, and registered under s. 27 LRA 2002,the transferee therefore vested in the legal estate in the first four named purchaser.
2) The equitable interest may be held by the co- owners as joint tenants or tenancy in commons. 34 (4) LPA 1925.
3) Factors to consider are the four unities; possession, interest, title and times
4) equitable interest can be held either as joint tenant or tenant in common. Their express statement to hold the beneficial interest as joint tenants is conclusive (Goodman v. Gallant).

5) Belinda letter "I want my share in the house to be bought out immediately" severed the joint tenancy by notice under s. 36 (2) LPA 1925.
6) It shows the correct intention immediately and not in future (Harris v. Goddard).To does this; it needs the consent of all the survivor parties.
7) It *is requirement to have notice to be sent to other equitable interest (beneficiaries) and* does not need to be signed (Re Draper's).
8) Belinda served the notice correctly as she posted them by special delivery post in line with s.196 (196) (4)LPA 1925.Such notice is deemed served if it is not returned by post office as undelivered. This presumes applies even if it proves that the notice never actually arrived at the destination. (88 Berkeley road NW9 (1971) Ch 648
9) In this case s.196 (3) 1925 is confirmed as the notice arrived at their destination. The fact that Anne's boyfriend forgot to give signed letter to other parties with equitable interest is irrelevant.
10) When Belinda died the legal estate vested in Carol and Anne by survivorship (joint tenant). She left her equitable interest to Ann in her Will so Anne will inherit Belinda's one quarter share as tenant in common.

576) Q: Explain Characteristics of tenancy in common?

A; This means that each of the friends can dispose some or all of her equitable interest \share during her life time or death to any one they choose (it does not have to be members holding equitable interest in the business of the trust.

The other co- owners have no right of survivorship i.e. when one dies, the will form part of her estate and her equitable share can be given to whoever she chooses.

That when the property is sold all the surviving tenant in common will be entitle to all the proceed. Shares do not need to be equal and it can be transferred freely

They serve the joint tenancy in equity interest when they declared "Unity of possession to use the property as business partners (Re; Fullers contract (1933) ch 652. (Goodman v. Gallant).

Tenant in common is also supported by their equal contribution (as opposed to unequal contribution in joint tenant. Payne v web (1874) LR 19 E9 26

The **legal estate** always remains **joint tenancy**, but the equitable interest will be held in tenancy in common by all five friends s.34 (2) LPA 1025.

They could hold the equitable interest as joint tenant or tenancy in common s.34 (4) LPA 1925.

Chapter 10

EQUITY AND TRUST(trustee, trust, Duress, gift, undue influence, shares, charity

577) Q; As the court cannot supervise the activities of every trustee, the prime responsibility for such supervision falls to the beneficiaries of the trust. They are expected to monitor the trustee's activities and to complain to the court if there is any breach---of trust". Peace and Stevens, Trust and equitable Obligation. OUP 6th edition, at P791
Critically evaluate the effectiveness of supervision of trust by beneficial

A; Trustee has power under TOLAT 1996 s.6, Trustee Act 1925 and 2000.

The rational of beneficiary's principles lies in the enforcement and therefore need a proprietary equitable interest in the trust property to be able to enforce the trust (fixed and discretional trust).Beneficiaries must monitor the fiduciary duties of the trustee at all time, it helps to balance power Re Shaw (1957). The right of the beneficiaries could vary by the trust as per s.31 and s.32 of Trustee Act 1925 and the Law commission report 2011.The court cannot monitor all trust, trust with certainty of settler\ testator intention, subject matter and object matter. The court rely on the beneficiaries (who the gift belong) to enforce the trust, if not the trustee owe no duty of care. In Murices v. Bishop (1805) 10 Ves JR 522 Sir William Grant MR said "Every trust must a definite object. There must be someone in whose favour the court can decree specific performance".

578) Q; What is the reason for beneficial principle?

A; The main reason for beneficiary's principle is for them to enforce the duty which must impose on trustees and without this, then there can be trust. It could be balance the power- trustee\objects. The theory may support private trust; fixed, discretional, outright gift, McHale v. Dolton, CF, Re; Barlow's and the condition precedent. However the theory does not explain charitable trust and Denney. Trust is obligatory and power is discretionary.

Beneficiaries, who are task to enforce trust, need to have equitable proprietary interest or just factual interest in enforcement Re Denney's Trust Deed (1969)

579) Q; Who is the rear owner of trust?

A; Trustee is invested with legal estate and beneficiaries have equitable interest and real owners of the trust property. It is therefore the interest of the beneficiaries who have "locus Stand" to enforce duty imposed on trustee. An unenforceable trust is void Re Astor ST (1952) Ch 534. Examples trusts in Re Shaw (1957) 1 WLR 729, Leahy v. A-G for New South Wales (1959) AC 457 were held to be void due to be absence of beneficiaries to enforce the trust.

580) Q; who enforce trust with a lot of beneficiaries?

A; Trust with an enormous number of beneficiaries example in McHale v. Dolton (1971) AC 424 which the class include about 110,000employees together with their relatives and dependent) are enforceable by individual beneficiaries even before being selected to have equitable interest.

581) Q; Explain Purpose trust?

A; In some trust such as purpose the beneficiaries merely need a factual benefit example the right to play sport) rather than the ownership of the property interest in order to enforce the trust.

Example if a beneficiary in a sports grounds have equitable interest, they would be able to end the trust under Saunders v. Gautier (1841) 4 Beav 115 and sell the land to developers. (Goff J's reference to Re Boyes. Factual interest could be "sufficient direct or tangible benefit" Beneficiaries of discretional trust possess locus

Standi to enforce trustee duties even before they have been selected which indicate that it is not necessary to have equitable interest in order to enforce a trust. In Schmidt v. Rosewood (2003) 2 AC 709, court confirmed that the power to enforce trust is not confined to beneficiaries with proprietary interest. The Privy Council recognised the rights of beneficiaries of power of appointment (who may not have equitable interest) to disclosure of trust documents as part of their right to enforce trust.

582) **Q:**What are some duties of trustee?

A: Trustees have a duty to be active in the management of the trust, they should watch over and correct the conduct of their co- trustee (Tonley v. Sherborn; Styles v. Guy) they will be personally liable if loss were coursed by their failure to monitor the trustee's activities. Some mismanagement of trust funds by trustee that beneficiaries to monitor include; Misappropriate trust funds. They must be forced to claim back (Foskett v. Mckeown), stolen money from trust subject. Trustee might give money to third party who may not be aware of where the money originated. In this case the beneficiaries or trustee will not succeed to obtain compensation from the recipient because he was unconscionable (BCCI v. Kindle.), If third party is innocent the relevant, the tracing rule to apply is Barlow Clowes v. Vaurghan. A third party could assist the trustee to break their fiduciary duties. Dishonesty test in Royal Brunei Airlines v. Tan. Trustee of a discretional trust are under a duty to select appropriate objects.

583) **Q:** What can beneficiaries do to incompetent trustee?

A; If beneficiaries found trustee to be incompetent, they could force the trustee to delegate the investment duties to an agent s. 11 Trustee Act 2000 (TA) the trustee may pay the agent out of the trustee's fund (s.32 TA 2000).Beneficiaries will monitor the trustee's duties; delegate in writing, provide a policy statement, reviews the arrangement and exercise the standard of care. 1 Ta 2000). Despite such arrangement, trustee can be sued if loss is caused by the breach of their duties although they are not vicarious liable for the agent's Acts.

Beneficiaries could force trustee to appoint a financial expert as additional trustee under s. 36 (60 Trustee act 1925 and pay him reasonable for professional capacity (s. 29 TA 2000). This must be in writing and agreed with other trustee.

584) **Q:** What are exception to the monitoring

A; Exception to monitoring are

Charitable trust is exception to beneficiaries' principle, they are valid although they do not have beneficiaries, and their enforcement is by the Attorney General. Charities must demonstrate public benefit and therefore justify enforcement at public expense. Anomalous purpose trusts are valid but unenforceable due to the absence of beneficiary's example Care of animal. (Re Dean (18890 (maintenance of graves and monuments (Pirbright v. Salwey (1896).Trustee with power of appointment (power of attorney) are not obliged to appoint any one and the court are unlikely to intervene compare to discretionary trust (Mettoy Pension Trustee Ltd v. Evans In fact the court acknowledged that exceptional cases ought not to be extended

585) **Q;** what is the beneficial principle?

A; The beneficiary principle avoid floodgate of beneficiaries court action against trustee, the court do not carry out intention of individual settlors who spend their money on non- charitable purpose. It is also possible for settler to identify an enforcer who is not beneficiary to the trust.

586) Q; How did Equity originate ?

A; Common law originates base on strict case laws, on the other hand, equity originated around 1408 and is regarded as prepared to go extra mile to be just, fair, reasonable, benevolent and conscience. The equitable presumption and give rise to undermine common law and hence "res Ipse loquitur" (infer) to be duress and undue influence

587) Q: Initially What was the judge based?

A; Most of the equity judgement was based on the judge's conscience which is their subjective opinion as there were no guidelines or rules which created uncertainty and difficult for lawyers to predict outcome of cases and led to the saying that "Equity varied according to the length of the Lords chancellor's foot".

588) Q: How do you define Duress?

A; Definition; Duress is common law doctrine characterised by illegitimate threat (physical violence or psychological), economic duress pressure which force coerce a party into consent to contract or varying contract, the individual have no practical or independent choice as decision forced on him\her and has to submit. It is difficult to differentiate economic duress and commercial pressure in business negotiation for contract.

589) **Q;** briefly explain economic duress?

A; Guidelines to determine economic duress was stated by Judge (Dyson J) in Carillion Construction Ltd v. Felix (UK) (2001) BLR 1, that there must be compulsion pressure which makes the victim lack practical choice. That this pressure is illegitimate and significance enough to force the person to enter into a contract or consent.

590) **Q:** How will you describe Equity?

A: Equity can be equated to economic duress where it becomes the judge conscience. The bar to rescind is "maxim" "equity will not assist volunteer" If one act outside the rule, equity always look to help the injure person. Equity is fair and just.

591) **Q;** Give Example cases of laws to support duress;

A; Barton v. Armstrong (1975) AC 104; in which threaten to kill Barton unless he buys his company's share. This is violence, illegitimate threat or pressure. The complainant acted due to fear.

592) **Q:** How can agreement be changed?

A: Atlas Express v. Kafco (1989) 1 ALL ER 641:Express went back on original agreement and put Kafco in a position that he has no choice but to accept the new deal (duress) NB that in this case Express offered extra on top of the original agreement which meant that they considered the new deal.

Williams v. Roffey; The parties renegotiated, and defendant promised extra money for the original contractual work to be done without duress. But it did emphasise payee must receive practical benefit without duress but there was not enough consideration. However, If the defendant is made to promise to pay for more money to do existing contractual duty without consideration's v. Myrick (1809) 2 Camp 317.

593) Q: Define undue influence?

A; Definition; Undue influence is equitable doctrine. It involves two parties with bargain powers. Actual undue influence is subtle whilst presumed undue influence is based on relationship of trust, honest and confidential, unlike duress, Undue influence can be legal threat.

594) Q; Give example of actual undue influence?
A 1)Claimant signed contract due to threat of going to court. Morgan el v. Drew (2005) EWCA Civ 507.Lord Nichols set out the guidelines for banks to take possession Royal Bank of Scotland V. Etridge (No 2) (2001) 4 ALL ER 499; 1) was the bank aware the loan

was for the husband sole purpose (business) which the wife has no interest.2) Did the bank insist to have private meeting with the representative of the bank and to explain the full extent of the risk. 3) The bank is to prove the extent of her (client) liability as surety. 4) Was the defendant warned of the risk she was running? 5) Confirmation of the surety understanding of the risk from a solicitor?

2)North Ocean shipping V.Hyundai Construction Co (Atlantic Baron) (1979) QB 705. A case where the claimant was forced to pay extra half way through the contract due to pressure. Claimant they lost the claim because the court stated the bars i.e. because they paid it, affirmation confirm and delay in making the claim

Is a case of presumed undue influence between two in relationship on gift, The court ruled that relationship about trust and confidence was not enough, and transaction must be readily explain how it was reached. Allcard v. Skinner (1887) 36 Ch D 145 at 185

595) Q; why are some rules in equity judgement.?

A; Equity produce rules to prevent duress and undue influence in relation to gift trust.

596) Q; what is some exception to equity rules?

A; As an exception to equity rule maxim "Equity will not assist volunteer" Milroy v. Lord), "Effort" rule (1952), Fortuitous vesting (Strong v. Bird (1874), DMC (Donatio Motis Cause) Unconscionability- Pennington v. Waine,gift or Will or trust can be declared void if the person\settler making it was persuaded to do so against his wishes (undue influence)

597) Q; what are the three conditions relate to a life time gift made in contemplation of one's death in DMC.?

A; Gift must be made in contemplation of death (Gardner v. Parker (1818). Gift must be condition of death of the donor; (Cain v. Moon (1896).

598) Q; what are the Fortuitous vesting four conditions?

A; Fortuitous vesting (Strong v. Bird (1874) set out four conditions whereby if an imperfect gift given during lifetime can be made perfect on the death of the donor because the original gift is invested in pure fortune. Properties must be transferred in correct manner example.

599) Q; What is the condition for transfer of shares?

A: SHARES- By completing and signed Stoke transfer forms Chattels must be deliver by hand or by deeds of gift. Land-There must be declaration in writing, s.1 LP (MP) 1989-s.52LP 1925 and then must be registered s.27 LRA 2002.Transfer of an existing equitable interest in land with s. 53(1) (c)LPA 1925.This must be in writing signed by the settler or an authorise agent.

600) Q; what are remedies in duress and undue influence?

A; in both duress and undue influence, there are no damages, the remedied is rescind, can order injections (prohibition or mandatory).

601) Q; What can equity do?

A: Equity Identify the right of the parties, order the defendant to perform his obligation, regulate exploitation transactions, is very hot on breach of confidentiality, not to disclose confidential information to others or breach fiduciary duty. Equity act firmly on invasion of privacy breach

Conclusion; equity principles is used in all courts .The judicature Acts 1873 and 1875 combine the common law and equity jurisdiction.

Scenario

In March 2006, Emmanuel decided to share his wealth among his family for tax reasons .He took the following steps during April 2006.

1)he spoke to his granddaughter Ifra, and said "From now on I am holding my apartment in Poole on trust for you until you get to the age of 21,when it will be yours "He later wrote a letter to Efra's mother telling her what he had don but took no further action.

2)Fahim also telephone his stoke broker, who held various public company shares holding on a bare trust for him urging the telephone conversation, Emmanuel instructed the stockbroker to transfer the shares to Emmanuel's son who is 25 years old. The shares have now been transferred in Hassan's name that is 25 years old. The share has now been registered in Hassan's name.

3) Emmanuel wrote to his son, Gazi," This letter is a transfer to you of my shops in Nottingham" Emmanuel owns two shops in Notting ham which are left to tenants. No further steps were taken.

4) In the same week, Emmanuel gave his share, certificate for his share in the family company, Edward

Ltd to his brother, Morgan, who has worked for the company for many years. Emmanuel told him that he wanted him to become the sales director of Edward Ltd. Morgan agreed and was appointed to the post. In June 2016, Emmanuel and Morgan quarrelled and have not spoken to each other since. Emmanuel is still registered as owner of the shares. A signed stock transfer form in Morgan's favour has been found in Fahim's desk at home.

5) In May 2016, Emmanuel began to fee unwell and was told that he had a terminal illness. Immediately he made a will which he appointed Ghazi to be his executor, left his "investment property to his with, Kali, and the rest of his estate to charity

6) Emmanuel spent the last few days of his life in hospital. He said to Hassan "If I do not survive, you are to have my diamonds, which are in safe deposit box at Ventnor's bank. Here is the key". Fahim has now died. Hassan has not taken the possession of the diamonds yet.

602) **Q:** Advice Ghazi whether the above disposition were valid and, if not what will happen to the property. Advice to executor (Ghazi)

A: Ghazi will have to identify properties\gift\trust are legally been transferred\form in accordance with the rules, where this is not met, assistance of equity tests may be invoked: “equity will not assist the volunteer” Milroy.v.Lord” “effort test” “ Will equity perfect an in imperfect gift”? “Re rose or considers other rules ;(Strong v Bird) (DMC) (unconscionability Pennington v.Wayne. ECT.

603) **Q:** What was his intention with regard to Granddaughter?

A; intention;_to create fixed trust for granddaughter (Efra)

604) Q: is this a varied trust?

This is valid trust but may pass “effort test” The fact appears to be valid express of the settlor intentions and he cannot change his mind. The oral declaration satisfied S. 53 (1) b of LPA 1925 confirmation of her having equitable interest which is enforceable, and the letter to her mum is written evidence of declaration in writing. The nature of this property is land; All three certainties comply (Knight .v. Knight (1840)3 Beav 148 Ch2. The trust was created in 2006 but the PAA came into force on 06\April\ 2006 therefore it is within the perpetuity period which is a life in being plus 21 when it will be vested (80 years). It complied with the beneficiary principal (Elfa can enforce the trust)

Fahim life time declaration of trust hold legal title in which Mary has equitable interest, and he set the terms as contingent when she is 21 years. It needs to be registered on notice in the deed.

When Emmanuel dies Mary will become the absolute legal and equity owner and at the age of 18 years she could end the trust (Saunders v. Volunteer).The trust completely constituted.

605) **Q:** What was the intention regarding the shares?

A; intention; company share gift to son (Hassan)

It is a valid vested as outright gift, is absolute and in possession (Milroy v. Lords (1862). It is implicit that the share transfer forms and the share certificates were handed to the agent (already signed or it was signed by the agent as per the settlor instruction and properly transferred.) otherwise he could not have got himself registered.

606) **Q:** Why is Emmanuel bound by the trust?

A: Emmanuel is bound by the trust because it is completely constituted and vested in Hassan. The fact that he is registered confirms that the legal title have been transferred to him. The oral declaration is effective because share is personality and complied with s.53(1)(c) LPA 1925.

607) **Q**; what was the intention regarding the shops?

A; intention: Gift of shops to son (Ghazi)

This is an imperfect gift. The correct formality for transfer of land is a deed to comply with Section 1 LP (MP) act 1989 is needed to transfer a legal estate in Land (s.52 LPA 1925. Legal title will actually pass to the done when she registered herself under section 27 LRA 2002. Mescal lv. Miscall (1985) 50 P &CR 119.If the land is unregistered then deed is relevant on the other hand if it registered then LRA 2002 registration at HM Land registry confirms ownership. (Compulsory first registration applies).

Since the correct formalities were not used there was not much effort done during Emmanuel lifetime, Ghazi cannot enforced the gift, moreover equity "will not perfect an imperfect". (Milroy v. Lord)The disposition is therefore not valid\not complete. However as Emmanuel executor, when Emmanuel dies, will equity perfect the gift? Does not satisfy all the 4 condition of (Strong v. Bird),

Emmanuel declaration was not made immediately before his death. It is unlikely equity will perfect imperfect gift "A judge consider, it failure will be added to the residue for charity and might perfect the gift. Re Rose.

608) **Q:** What was the intention of the company shares?

A: intention: company share gift to brother (Morgan)

This is incomplete constituted and imperfect gift. The correct way to transfer share is for the settlor to sign stock transfer form, add it to the share certificate, and hand them to the done to register with the company as a shareholder and legal title to him. (section 53 (1) (c) 1925. gift was not completely constituted because Emmanuel did not hand over the completed stock transfer form section 1 of the Stock transfer Act 1963 to Morgan hence the legal title was not passed on to him. The transfer was valid because share certificate was delivered.

609) Q; Will equity rule suffice?

A: No. Because Emmanuel has intentionally not done enough, and the evidence is clear (quarrelled and have not spoken to each other since Emmanuel promised). This can be construed that Emmanuel (donor) might have revoked the offer. During the life time equity do allow donor and settlor to change their mind at any time before formalities are complete thereby preventing them from being bound by rash action Did he changed his mind during lifetime?

610) **Q;** When Emmanuel died, will equity take

A; presumption that Morgan would have accepted the position of sale director on the promise of being share holder and a director?

It is presume that one cannot be a director without being a shareholder. (T.Choithram v. Pagarani), Pennington v. Waine). This presumption might be rebutted because Morgan had been working for the company for long time and one would assume he already have shares in the company. Or will they consider that the fact that the share certificate delivered to Morgan , stock transferred forms signed but not given to him to register himself in the company. Which they might Will equity perfect this on rule of unconscionability. Pennington v. Waine (2002)EWCA Civ 227. This case conflict with "effort test" and the equity decision must be on balance of probability. Considering the above constructive argument, this TMA will not determine the outcome of equity.

611) Q; what was intention regarding property?

A; intention: Investment Property gift to wife in (Will)

This is a perfect gift (devise or realty) provided the Will meet formality. As testator intended an immediate transfer of the house. His intention continued until his death Re Gonin, the gift is regarded as completely constituted. For Will (or testamentary trust) to be perfect, it must complied by section 9 of the Will act 1837, it must be in writing, the testator had to have signed it in presence of both witnesses, and the witness have to signed the Will in testator presence. If there is any doubt equity will consider was contingent of his death. : (Strong and Bird), all 4 conditions are satisfied and passed "effort test" (Re Rose) (1952) Ch 499, and the three conditions of DMC. To transfer to Kali when Emmanuel dies, a deed to comply with Section 1 LP (MP) act 1989 is needed to transfer a legal estate in Land (s.52 LPA 1925. Legal title will actually pass to the done when she registered herself under section 27 LRA 2002. Ghazi being the executor of Emmanuel Will have grant of probate as deceased PR (personal representative all Emmanuel estate legal title will be transferred to him by assent. his priority is to pay any Emmanuel debt, inheritance tax and carried out the valid disposition.

612) Q: What is the intention on charity?

A; The intention is residue gift to charity.

As this is in Will properly constituted, is perfect gift, the testator gave the executor a discretion trust but is not certainty what the object or who beneficial is. This assignment will presume that either the executor knew testator choice, or he could make discretional decision.

613) **Q**: What was intention on the chattels?

A; The intention is gift of chattel (diamond) to son

Is not perfect gift as he did not amend his will by codicil, but equity may perfect the gift?

To give a perfect gift, it is necessary to declare the gift effectively and constitute the gift by transferring to done by delivery or deed of gift. This did not happen during Emmanuel life time hence is incompletely constituted as the legal title remained with the settlor\testator and he indented an immediate trust and would be unconscionable for him to revoke the trust (gift). T.Choithram international SA v Pagarani (2001)2All ER 492. The oral declaration is valid as chattel transfer is personality and it satisfies section 53 (1) (b) LP 1925.

Diamond was appropriate delivered he gave him the key to the safety deposit box and directed him where to find them Woodward v. Woodward (1995). His intention which continue to his death) and his death was within near future Re Graven (1937), Moreover the gift was contingent "If I do not survive, you are to have my diamonds" It was condition of his death (Gardiner v. Parker (1818).

It satisfies DMC, a gift in contemplation of death. All three certainties satisfied (intention, object and subject matter) also all the three condition of DMC. The gift then becomes absolute when Emmanuel dies (Sen v. Headley (1991) and may pass effort test. Re Rose. There is no statutory requirement and the direction given by testator is obligation.

Lord Lindly said "When once the possession is changed it is too late to revoke" Re; Gonine (1979) CH 16 because the gift was incompletely constituted.

Chapter 11

JUDICIAL REVIEW (traditional, proportional, Grounds Impropriety, remedies, irrationality, proportionality, hybrid, narrow, mixed)

614) Q; "The difference in approach between the traditional grounds of Judicial Review and the proportional approach may ---- sometimes yield different result--- This does not mean that there has been a shift to merits reviews". Lord Stein in R (on application of Daly).v.Secretary of state for the home department (2000) 2 AC 532.

Critically evaluate Lord Steyn's statement .Explain proportionality approach and analyse the extent to which approach differs from the traditional grounds of Judicial Review in particular irrationality.

A; To critically evaluate Lord Steyn's statement, compare and contrast proportionality and tradition approach of judicial review approaches, judgement and perceived problem with dishonesty.

Judicial review allows individual to challenge public body\ Public Authorities such as local authorities, tribunal, quangos, inferior court etc.

UK incorporated HRA 1998 into the statute, using HRA section 2(1), 3(1), 3(2b), 4, 19(1b) and in line with the four conditions to interference with the qualified rights (example 8, 9 10 11) which must be lawful, serve legitimate purpose, be necessary in democratic society and none discriminatory. The state is expected to balance public interest to individual.

By 2013, the court had declared 28 HRA 1998 as incompatible with the statute; parliament had to remedy those (14 resulted changes in the law). Therefore Lord Steyn statement made in 2001 is fair. He was supported by Sir Thomas Bingham, MR in R.v. Ministry of defence ex parte Smith (1996)1 ALL ER 257) "The more substantial the interference with human rights, the more the court will require by way of justification before it is satisfied that the decision is reasonable" "in order words, the court scrutinise Public Body decision under review much more closely where proportionality Human Rights are in play.

615) Q; What are the Grounds to challenge in Judicial Review?

A; Lord Diplock (in CCSU mentioned three traditional grounds of challenge; procedural impropriety, Illegality, irrationality. Human Right Act 1998 is based on proportionality.

616) **Q**: What is the procedure for procedural impropriety

A; The requirement of procedural fairness in proportionality is linked to traditional rule of Law include natural justice; Bias (Indirect and direct).Fair hearing (standard, types and cope reason, legitimate Expectation (procedural and substantive) right and benefit. Applicants must be “standing” (Locus Standi) or sufficient interest include direct victim (s.7 HRA or s.3 of SCA 1981), 4) collateral. 5) Timing which must be promptly without undue delay (SCA 1981.s.31 (6).case laws (Hardy) (Caswell). Claimant must follow the right procedure for review as per SCA (Supreme Court Act) 1981 s. 31.2), Civic procedure rules.54

617) **Q;** What is the remedies

A; (Must choose right remedies), Public law use “prerogative” orders; quashing, prohibiting, mandatory request right remedies as per s. 31. (1a, b, c), and Civil procedure Rules (54 .6). Private law; Injunction, damages, declaration of incapability. In proportionate one can claim under section 8 of HRA.

Ultra-Varies (Mc Cathy and Stone), Error of law and Ouster clause (Anisminic) jurisdictional error of fact Khawaja) fettering of discretion, wrongful delegation, unauthorised purpose, fettering of discretion, Consideration, (Appendix A to G)

618) **Q**; Explain irrationality;

A; In Judicial review, parliament expects the executive to use power conferred on them in rational way, the court will be looking for any irrationality in the public body decision, implementation of natural justice, hence it require a very high degree of threshold.

Lord Diplock in (CCSU) (1985) in council of civil service union's. Minister of civil service (1985) AC 374. Decision must not be as "so outrageous that it defies logic or moral standard that no reasonable public body would have made it". Additionally Lord Green commented on irrational decision as "—so unreasonable that no other reasonable decision maker could have come to it" (Wednesbury 1948) in Association provincial picture house Ltd v.Wednesbury corporation (19480) 1 KB 223.

619) **Q;** Comment on proportionality

A; This is a European principle incorporated into the UK statute and requires that all public authorities including the courts must comply with public authorities including the courts, must comply with convention right when making decision (HRA 1998 s. 6).

Proportionality provided an additional dimension of change in judicial review aim to protect the individual right by controlling the use of executive powers which must be against bias; right for fair hearing and abuse of power (natural justice)

Proportionality has built in mechanism which allow the court to use its power to thoroughly examine or go further detail where human right review comes to play. At the same time to consider alternative measures aim to inflict less damage to right.

620) Q; What are the test for proportionality?

A:The three-stage test of proportionality in Judicial Review by Lord STYNE; ”---whether 1) the legislative is sufficiently important to justify limiting a fundamental right 2)The measured designed to meet the legislative objective are nationally connected to it 3)The means used to impair the right or freedom are no more than is necessary to accomplish the objective”

621) Q; Compare Irrationality and Proportionality

A; Whilst irrationality (originated from common law principles) measures must be upheld by the court, Proportionality enables the judicial review wider alternative measures in reviewing executive decision. Traditional approach to Judicial review do check that decision has approach the question in the right way and procedure is correct, but doctrine of proportionality is instrument of the court to determine whether decision maker has infringed convention right. (Belfast city council .v.Omits behaving ltd. (2007) UKHL 19.

622) Q: What is the requirement for procedural fairness.?

A; The requirement of procedural fairness in proportionality is linked to tradition of the rule of law and has some similar elements; must be open and fair hearing, absence of bias, correct application of the law, ability to guild action distinct between public and private law.

The methodology approach to proportionality or the idea has not yet fully decided by the UK Supreme Court as they had been inconsistent.

623) Q: What is the leading case in proportionality?

A: The leading case in proportionality is R. (on the application of Daly) v.Secretary of state for the home department (2001) 2 AC 532. In 2007, 4 more elements were added in a case of Huang and others. V. Secretary of state for the Home department (2007) UKH11.

Lord Steyn used proportionate to propose legislative objective to meet fundamental right in De- Ferias .v. Parma net Secretary of ministry of Agriculture, Fisheries, land and housing (1999) 1AC 69 (privy council case).

UK courts have considered proportionality to be similar but recognizable deferent from irrationality approach .In conclusion, this essay supports Lord Steyn statement.

624) **Q;** what is mixed case?

A; is cases involve public and private law e.g. Cooper V wands worth board of works (1863) 14 CB N5 180

625) **Q;** name public departments which can be review?

1) **A:** government department
2) Local authorities
3) Tribunals
4) guanos
5) Inferior courts such as magistrates

626) **Q;** name cases where private bodies could be review?

A; if it is regulated in public system e.g. Advertising standard authority, press complaint commission, exempt R.V. panal on takeovers and mergers, ex parte Datofin PLC (1987) QB815.

627) Q; explain citation comparing traditional and modern

A; 1) traditional remedies was called "prerogative orders" now the crown proceeding
1947 in name ("R.V") and claimant pay the cost. Now traditional citation. R. on the application of claimant. V.public authority. R.V.public authority, EX parte application.

628) Q: Who used to be called respondent?

A; traditionally the public authority defending the case used to be called respondent and private individual called applicant. Since October 2000 this has changed to claimant (individual) and defendant (public Body).

A; ex parte used to represent that proceeding can be brought without service on application notice on the respondent/defendant this is now replaced by e.g. R on the application of claimant V. Public authority.

629) Q;who does statute provide for appeal?

A; decision of local authority can be appealed to minister in charge.

A; decision of government department can be appeal to a Tribunal. These two could be rehearing the entire case.

630) Q; what is the function of the judicial by Eminent Lords?

A; Lord Hailsham described the courts (J.R) function as being to ensure that the individual receives "fair treatment, natural justice". Lord Brightman said that it should be concern with decision making process not thee decision.

631) Q; what has changed between the state and individual since Dicey era (1866)?

A; the creation and development of welfare state, the increase of encouragement of the state into our lives and joining of the human rights act 1998.

632) Q;what can the judicial review do?

A; They can only review decision which are concern with public law and cannot alter decision made by public body although they can quash, prohibitory injunction, that the public authority act legally, rationally and follow procedure.

633) Q; what is "standing" in judicial review?

A; this use to be known as "locust standi" it means that the person must have sufficient interest in the decision in the application/decision to be reviewed.

634) **Q;** who can apply judicial review and quote case law?

A; must be right person to seek right remedy in a right proceeding (HWR Wade and CF Forsyle, administrative, 8th edn p287

635) **Q;** what are the requirements to challenge decision of public authority?

1) **A;** Claimant must follow the right procedure for review as per senior supreme courts act 1981 5.31.
2) Claimant must request right remedy as per 5.31
3) Claimant must be "standing" (locus standi) sufficient interest under 5.31.

636) **Q;** on what grounds are claimant applications refused?

A; delay in making a claim/application statutory exclusion of review, public interest in upholding a decision.

637) **Q;** Quote one case of judicial review by Lord Lane?

A; in case R.V commission for racial equality, ex parte cottell and Rothen (1980) IWR 1580 described judicial review as natural justice to be like an "unruly horse".

638) **Q;** how and what procedure is judicial review known as?

A; judicial procedure known as the claim of judicial review regulated by 5.31 of the senior court acts 1981 (sca) and part 54 of civil procedure rules (1998)(CPR)

639) **Q;** what other way can judicial review obtain?

A; collateral: addition but subordinate one can obtain review collateral as incidental part of private law. The present review procedure was in 1978 and amended in 2000.

640) **Q;** name the two main procedures in judicial review?

A; 1) permission (formally leave) to apply

2) Statement to support formally (affidavit)

641) **Q;** what is the difference between private and public law?

A; private law deals with matters between individuals whilst public law deals with individual and state which come under judicial review in administrative court.

642) **Q;** what is the judicial review concern?

A; it is not an appeal court, its concern to make sure the public body/public authority decision has been made correctly, decision made by right person, using the power correctly and in the correct way. The court is not concern whether the public authority decision is right or wrong and their decision itself is not irrelevant. In short judicial review is only available to test the lawfulness of the public bodies

643) Q; which bodies are subject to judicial review?

A; government departments, local authorities, tribunals, quangos and inferior courts e.g. magistrate court and private bodies which exercise public function.

644) Q; how could you recognise cases of judicial review?

A; prior to October 2000, cases use to be cited as RV. Public authority (name), ex patre (applicant name) e.g. RV. Panel on takeovers and merges, ex parted datafin PLC (1987) QB 815.

The RV represents the crown, the ex parte means that proceeding can be brought without serving application notice on the respondent (now defendant).

645) Q; what and give example of the new citation?

A; R on application of claimant, V. Public authority e.g. Lloyd V. McMahon (1987) 1 A11 ER 1118

646) Q; what procedure one has to follow?

A; must strictly follow procedure set by SCA (senior court ACT) 1981, 5.13, or civil procedure rules (CPR 54).

647) Q; name the three requirements for challenging a decision by public bodies?

A; application made under SCA (senior court Act 1981) section 31 by claimant who has "standing " or "locus stand" means has sufficient interest.

B; must state remedies sought under SCA 5.31 or CRR 54.

C; follow right proceeding of SCA. 5.31 or CPR. 54

648) **Q;** what is the different in procedure between judicial review and private law, the judicial review?

A; 1) the procedure consists of two main features: apply for permission (was leave)

2) Statement in support (was Affidavit)

The application for permission is often reported in the press, the judicial review may not be given permission because wrong procedure chosen.

649) **Q;** what document one need to lodge formal complaint?

A; claim form complete fully, state grounds and remedied sought, statement in support.

650) **Q;** what else must be in the statement?

A; must state everything for or against if not after to come to attention the remedies will be set aside. The design of the form to decide swift decision if the/ whether public authority acted lawfully.

651) Q; why statement use?

A; it helps swift decision concern with issues of law not fact.

652) Q; what are the remedies under public law?

1) **A:** Quashing orders
2) Prohibiting orders
3) Mandatory orders.

653) Q; what are the remedies under private law (before 1978)?

A; The following remedies can still be used under private law.

1) Declaration (that decision is void)
2) Injunction similar to prohibition but this could be part of the decision whilst public law deals total.
3) Damages.

654) Q; name decision makers subject to judicial review?

A;1) public bodies and public authorities (note that these are synonymous –court of appeals R (on the application of beer) V. Hampshire farmers market LTD (2004) 1 WLR 233.

2) Private obligations of public authorities (public authorities only by the public law)

3) Public functions of private bodies.

4) Hybrid authorities.

5) It look at "does the body exercise a public function? Traditionally, judicial review only look at the source of power (statue or contract)

655) **Q**; what is a hybrid authority?

A; private body operating with sufficiently public function and its decision reviewable.

656) **Q;** how is a civil procedure rule?

A; civil procedure rules (51 1998 / 3132) rules part 54 (54.1 to 54.7).

657) **Q;** why are judicial review not available to others?

A; 1) if the body has no public function

2) applicant must satisfy the statutory test known as standing or "locus standi" or sufficient interest.

3) cases on standing where pressure group such as green peace or public-spirit citizen or busy bee people might be able to challenge public authorities.

4) delay application for permission must be made within specific time (3 months) in accordance to SCA 1981 5.31 and CPR part 54.

5) exclusion of review i.e. ouster clauses, ouster clause is where by parliament protect some public bodies by ouster clause example, a decision shall not be called in question in any legal proceedings.

6) time-limit clause, in this case the time limit may expire but due to public interest, the review may go

ahead, e.g. RV. Secretary of state for environment ex parte ostler (1977) QB 122 or Smith v East Elloe district council (1956) AC 736.

7) Immune from judicial review decision under royal prerogative powers by the government such as national security, international law, declaration of war, appointment of ministers or granting of honours, granting of mercy.

658) **Q;** cite the case to support delay prevent judicial review?

A; RV. Stratford-upon-Avon DC, ex parte Jackson (1985) I WLR 1319.

659) **Q;** what entails revision of judicial review in 1978?

A; it became specialist procedure for resolving public law issues traditionally or prior to this private law issues were used.

660) **Q**; what case resulted private law remedies and what were they?

A; ridge .V. Baldwin and Anisminic – remedies – declaration and injunction.

661) **Q;** why was judicial review procedure reformed in 1977/8?

A; Lord Diplock said "to remove the defects in the old procedures".

662) **Q;** in O'rielly .V. Mackman (1983) 2 AC 237 what significance?

A;1) it distinguished between public law and private law procedure in judicial review.

2) Private law in judicial review procedure applicant evade safeguards impose against groundless, tardy or numerations decision.

663) **Q;** explain exclusivity rule (modern)

A; in case in Orally .V. packman (1983) 2 AC 237 the house of lords in 1983 introduced exclusivity rule in order to channel all public law cases into the new procedure of judicial review.

664) **Q;** name the two exceptions to exclusivity rule?

A; 1) where none of the parties object using private law.

2) where the invalidity of the decision being review arises as a collateral issue in private right claim collateral: addition but subordinate.

665) **Q;** what is the broad approach of judicial review on exclusivity?

A; where no private rights bare at stake.

666) **Q**; what is the narrow approach?

A; allow public law issues as were as mixed cases to be heard.

667) **Q;** name mixed cases which can be bought to judicial review?

A; private law (trespass) public law (ultra vires byelaw) criminal law and public law (raise in criminal case proceeding not JR)

668) **Q;** in modernised J.R, there had been an increase of reason to refuse compared to tradition, name some?

A; delay, lack of standing, no public function, issue not justifiable, ouster clause, discretion of the court, exclusivity rules applies – a pure private law case, need good administration.

Chapter 12

CONTRACT LAW (offer, Acceptance, consideration, clauses, UCTA, test, express)

669) Q: Name the three elements for formation of contract.

A: Offer and acceptance=agreement

Example a proposer (offer) and agree to proposer (acceptance)

670) Q; Explain offer

A; OFFER; the person must be willing to be bound if accepted

There must be certainty in the offer.

671) Q; Explain Acceptance

A; ACCEPTANCE; final unqualified assent to the terms of the offer. This must be communicated to the off error.

672) Q; Explain the three ways to terminate offer?

A; 1) Revocation (withdraw the offer) this must be communicate to the offered if not the law regard it as acceptance.

2) Rejection this means it put an end to the offer and cannot change their mind.

A counter offer implies rejection of original offer.

In some case the offeree wants more information before accepting (this exploration is not rejection)

3) Laps; this is when the offer is only open to specific time and no acceptance before the time. (If no time is stipulate then the law state that it laps after reasonable time.)

673)Q; Explain intention to create legal relations?

A; If there is disagreement of if there was intention to create legal binding, the court has to decide objectively. Also consider commercial (the law presume that it is legal binding unless the fact show otherwise)) and domestic (the law start that it is not legal binding unless otherwise) agreement.

Facts, the amount involve, the relationship between the parties are considered in deciding if there was intention to create legal relationship.

674)Q: Explain consideration?

A; Consideration is to hold the other party you need to provide something in return. Example if one party give a product and the other one give money in return is regarded as consideration.

There must be consideration for promise by the other party

675)Q; What is Adequacy of consideration;

A; It means that (The value does not have to be same amount) is the amount. The law doesn't question the adequacy of consideration or value of the agreement.

676) Q; What is sufficiency of consideration?

A; Is the sort of thing it is) is what is being provided appropriate to the subject matter. Example money, goods and services may be provided in exchange for the promises

677) Q: Give brief explanation of exception clauses

A; Defendant aim is to pass the risk to the defendant and attempt to disclaim any liability of breach of contract.

Common law test is that if the exception clause is incorporating (if contract is signed) in the contract then is binding.

678) Q: Explain UCTA (unfair contract trade Act 1977)?

A; Statute; UCTA 1977 to deal with onerous or unusual terms. UCTA does not affect the common law (It must be transaction during the course of business) UCTA applies to commercial transactions.

1) UCTA could prevent the defendant using the term.
2) Or the defendant clause may not has effect on the term\claimant
3) Or subject the term to requirement of reasonableness test. That it must be fair which is judge by what the parties knew or what they ought to have known prior to the contract?

679) Q; What is reasonable test

A; Reasonable test is test of incorporation into the contract (that is before contract was breached not reasonable of reliance (after the breach)

680) Q: What Factors considered in reasonable test

A : include; 1)bargain power of parties 2) if clause is in small print so that the claimant could not see\know about it.3)worth of parties i.e. who can pay the cost considered the insurance cover of the parties.

The court will consider a number of factors of the case.

681) Q; Who does the Unfair terms Act 1999 applies?

A; The Act Applies to consumer transaction which provides systematic control fair terms including exclusion clause

682) Q; Outline how the Act prevent unfairness?

A: The Act prevent unfair act on the consumer, by considered; consideration, timing, consistence and contra preferential rule.

683) Q; Explain consideration?

A; Consideration; signed contract means you agree to be bind by the terms and NOT that you have read and understood them.

684) Q; Explain timing?

A; TIMING; Notice must be given before or at time of contract

685) Q: Explain Consistence?

A; consistence; between the parties of what had been practice previously as an acceptable between the parties.

686) Q: Explain contra preferential rule?

A: Contra preferential rule is rule of construction that is If there is any ambiguous in the wording of the clause, and in most cases it goes against the defendant.

687) Q: In relation to terms of contract what does consideration mean?

A; Construction of contract; This relate to the content of the contract

688) Q; What does Express mean in term of contract?

A: Express. is what the parties agree. If possible the law avoid interfering with express terms. The exception is terms that contains criminal activities or immoral means, or commercial organisation who fixed prices or dictates environment. The court would not enforce them if the terms work against public interest.

These terms include exception clauses especially when it disclaims all limit of liability.
Exception clause cannot disclaim liability on personal injury or death.

689) **Q;** When is reasonable term use?

A; Reasonableness test. This test is used where there is disagreement in exclusion clauses.

690) **Q:** Name one problem with regard to express terms of contract?

A: Small print is one of the problems.

691) **Q;;**Name another problem with express contract?

A; Other problem is whether the terms are regarded as part of the discussion or terms. The court has to find out the intention of the parties.

692) **Q**; What does Incorporate mean in contract?

A; INCORPORATE into contract means that if it is sing then is binding. Exception is if one is trick or undue or under duress to sign.

693) **Q;** What is reasonable notice in express terms?

A; REASONABLE NOTICE is where the contract is not signed but the defendant wants to rely on it, the defendant must show that reasonable notice was given, and the claimant attention was drawn to it earlier.

694) Q; What are the four main categories of implied terms of contract ?

A: These are 1) Custom 2)Necessary,3) Persistence, 4) Statue

Also the Intention of the parties,

695) Q; What is customs?

A; ; 1) Customs (well known in particular trade)

696) Q; What is necessary in contract?

A; NECESSARY for the particular contract example health and safety in employment contract.

697) Q; What is persistence in implied contract?

A; persistence agreement can be presume as part of the parties norm

698) Q; Give an example of statute?

A; Statue example SGA... s. 13 goods by description, s.14 that goods be of satisfactory quality (relate to commercial), s.14 (3) fit for the purpose.

699) Q; What do one mean by intention of the parties?

A; The intention of the contract. Especially the words use in the contract

700) **Q;** Briefly explain some contract obligation of the parties?

A; The contract obligation of the parties include:

1. CONDITION; can terminate and claim damages because it is repudiate breach of contract.
2. WARANTIES; can claim damages but not terminate the contract.
3. INNOMINATE; this depend on the seriousness of the breach. Can terminate or only claim damages.

Chapter 13

WILL

scenario

You have been consulted by John Hunter and Kiahna Pirie regarding the will of their late mother, Bernadette Hunter. John and Kiahna tell you the following;

Bernadette died a week ago , age 90, in a nursing home where she had been living for the past six months, She was an independent lady but find living on her own impossible owing to increasing frailty and forgetfulness. On the advice of her doctor, who diagnosed the onset of early dementia, she agreed to go to nursing home .John and Karen, who visited her weekly. Said she was happy there but sometimes confused. She also had her “good days”, when she was perfectly lucid.

Edna had made a will in 2006 leaving her entire estate to John and Karen, her only relative. After the funeral, they were astonished when Kate Smith, the nursing Home owned, showed them a new will, made three months before Edna’s death. This new will

- Revoked any previous will
- Gave a small legacy to charity, and

- Gave the rest of her estate (worth approximately £500,000) to Patricia

A new one page will have been word processed in the nursing home, apparently signed by Bernadette at the bottom of the page, and witnessed by two employees at the home, although there was no attestation clause.

John and Kiahna cannot believe this is what their mother would have wanted, and wish to challenge the recent will.

You have been consulted by John Hunter and Kiahna

Advice, with reference to deciding cases and statute, whether John and Kiahna could challenge the recent will on the following grounds and assess their chances;

a) Lack of due execution

b) Lack of mental capacity

c) Lack of Knowledge and approval

d) Undue influence

e) Under the inheritance (provision for family and dependants) Act 1975 and explain why this ground might be less suitable.

701) Q: How do one view this ?

A: From the facts, one might view this case with deep scepticism, breach of duty of care by the sole beneficiary and the will be invalid.

In advising John and Karen, they will be interviewed for some clarification include; did Bernadette knew or any knowledge and approve the will? What reasons that would make Bernadette to exclude them being the only relatives in favour of strangers who have only cared for her for three weeks? Her testamentary capacity? Do they suspect forgery or fraudulent, ethnicity of the signature? Answers to these and more will lead to the type of investigation which might include medical expert, handwriting expert act.

702) Q: What is the starting point?

A; To look at the execution of the will;

The starting point in this contended matter is to investigate if the Will document had not been properly executed.

703) Q: Explain the terms for a will to be varied?

A; For a Will to be valid, it has to satisfy s. 9 of the Will act 1837 c.26 which state that;

a) "It must be in writing and signed by the testatrix (Edna) or by some other person in her presence and by her directions". How can a demented person give direction?

b) "That the testatrix intended by her signature to give effect to the will". (Was the signature forged, did she know what she was signing or was it typed and given to her to sign under undue influence?

c) The signature is made and acknowledged by the testatrix in the presence of two or more witnesses present at the same time, each witness either, attest and signs the will acknowledge her signature and in the presence of the testatrix (both not necessary in the presence of any other witness.

d) But no form of attestation shall be necessary.

704) **Q:** How do you check the authencity of the Will?

A; To investigate, copy of the Will to look for precatory words, check the nursing home staff rota if both the witnesses were on duty at the same time of the date of their witness and also to interview the witnesses. View the health assessment record, the dairy input of Bernadette entry about her. A hand writing expert to investigate if Bernadette signature was genuine or been forged. There is no evidence that the employee's witnesses were present at the same time, which must themselves, signed the will or acknowledge signatures in Edna's presence.

705) Q: What happen if it is prove that the testor signature been forged?

A; If it proven that Bernadette signature has been forged then it is conclusive irrefutable that they will had been forged and does not matter the burden of proof (Supple v. Pender (2007) EWAC 829. Even if the expert rule that the signature was not genuine, Kate could argue that the expert express opinion evidence was qualitative and not quantitative

Assessment of the genuine might also on the view taken of the credibility of the attesting witnesses Bernadette signature. The witness might give evidence that they saw decease signed the will (Sherrington v. Sherrington) (2005) EWCA Cave 326. Were the two witnesses under duress or did not intend to attest the signature of Edna? Furthermore, how could Bernadette being diagnosed with dementia gave instruction, knew and approves the content of the Will?

the process by which a testatrix's will is made legally valid is that it must be signed at the end so that no one can add anything more.s.9 Will Act 1837.In this case Bernadette allegedly signed at the bottom of the page, and as the beneficiary was in possession of the Will and could add more content after Bernadette executed it. In

Sherrington v. Sherrington (2005) EWCA Civ 325, the judge said when a Will contain the decease, witnesses signature and an attestation clause the presumption of due execution would prevail for policy reason" In the absence of the strongest evidence, the testatrix signature on the Will, the attestation clause and underneath that clause the signature of the witness. There was no attestation clause in Edna's Will. Kate will argue under s. 9 of the Will act 1837 state "no form of attestation shall be necessary" This is an evidence that Home owner who word process the will might not have legal qualification or experience in law.

706) Q; Is there any suspicion?

A; Referring to the Mental Capacity Act 2005 ss.1 &2 test of lack of capacity, and the circumstance will reveal common grounds of suspicion?

1) Kate prepared the will and she alone benefited albeit a small legacy to uncertain charity. She would be expected or burden to satisfy the court on balance of probabilities that they will express the true will of Bernadette (Wyniczenko v. Plucinska (2005) EWHC.
2) No evidence that Kate explain the terms of the will to Bernadette who only lived another three months after

the alleged will executed.(post mortem for the cause of death to eliminate murder)

3) Kate did not inform the only relative, John and Kiahna of the change or her intention to change of Will who visited weekly.
4) No evidence that Bernadette knew and approved the content of the will (Barry v. Butlin 12 ER 1089, Wintle v. Nye (1959) 1W.L.R 284 applied.
5) Possibility of forgery, fraud. Supple .v. Pender
6) There was no reason for Bernadette to disinherit John and Kiahna who are her only relative and care for her for years.
7) The owner breached the duty of care owe to Edna, as it is requirement of the care standard and the term of registration for nursing home owners \managers to request the next of kin or summon a lawyer to independently interview patient in such circumstances.
8) The beneficiary has only known Bernadette for three months before the Will executed and died three months after.

707) Q: Give a case law on suspicion?

A; Viscount Symonds said “It is not the law that in no circumstances can a solicitor or other person who has prepared a will for a testator take a benefit under, but the fact create suspicion that must be removed by the person propounding the will---- the degree of suspicion will vary with the circumstances of the case----"Wintle v. Nye.

In conclusion, to excite the suspicion of the court and therefore nursing home owner have the burden of proof that the Will was executed with the knowledge and approval of Edna. Considering aforementioned, the will is therefore not legally executed.

Chapter 13.1
Mental Capacity (WILL)

708) Q; How do you deal with the mental capacity aspect?

A; Dementia is mental disorder characterised by forgetfulness, disorientated to time place and person, Impairment of cognitive functions. The mental capacity Act 2005 s.1(1) and s.2(1) gives definition of when a person is able to take decision, and how decision could be taken on their behalf in their best interest if they are unable to do so.

709) Q: Give a case law relate to mental capacity to sign a will?

A: The issue here is whether Bernadette has sufficient mental capacity to make decision i.e. testamentary capacity. References from statute, mental capacity 2005 Act, from common law in Bank v. Good fellow (1870) LR 5 Q 549and Parker v. Filigrat and supported by other case laws.

710) Q: Give any difference between statute and common law?

A: There is evidence of disagreement between statute and common law. In Walker v. Baldwin (2004) EWHC, the judge argue that “The Act was inappropriate to evaluate whether a deceased had had capacity at the time of making their Will

711) **Q;** What is the test use in assessing mental capacity?

A; the correct and the only test for testamentary capacity where what was issue was the validity of the will executed by a deceased was the common law test set out in Bank v Goodfellow.

1) Testatrix understand the nature of the act and its effect
2) Understand the extent of the property he was disposing. Comprehend and appreciate the claims to which he ought to give effect and with a view of latter object.
3) No disorder of the mind shall poison his affections, pervert his sense right or prevent the exercise of his natural faculties.

712) **Q:** How do you use the bank test in assessing this scenario?

A; To apply Bank test to Edna, Her progressive dementia affected her faculties and such magnitude decision is too much for dementia person, she would not have the knowledge to appreciate facts example, how did

Bernadette know her property worth £500,000 and chattels act she had? It can be argued that when she made the first will, her testamentary capacity was greater as she was not diagnosed of dementia and hence valid will, but Kate will argue for the new Will that Bernadette had her good and bad days and partial unsoundness does not affect the operating on the mind is not sufficient to render her incapable of disposing of her property (Banks v. Goodfellow). And quote the judge in Burns v. Burns (2016)EWA,that despite show signs of mental impairment at the time of making the Will, Bernadette had the requisite testamentary capacity to know and approve the Will content.

713) **Q;** What is the golden rule for mental capacity testor?

A; The golden rule that a testor whose capacity might be doubtful, a solicitor should have been called to draw up the Will who would have interview Bernadette several times, and obtain medical assessment to establish her understanding and knowledge of the act which would have had some air of genuinely (Parker v. Felgate), before Bernadette make decision.

714) **Q:** How would you conclude this case might be?

A: In conclusion, applying the symptoms of dementia, rules of the common law and statute, Bernadette would not have testamentary capacity.

In the absence of evidence from John and Karen, nursing Home owner and the two witnesses, of Bernadette mental faculties, the doubt about her testamentary capacity will exist, from reasonable person looking at the case objectively the absence of provision for her children was unreasonable (Coventry v. Coventry) However, in Burns v Burns, the Judge commented that "the rule was a prudent guide for solicitors and not a rule of law".

715) **Q:** How do you deal with lack of knowledge and approval ?

A; To apply Banks v. Goodfellow, it is essential that Bernadette understand the nature of the content of the Will and its effect, comprehend and appreciate the extent of property being dispose of. Bernadette has had increasing forgetfulness and with the symptoms of progressive dementia which include lack of short-term memory, she might not even know the subject matter and could not have approved them. She was in physical and mental fragile to know and approve the will. (Greaves v. Stolkin (2013) EWHC

No evidence that Bernadette was capable having knowledge, that she was free of dementia symptoms as to be able to have a will of her own to in the disposition of his property and to act upon it. Or she gave instruction of the content, neither was the content read to her for approval. Kate might argued that, In Simon v. Byford, the judge commented" the law upheld the right of the elderly to leave their property as they choose, even if their mental faculties has decline considerably". This can be rebutted that the law is there to protect the vulnerable from being exploited by fraudulent people, moreover the case referred to family beneficiaries where the testator only change the proportion of the benefit to his children.

716) **Q;** How will conclusion might be?

A; From the fact, Bernadette clearly lack knowledge of the content of the alleged Will. There is no certainty of the type or the value of the subject matter, no mention of chattels, shares, personal, fixtures, and no valuation carried out on any of the subjects. There is no evidence that the will was made in contemplation of her death (Strong v. Bird), she was not physically ill although frail and died only three months after executed the will. The gift to charity is imperfect as it lack certainties of intention, subject and object matter or the purpose or amount to be allocated, therefore presumption cannot be used and initial failure cy-pres applied.

In conclusion, considering the test in Bank v. Goodfellow and Parker v. Felgate, it can be irrefutable conclusion that Bernadette did not know and approve the content of the will and is invalid.

717) **Q;** What do you think of any undue influence?

A; Considering Bernadette age, physical and mental condition was lonely in her house but now being supported by staff, it is obvious that she can be easily influence by nurses. Undue influence is equitable doctrine which involves two parties with bargain powers. Actual undue influence is subtle whilst presumed undue influence is based on relationship of trust, honest and confidential.

718) **Q;** Explain how undue influence could be inferred?

A; There could be actual undue influence of threat Daniel v. Drew (2005) EWCA Civ 507. Unlike duress, Undue influence can be legal threat, but the court turns to support the weaker party example in Royal bank of Scotland v. Etridge (No 2) (2001) 4 ALL ER 499.the court ruled in favour of the wife against the Bank

Kate holds the balance of power and her influence might have prevented Bernadette from having a choice to exercise an independence judgement in respect to decision or transaction and expert opinion would be valuable, but Kate will argue that expert could be caused of taken too high a standard for testamentary capacity and given undue weight to unreliable expert evidence. Sharp v. Adams (2006) EWCA 449.

719) Q: What is likely argument by the next of kin (John and Kiana)

A; John and Kiahna argument would include Bernadette lacked testamentary capacity to make the disputed will and did not know and approve the contents and that it had been procured by undue influence by unwanted pressure and coercion on the part of the sole beneficiary in executing the will. Corduroy v. Cranfield (2011) EWHC.

On balance of probability considered, no reason to disinherit her only relative John and Kiahna from her previous will and executed new will, in favour of sole beneficiary, and this can be construed only to happen due to undue influence (Shomberg v .Taylor) and Coventry v. Coventry (1980) Ch 461, the court supported such suspicion. It can be argued that in the absence of evidence and prove from the sole beneficiary, it is submit that they Will did not express the wishes of Bernadette and she was coerced into signing unknowing what she was signing. (Wingrove.v.Wingrove (1885) 11 PD 81 in this case it established undue influence to invalidate a will.

720) **Q;** What might be possible conclusion?

A; In conclusion It is also possible that her signature had been induced by undue influence and that the sole beneficiary had manipulated and controls Bernadette to submit for her signature, consider the short duration (three months) Bernadette would have been under undue influence to the extent that the sole beneficiary of Bernadette will would have poisoned her mind against John and Kiahna such as making untruth accusation against them in order to change her mind (Edward v. Edwards 92007) EWHC 119.The will is not valid.

721) **Q;** What about inheritance (provision for family and dependants?

A; This Act does not relate to the issues in dispute, that is the invalidity of the will. The information in the inheritance Act is not helpful in advising John and Kiahna as there is insufficient information about their circumstances. Are they independent or relied on their mother for financial maintenance?

It deals with an award under the inheritance and its effect on state benefit. And relate to living people, not payment under inheritance. None of the sections s is applicable

722) **Q:** What is your conclusion on this scenario?

A: There is no arrangement in the will to pay inheritance tax, debt payment or residue. The requirement for perfect gift is not satisfied. Bernadette mental capacity is in doubt, there is no evidence\prove of Bernadette knew and approve the will, no reason for her children being excluded from the Will, No certainties of the subject matter, object matter and no intention to create the will, the will is not properly executed and therefore not valid. Equity will not help Kate as it will fail "effort" test.

Chapter 14

Theft/ Honesty

723) **Q:** What is dishonesty?

A; A; "Dishonesty is something which layman can easily recognise when they see it" due to cultural, social and law or moral different in country of origin. (criminal law revision committee s.39 state)

There is partial definition of dishonesty in the statue (Theft Act 1968 s.2 (a, b, c).and is mainly the mens rea or the cognitive of the mind test which formulate the characteristic of the individual action or conduct. It gives three negative provisions situation if available then "D" is not dishonest, Judging dishonesty include; Ghosh and lie test, interview by police, being examined and cross examine in the court. The fact of the case must be scrutinised

724) **Q:** Explain Gosh test?

A; R.V. Ghosh (Deb Baran) QB.1053- 1982) 3WLR 100 CA (crim. Div.); Ghosh test had been recommended usage because it forms of mens rea of many offences against properties such as theft, fraud by false representation, burglary and robbery this use objective and subjective test. In fraud Act 2006, explanatory (notes 10) indicated the use of Ghosh by juries.

725) Q: How does the Julie use the Gosh test?

A; 1) The Jury judge dishonesty if that according to ordinary standard of reasonable and honest people they think defendant is dishonest (this is objective). If yes, Juries ask.

2) The jury should then ask themselves whether the defendant realises that reasonable and honest people would regard what he did as dishonest (subjective) think. If yes defendant is guilty.

726) Q: What is the initial test in Gosh?

A: interview \examination.

The initial test of the defendant dishonest is when the police interview defendant. During the examination and cross examination of the defendant under oath in court is to help the Juries to use the Ghosh test to judge.

727) Q; Explain theft Act?

A; Theft act 1968.

It is very important when considering cases of dishonesty to refer to the element of theft act 1968 s.2 (1) and to consider the **facts** of the case. Example in R.v. Gladstone Williams (1984) 78 Cr App R 276 decided you were to be judged on the facts as you honestly believe and did not have to be reasonably.

Judging from the law on theft Act 1968, R.V. Gomez (1993) 1 ALL .E.R.1HL and recent case of R.V. Hanks (2001) 2 AC the House of Lords place more emphasis on the concepts of dishonesty in the law of theft rather than element of proportion. Section 2 (1) objective, (subjective s.2 (2)—i.e. foresee or ought to have foreseen)

728) **Q:** What does the theft Act section 2a,b,c, relate to

A: According to Theft Act 1968 s.2 (1a, b, c,) relate to the person belief and if any of the three elements is established then the defendant is not dishonest

Section 2 (1a) Right to deprive a person of his property because you thought it belong to you (subjective) even if the property belong to somebody else (Defendant has the right to take it back

Section 2(1b) one may take some body property without consent directly but believe the other would have given consent example "A" bought a football ticket and told "B" that he would not go and left it on his desk."B" then took it and left money in place reasonable believe that “A” would have given his consent.

Section 2(1c) to take the property because the owner cannot be found despite reasonable steps taken. Example if one finds a watch on the street and has no sign of which it belongs to. (If however the owned might put request in local paper and the person read it he\ she must return the watch if not from that moment the person would be dishonest if is not return to the owner.

Section 2(2) relate to the person willingness to pay (he took the money from the till of Book maker and state that he in turn to pay. Personally it requires an integral element of deceit in dishonesty conduct.

729) Q; what is lie test use for?

A; Lie test; this could be used but they are unreliable, and court are reluctant to accept the finding.

730) Q; what problem is with Gosh?

A; the perceive problem with the Gosh test is not automatic as is inconsistent. Some problems judging dishonesty had been highlighted by the law commission, eminent people, and especially honesty and morality in decision making, the Ghosh test is likely to include Moral judgement these would lead to unlawful criminal conviction (as moral may play part in the juices mind, either expect higher or lower moral of the defendant compare to themselves. And might not consider defendant culture or background (when using subjective test)

I with the Law commission suggestion that , law should say what is forbidden and what should be affirmed by moral concepts and the apply then law by coming to factual conclusion not moral ones. In the absence of such approached and by following Ghosh to the letter (which sometimes found unworkable) it would lead to endemic inconsistency between juries.

731) Q: How is honest judge?

A; Honest and dishonest is judge according to the law of the state, and when one travel to another country and not aware of the rules and laws, the person's mind is clear but the conduct within the new country might be lodged as dishonest discretion must be exercise in this situation.

There must be legal definition of dishonesty with elements, Actus Reus\ mens rea of dishonest for Jury. Example recklessness frauds have legal meaning, too. To make reasonable decision of criminal liability on the defendant.

732) Q; what does the Law commission say about the Gosh?

A; The law commission in 1999\2002 challenge Ghosh as a concern saying "reproves determination of criminality a normal judgement of the conduct and mental state of the defendant" but still Ghosh remain in practice unproblematic.

It can be argued that Ghosh test has presented no problems since 1982 and people are likely to agree with the law commission that modify, or reject will cause more harm than good. There are many miscarriages of justice due to juries misjudge or include their moral instead of using the law.

733) Q; what does professor Glanville think of dishonesty?

A; Professor Glanville Williams support mind set as he said honest or dishonest is "special mental state"

734) Q: What is the Supreme Court definition of dishonesty?

A; The Supreme court stated that the meaning of "dishonestly" is matter of law for the judge which is " with disposition from a person what is right" This bring question of discretion and can be found in R.V. Salvo

(1980).v.R.401,432,R.v.Brow (1981).v.738,R. Bonillo (1981).v .R 633.

735) Q; what did professor dicey regard dishonesty?

A; Judging dishonest need discretion which Dicey feel that it must be narrow yet Joseph Raz and Lord Diplock wanted wider discretion which is more likely to cause injustice. Lord Bingham states the use of law in judging dishonest and not by discretion.

736) Q; what is your view of dishonest test?

A; the existing means of judging dishonest, using Ghose, theft Act 1968, interview and examination will stay with us for long time and the argument of pro and con, miscarriage of justice will continue.

Chapter 15

PUBLIC LAW EUROPEAN LAW

Scenario

JAMES Osei is a leading campaigner against the role played by faith schools in UK's education system, arguing in favour of a secular education system. In this context, state schools are state funded schools that teach a standard curriculum, but which have a particular religious character or formal links with a particular faith. The following article has recently appeared in the Eastbourne Echo, a local newspaper.

The article is accompanied by a photograph and his daughter arriving at St. Mark's Church of England primary schools. The face of his daughter has been blurred to protect her identity.

Although James accept the article and the photograph are factual correct, he has commenced preceding in the high court alleging that his right to privacy had been infringed. Assenting that his right to freedom of expression, The Eastbourne Echo intends to defend this claim. Explain, to reference to relevant case laws, the basis on which James will bring his claim and the basis on which the Eastbourne Echo will defend it.

James's school Scam (This is a newspaper article)

James Osei has been a critic of faith schools for many years and has been a vocal proponent of the benefit of non –religious education. Well, James may have undergone conversion! His daughter, age 7, has recently started attending St. Luks Church of England Primary School, One of Eastbourne most sought-after school-and a faith school. A parent at St. Mark's Church of England primary school told the Eastbourne Echo that James and his daughter quietly started attending St Luke's Church a couple of years ago so that the young girl could get a school place. As soon as she got a place, they never set a foot in the church again!

It seems James no longer believes that faith schools are so harmful after all. He should clarify his position.

737) **Q;** Outline the approach that the High court will take when considering the claim.

A; The first thing is to outline the submission of both claimant and defendant supported by relevant authorities, statute, common law EHRR The case is complicated because of the claimant's daughter photograph which has raised conflict between freedoms of privacy against paparazzo's freedom of expression.

738) Q; what argument might James present?

A: James may present the following

Although the daughter face was blurred, the father was seen holding her hand, this make it easier to identify her when she is dropped and picked by the father. Eastbourne Echo newspaper did not obtain consent from the parent to photograph the daughter which is breach of confidence or refer as breach (private information) and also breach Article 8 (freedom of private life. James had been a campaigner for faith school, make him a public figure but he expect "reasonable expectation of respect for his family private life". James would argue that the welfare of his daughter is paramount and would seek injunction that taking and picking his daughter from school would not be targeted by the media to take photograph in public places without written consent from the parent.

James will quote; Dame Elizabeth Buttler-Sloss in X .v. Netherland (1958) B EHRR 235; Botta .V. Italy (1998)26 EHRR 281. "What to be taken into account is fragile mental health of James daughter which has been affected"

James can quote Judge Tugendhat who said, “Freedom to live as one chooses is one of the most valuable freedoms”. James may seek injunction and financial compensation.

739) Q; What might the newspaper defend the claim?

A: Echo news paper

This is a case where James morality draws into question.

Human Right Act 1998 Article 8 and 10 which James quoted are not absolute they are qualified for democratic society. Under Article 10, it is morality and reputation and privacy issue, and the newspaper was right to demand if James view on faith schools has changed. That ECHR allows member state to deal with moral whether his choice of moral is good or bad.

The press freedom of expression is to make the public aware the behaviour of public figures like James who has divided the local school community with his charismatic campaign is already in public domain.

James is not ordinary private person as his ideology had impact on the public and is right the public to know his current moral or change of belief.

Newspaper protect the democratic right of others who might already been condition by James opinion.

Baroness hale made a comment about Naomi Campbell "------ There is nothing essentially private information nor can be expected to damage her life—"this is because Campbell is a public interest.

Similar case in Von Hannover .Germany (No2) (2012) EMLR 16.The conduct of other members of society as being socially harmful or wrong, media is allow freedom to criticize or make the public aware within the limit of the press code. James and his daughter daily activities of trip to and back from school will not give them expectation for private life. He caused morality harm to the public and that their picture and article is to protect morality which is based on share morality by majority in the community.

740) **Q:** What will the court consider?

A; what is the information being sought to be protected? How important is it to protect them?

How important is the family in the community?

Is there a risk? If so thus that risk displaced the right of free expression \information about James without court rescue. Is there any perceived risk to justify placing confidence above freedom of expression?

741) Q: what is the likely Judgement in court?

A: Court decision

It also call into play how the court will try to find balance to compromise within the EU Article 8, 10 which both parties have actually emphasise in their submission.

742) Q: What will be the aim of the court?

A: The court weighs and must strike a fair balance between the competing interest protecting the individual against arbitrary interference to his family life and the broad general principle and importance of convention right to the freedom of expression, by the press and other media.

743) Q; what consideration the court will take regarding the press?

A; as Lord Woolf stated in A.V.B (2002) WLR542 "the existence of the free press is itself desirable and so any interference with it has to be justified".

The court might take the view that it is not the journalist to undermine human right or court to refuse to enforced them on the ground of moral disapproval. The protection of moral (R. V. Handyside (1976) 1EHRR 737**.**The court might avoid restraint on the freedom of the press without vital scrutiny, the court has the right to protect the public from being corrupt, the law always make decision to protect vulnerable people such as children.

744) Q; what cases might be used by the court in making decision?

A: Appeal court case (Murray) support James that every day public activities still attract a reasonable expectation of privacy especially for children.

Article 8 give James right to respect for private life, article 10 provide the newspaper freedom of expression, and Article 3 prohibition of psychological torture of the daughter, this will then engage Article 8 and 10. Dame Elizabeth Butler – Sloss made it known that the Human Rights Act 1998 are not directly enforceable against newspapers as they don't come within the definition of public authority. Parliament has great importance of article 10 and protection of freedom of expression, inter alia for the press and for the media.

In Campbell .v. Mirror group newspapers (2004) UKHL,22,(2004) WLR 1232.Dame Elizabeth Butler – Sloss granted life time injunction in X (Mary Bell) and another news group newspapers and another (2003)

EWHC QB1101, (2003)EMLR 37 in which the court protected her.

745) Q; Outline the jigsaw of judgement?

A: The newspaper had published article about James in circumstance that clearly highlight details about his daughter. It is this information of photograph of her, James argued that the newspapers had over stepped the line. Is the school detail confidential? Is it in the public domain?

In T and Yv the Netherlands (1985) 8EHRR court found that a threat to life\threat to safety, is James ----that both his and his daughter in danger should the court not allow the freedom of expression? ----the fundamental right is show to them as per Article 10 (2).

Would James and his daughter be subjected to revenge attitude? If that is genuine possibility the balancing the various Article and to be evaluated with great care.

746) Q: what does Article 8 protect in this case?

A; Article 8 protect individual against arbitrary interference by newspaper. Whilst Article 10 covers "the convention right to freedom of expression" one might have particular regard to both Article 8 and 10. There are many measures the court can used to protect their private life including appropriate respect to the position of the press and their right and duty to be free to publish.

747) **Q;** what does the court consider press code?

A; The court aware that press code is not adequately to protect them as the court might take the view that the risk is too great to rely on the voluntary press code and the provision of the protection from harassment Act 1977 might not be strong enough to protect them.

748) **Q:** How will they consider children involvement in this case?

A: The one thing that concerns the court is, we have a young child effectively identify by reference to the father's name and school .The photo also assist identification. Are school details confidential? Is there possibility of harassment? The main point claimant has doubts about the article and photos since the article has already been published have that horse not neigh already butted.

The court have compelling reasons to protect any information possible leading to the identity or future where about of James daughter. (Include photograph and characteristics and will issue global injunction to protect daughter from the media; her appearance and address education, outdoor and indoor activities without the consent of the parent up to age of 21. A financial compensation of about £20,000 for the daughter. The court will allow the press to continue dealing with James as any other citizen.

Scenario

"(In) many matters concerning Human Rights balance falls to be struck between the right of individuals and the general public interest concern... as Williams stated in his seminal book on public order (keeping the peace (London 1967), the law in this area is a "compromise "that seek to balance the competing demands of freedom of speech and assembly on the one hand and the preservation of the Queen's peace on the other"
Elliot, m. And Thomas (2014) public law (2nd edition), OUP, Oxford, 783.

749) Q: Discuses this statement.

A: There had been many occasions when conflict between statue and EU articles, the judicial have to find balance to satisfy both authorities

Judicial achieves by using appropriate interpretation, exceptional circumstances discretion, proportionate, declaration of incompatibility, and restriction in the law making. Such compromise helps to provide fairness to both claimant and defendant. Some laws are not being repealed allow the executive access.

Chapter 16

Police

750) Q; Name some police powers?

A; The following are some powers for the police aim to control violence or suspected in protesters within the Public Order act 1986; Section 1; "A person using unlawful violence can be arrested and charged". Section 2, "an offence under violent disorder can attract maximum of five years imprison". Section 4 gives the police power to arrest and charge for anyone who use threaten behaviour with intent to cause immediate unlawful violence

Section 11(1) require protestors or public meeting to give notice of at least six days to police before the meeting, (s.11 (6).This allow the police to research and to make contingent plans for any eventuality, unexpected violence with opposition act. Section 12; allow the police to direct route and impose conditions prior to the meeting. whilst Section 13 gives the police power to ban processions if police suspect any problem underSection14 give the police power to limit the number of protestors especially on picket line to avoid any serious public disorder (for public assemble),whilst section 14A permit the police to ban trespasser assembles and to criminalise meetings on somebody private land without consent. Article 11 support limiting protestors to peaceful protest\assembly, it also create a positive right of freedom of assembly and freedom of association and requires police to protect lawful protestor. Section 16 gives the police the power to give direction and to define picket line and the highway. Section 18 give powers of arrest for incitement of racial hatred as defend in section 17.Section17 to 23 give the police direction and power as were as their limitation in dealing with threaten, abusive insulting behaviour incitement to racial hatred.

751) Q: How are police treated if they break the law?

A; they are also treated like any citizen if they break the code of duty and hence to scrutiny and judgement in court. Police must only Act lawfully within specific legal powers. Some police powers are discretionary which can give rise to be challenge for illegality in their duties such as arrest, interrogation or if they failed to follow procedure or being irrational. Police arrest must be within s.24 (2) or section 24(3) of PACE 1984 or section 24 (5) police must give reason of arrest as soon as possible There are limitation to go with the power that they had been given but Complaint against police include;

disciplinary charges under police conduct regulation 2008, use of unduly force, abuse of authority, victimisation unreasonable discrimination, disobedience to lawful order

752) **Q;** Give example of police and protesters?

A: Police oppressive behaviour towards protesters could lead to police facing criminal charge. The following are some various cases regarding protestors in which police had been guilty (Kremlin. V. Gardener (1967)2 QB 510.A protestors who assaulted a police officer for unlawful arrest was given compensation under section 89.A defendant who police unlawfully refused access to a solicitor prior to interview resulted the evidence void and protestors were paid compensation under section 58 of PACE (Ireland V .UK 1978)2 EHRR 20 article 3.Beatty .V. Gill banks (1882)9QB308 Salvation Army marching were a lot of protestor's ahead .V. Percy (1995)1WLR 1382 this is a case where by the court said that there must be a violence or threaten of violence before the court arrest protestors.

753) **Q**; Give an example cases involve protestors and the police?

A: Redmond-Bate V. DPP (1999) Cram LR 998; protestor arrested and convicted for obstructing police officer. Ashman and Harrumph V. United Kingdom (2000)29 EHRR 241 (Binding over orders).In Arts fur Das Leben. V. Austra (1991)13EHRR 204 ECTHR state "State may infringe freedom of assembly if it does not take positive measures to protect the exercise of the Right of assembly.

754) **Q;** Do the court sometimes compromise?

A; Sometimes Court allows compromise when dealing with cases involve police example Lord Irvine said that protestors can use public highway as long as this is peaceful and lawful and not intimidating others.

Chapter 17

CONSTITUTIONAL LAW

755) Q; what do you understand by convention?

A: "Conventions are practices that have not been written down as rules but are followed as a matter of tradition. As result as the way in which the UK constitutional practices have developed, a convention may well contradict the strict legal position" *Joneses. (2012)Public law. In Slorach, S. (ED) foundations in context, college of law publishing Guildford, p203*

756) Q; Explain how convention is linked to UK constitution?

A; Convention has followed tradition and is link to some of the elements of constitutional significance.

757) Q; Give an example of how tradition is link to convention?

A; Example Magna Carta 1215 gave power to the monarch; trial by Jury individual right, government action must be within the law. Bills of Right 1689, limit the monarch powers, freedom of speech within parliament. In 1603 England and Scotland share monarch, Act of settlement 1707 union between

England and Scotland rules of succession to the throne, monarch being the head of the state for common worth countries. Parliament act 1911 and 1949 that the will of the electorate prevail over unelected House of Lords. Devolution of Wales started in 1284 and with union 1536.union with Northern Ireland 1541. Legist ration for Scotland, Welsh, Northern Ireland in recent years. European convention 1972 and human Right 1998. (P59)

758) **Q;** Is convention legal?

A; Convention is non-legal gentlemen agreement between two or more bodies or individual whereby the rules are implemented but cannot be enforced the judiciary

759) **Q;** Are there some element of legal and politic?

A; Convention have degree of constitutional elements which is legal or political, hence breach of the convention will result breach the law. Occasionally the court may contradict the convention non legal to legal position the court or different judge's interpretation and applying to the facts of the case may be different. The judicial to keep government action within the law and enforce the will of parliament view of how right should be balanced. Right are convention rules and matters be absence in Legist ration.

760) Q; How did Marshal and Moodier define constitutional convention;

A; There are various legal definitions of constitutional convention; state. ".....rules of constitution behaviour which is considered to be binding by and upon those who operate the constitution but enforced by the court which are not...or parliament". (P76) (Marshal and Moodier problems of the constitution (1971) but not binding on ordinary citizens. Convention values include legal certainty, personal liberties and due process.

761) Q: What is Characteristic of constitutional convention?

A: Characteristic of constitutional convention is summarise by Sir Ivory Jennings as "the flesh that cloth the dry bone" And must pass three tests must be passed before a convention existence recognised 1) there must be precedent 2) No binding rules .3) There must be reason for the rule. (Sir Ivory Jennings (the law and the constitution 1959). (P76-77). Parliament is retains supremacy, protect the convention, the breach of a convention breaches the law make and review the law, separation of power, unwritten, no single authoritative, unitary, monarchical, flexible, fused power.

762) Q; what source is U.K constitution convention?

A: UK constitution convention is made up from various of sources; Legist ration, judiciary, Royal prerogative, the law and custom of the parliament, the European union law and European convention on human Right (P.122-125), devolution (P.133-140), non- legal include convention Authoritative works; Persuasive. For example the enforcement of the law and custom of parliamentary privilege of the House of Lords.

763) Q; what is the purpose of convention?

A; The purpose of convention is for everyone to respect and observe the principle of the constitution expressed by the will of the House of Commons in the first instance, and ultimately the will of the nation as expressed through Parliament.

764) Q; Name some function of constitutional convention?

A; The core function of traditional approach that constitution convention rules establish and regulated the entire system of government includes legal machinery.It provides some flexibility and discretion, example; it had been a custom for the chancellor to deliver budget in March\April but between 1993 to 1996, it was delivered in November. Never the less Statute may override constitutional law. Example Modzimbamuto. V. Loudness-Burke (1969) 1 AC. (P.85, 92).

765) **Q:** Give example of convention relating to international law?

A; Convention form the basis on international law such as the European convention gives sense of belonging to fundamental understanding of human right (1998). There will be constitutional crisis to disregard them (OU 107). Another example is that the cabinet minister is not allowed to criticise other ministers in public cabinet minister may choose to resign instead of breaching this convention rule.

766) **Q:** What part is play by UK monarch and the parliament?

A: By convention the monarch has to give Royal assent to bills after it has passed through the Houses of common and Lords as it has been tradition. Members of parliament are held responsible for their action. Judges are not to be active in any political party. There is a notable convention between the houses of parliament the Crown and judicially which are observed as traditional.

767) **Q:** why must convention rules is observed?

A: The reason why convention rules must be observed, is obeyed to legitimate the exercise of power "They make the legal constitution work; they keep it in touch with the growth of ideas "by Sir Ivory Jennings (the law and constitution 5th end, 1959 convention in UK. It. (P.82-83) requires the public officers to follow the convention rules or in effect convention rule go hand in hand with the job." The rule of the game" (P. 82) the office holder is impliedly agrees to be bound by the rules. Sanction will be applied if convention rules are broken. It avoid unlawful act, illegal, irrational, procedural (unfairness) obey 1998 of Human Right Act.

768) **Q:** What will happen if convention rules are disregarded?

A: There will be constitutional crisis if convention rules are disregarded because the main areas of the government activity are regulated by convention rules which dictate rules of how the content of constitution is operate. SEWEL convention in July 1998 "The Westminster government will not normally pass a Legislation in relation to devolved matters in Scotland without the consent of the Scottish parliament, (P.. 77)) devolution matters are convention not lawn

769) **Q**; what happen if member state failed to observe the convention rules?

A; although the European treaty restrict national sovereignty and UK may choose to pay penalty instead of observed certain things according to traditional therefore.

770) **Q**; what are Royal prerogative powers?

A: Royal prerogative is absolute powers which the Monarch historically enjoy at common law-"----the residue of discretional or arbitrary authority of an Act of Parliament is done in virtues of this prerogative (*An introduction to the study of laws of the constitution 1885 by Dicey)*

771) **Q;** Give example of how the parliament deals with issue of convention?

A; Lord Salisbury was the last peer to hold office as prime minister when he resigned in 1902. Monarch have act according to convention precedent as tradition where by the Queen\King appoint the prime minister until 1965 convention demand leader of majority party at general election to present his manifesto to the monarch for royal assent and to be appointment as prime minister. Example 1923 King George V appointed Stanley Baldwin as prime minister despite Lord Curzon being the party choice. In 1940 King George V1 appointed Winston Churchill as prime minister despite party choice was Lord Halifax. In 1963 Peerage Act (that prime minister appointment ceased to be from House of Lords. From 1965, the precedent set in 1963 by House of Commons majority party chooses the leader as prime minister

772) **Q:** Can the court change Legislation?

A: No Because of the doctrine of parliamentary supremacy UK court has no powers to review Legislation. Picking v. British railway board (1974) AC 765. (P.111) a problem may arise when parliament makes the Act no longer effective by; express repeal or by implied repeal. If convention is broken, the government institution or the public opinion will apply formal sanction and remedy need to be sought quickly. Court can disregard any Act which parliament no longer intends to be effective. When convention conflict with law, the court are bound to enforce. (P65)

773) **Q:** What happen when there is link between member state laws and convention rules?

A; Sometimes there may be link between the legal laws and the convention rules and might be used in the court in such case the Supreme Court adjudicate. Example Attorney-General's. Jonathan Cape Ltd) 1976) QB 752-i.e Enforcement of convention rule (whether the government could stop the publication of the former cabinet minister Mr. Richard Crossman diary. Carltona.V. Commissioner of works (1943)2 ALL ER 560, whereby civil servant signed document to purchase a land in a wartime for minister. Example; R.V. Secretary of state for the home department ex parted Chehak (1991) 1 WLR 890.Chadian. V. Godin-Mendoza (2004)2 AC 557-Lord Steyn (P 124) (that homosexual treatment the same as the homosexual in considering inheritance of tenancy).

774) **Q;** how is convention rules protected?

A: Convention though not a legal rule, are protected by Legislation; example section 3 and other provisions in the European convention to protect the Human right 1998 and all member counties in the EU to regard fundamental Right as a primary polices. There is no legal obligation to amend or repeal a conflicting

Legislation but there will be political pressure on parliament to do so.

775) Q: What happen if there is conflict between member state and convention?

A: In event of EU and UK statue found to be accidental conflict, the former prevails section 2 (4).example R.V. secretary of for transport ex parte Factor tame (No 1) (1990)2 AC 85. (P.65) Section 3 of the Human Right 1898 state "so far as it is possible to do so, primary and subordinate Legislation must be read and given effect in a way which is compatible with convention".

Chapter 18

HUMAN RIGHT

776) Q; When do the courts take notice of EU treaties?

A: European Union treaties does not operate as a legal limit on member \UK parliament rare convention rules "We take no notice of treatises of European Union until they are embodied in laws enacted by parliament and then only to the extent that parliament tells us" by Lord Denning in Blackburn. Attorney general (1971)2 ALL ER 1380 P142

777) Q: What happen to Magna Carta?

A: tradition approach which started over 800 years ago (Magna Carta 1215) is still being observed and failure to continue in my opinion will result constitutional crisis

778) Q; Explain rule of law?

A: Rule of law is the main principle of any country constitution; there are three elements of rule of law; according to professor Dicey;

1) No retrospective or arbitrary
2) Equality
3) Government must be bound by rule of law

779) Q; Explain constitution of a country

A; A country might have written or unwritten constitution

1) A written constitution is the country's supremacy which protects the right of individual and may contain Bills of Right.
2) Unwritten constitution such as the UK, their right is created and protected by the courts (common law) and by parliament who enact statute law which expressly created and protects human Rights.

780) Q; Explain Bills of Right in constitution?

A: In written constitution, fundamental human rights are in the Bill of Right which makes it difficult to change without going through special procedure.

Since UK is unwritten constitution, there is no Bills of Right, the parliament supremacy means that parliament can make review law as it please, No one can override statute, and parliament is bound by the rule of law

781) Q: When European convention was first created?

A; European convention was first created in 1950 after the Second World War to prevent the atrocity of Nazi of Nazi behaviour.

All member state accepted the principle of rule of law within the convention frame work of protection.

782) Q: What is Standpoint?

A; is point of view. All the EU countries have variety of moral standpoints.

783) Q; what approach was convention drafted?

Convention was drafted in general approach call "open ended" drafting which allow member country to interpret as cases arise. Convention addresses certainty or Right.

784) **Q**; what does open ended constitution means?

A:"With the open-ended EU draft" and parliamentary supremacy means that any future government in UK can do and undo the work of earlier\ previous government. To make it difficult to undo, UK government have ingrain the right in the Act within the legal system.

785) **Q:** How can one repeal law in UK?

A: There are two ways to repeal laws in UK

1) Express
2) Implied

Chapter 19

EUROPEAN LAWS

786) **Q:** Name types of Human Rights?

A; There are two types of human rights; Absolute and qualified

787) **Q:** What is absolute right?

A; These are the right that member states have to observe strictly and cannot be interfered with by state (may subject have limitation).

788) **Q:** What are impose to member state in Human Right?

A; Human right Article can impose restriction and create obligation on member states to prevent breaches of the Human Rights.

789) **Q;** Give example of absolute rights?

A; Article 6 Right to a fair trial

Article 3; Prohibition of torture, inhuman, punishment, degrading treatment.

Article 2 Right to life.

790) **Q;** what is qualified Right?

A; these are flexible to interfere with

791) **Q:** Give example of qualified rights?

A; Article 10; Freedom of expression (Libel and slander)

Article 11 Freedom of association (terrorist, security)

Article 8 Private and family life (children at risk)

Article 1 part 1 Peaceful enjoyment of property (compulsory purchase)

Liberty and security of the person.

792) Q: How many rights are qualified rights divided?

A; Qualified right is divided into two parts.

793) Q: Using Article 8, explain the part of qualified rights?

A; Most of the qualified rights has two rights, and element.

794) Q: Explain the part of Article 8?

A: First part is the expression of the right and it is set out in the same way as absolute right

The second part is divided into three legally distinct sections known as element.

795) Q; what does the first part of the second part of Article 8 state?

A: The first part of the second part state being the first element "it can only be interfered by public authority if is in accordance with the law. (For UK, the laws are statute or common law)

796) Q; what does the second element of second part of section 8 state?

A; The second element state “The right can only be interfered by public authority if interference is necessary in the democratic society”

797) Q; what does the third element of second part of section 8 state?

A; The third element set out the legitimate aim for the member state to interfere

798) Q: What are the legitimate aims might consist of?

A; Most member state legitimate aim under Article 8-part 2 element three include

1) National security, public safety and the economic wellbeing of the country
2) Protection of disorder or crime, the protection of health or moral.
3) The protection of the rights and freedom of others.

799) Q; What happen in Judicial Review

A; in judicial Review, the administrative court will

1) Consider what is prescribed by law
2) Consider the legitimate aim of interference
3) Consider if is necessary in a democratic society.

800) Q: Who decide the article?

A; Domestic court decide what the article of the convention mean and how they do this.

801) Q; What are protocols?

A; The right that only have an article number were part of the original convention, any later additions or amendments to the original convention right are called protocols

802) Q; What does HRA section 3 allow member state?

A; The 1998 of the HRA section 3 has given the member state the power to interpret the Act for remedial measure and compromise and proper implementation of the HRA laws.

Most of the Articles EU laws and UK statue and common laws have built in restrictions example Article 8(2), 9(2) and 10(2) which helps the court to find balance on some define grounds, such as POA (police order Act 1986, Criminal justice Act 2003.

803) Q: What happens when there are conflicting HRA Articles?

A; Another provision aim to strike the balance or compromise two conflicting Articles is the use of proportionality test Baroness Hale found out that it is easier to apply proportional if there are only one convention rights than two conventions as she said "---- the proportionality with one has to be balance against the proportionality of restricting the other"

804) Q; what does the EU law section 4 allows?

A; EU law section 4 of the Act allows member state; higher court to declare the EU law not in compatible with the statue (Act of Parliament). Example between 2000 and 2013 there were 28 declaration of incompatibility of which eight were overturned on appeal, remedial to four of the law and no decision was done on one, fourteen resulted change of the law to render them compatible.

805) Q: Give example of the House of Lords on compromise on EU law?

A; Lord Steyn made a bold comment about this compromise "----the court had not been using their powers under section 3 sufficiently, if they had used a broad, purposive approach to statues that appear to conflict with the conviction right, they would have avoid the need to make so many declarations of incompatibility". He was supported by Baroness Hale in Campbell. V. Mirror Group Newspapers Ltd (2004)2 AC 457 said "--- the court not only can but must balance the competing convention rights of the parties"

"Dame Elizabeth Butler-Sloss in a case X.V. Netherlands (1985)8 EHRR 235 and another case of Mary Bell, she went to the extend first thing that is considered in exceptional circumstance just too struck balance.

806) Q; Explain what powers the police have in English law to control the conduct of protesters. and evaluate how Articles 10 and 11 of the European conservation on Human rights (ECHR) and the human Right act 1998 seek to balance the competing demands referred to by Elliot and Thomas in the scenario?

A: United Kingdom police is part of executive and is a public authority, and have wide powers to carry out their function to enforce the laws and to keep public peace. Prior to the Public Order Act 1986 (POA), the highway Act 1980, the racial and religious haltered Act 2006, OAPA (Offence Against person Act) 1861; sections 47, 20 and 18

807) Q: What are the powers to control protestors?

A: Criminal Justice and Public order Act 1994, 2003. European Union convention 1972, PACE (police and Criminal Evidence) 1984. European Union of Human right 1998.

With reference to the specific powers to control conduct of protesters and the evaluation of the Human Right Act, Article 10 (freedom of expression and press) and 11

(Right for peaceful assembly and right of freedom of association),both with limitation for the protection of others ,aim to prevent disorder and crime.

808) **Q:** How are freedom of expression protestors protected

A: Although the legally, pre-arranged freedom of assembly and expression protestors are protected by police. It can also be argued that the police prevent freedom of the opponent by arresting them. Both articles are qualified means that member state can make adaptation as per section 3. In democratic society, the protestors who have followed the procedure in accordance to POA (police Order Act 1986). The EctHR allow police to take positive measures to protect the exercise of right (Platform "Artze fur das Leben ".v Austria (1999) 13 EHRR 204.

809) **Q:** Why are some UK laws not repealed when new laws are enacted?

A: In UK, despite new laws being enact by parliament, the common law powers were not repeal which allowed the police sometimes to use them as they are more flexible and easier to implement despite been uncertain.

810) Q: What does UK stand with regard to Bill of Right in EU?

A: The fact that UK embedded statute into the convention gives it partially Bills of Right with the convention.

Never the less the UK constitution is written so no Bills of Right as Parliament supremacy (although this can be argued due to UK laws that it has to be satisfied.

811) Q: When was UK Bills of Right?

A; UK had bills of right in 1689 in the Glorious revolution

812) Q: Are EU member state legally bound member states?

A: The constraint on UK by ECHR and other members are not legal but are political.

813) Q: Which Article deals with EU interpretation?

A: Section 3 of HRA gives obligation to member state to intemperate the rights in the direction on section 3.

814) Q: What does the court have to consider during interpretation of HRA laws?

A: During the interpretation of HRA by the courts, they have to consider the intention of Westminster Parliament which call for the court to adjust their traditional roll but at the same time abide by section 3 rules

Confliction might be crown approach in a constructive interpretation but section 3 always must be upheld if it apples

815) Q: What is the last result for member state if they cannot agree with the EU laws?

A: If a member state cannot agree the terms of EU laws, then they must declare it as incompatible using section 4. Never the less section 3 is usually preferable

816) Q: What must member state minister do with incompatible law?

A: Section 19 requires the responsible minister to state any new law that is compatible to HRA section 19(1b). If the minister cannot make these declarations that he\she must say so.

817) Q: Who is allowed to use section 4?

A; Only High or Higher courts can declare a statue incompatible to EU law. Once this declaration is made, then the EU law override the statue. This is why parliament has to apply remedies in order to maintain parliament supremacy.

818) Q: What happen if verdict is declared unlawful?

A: If court can declare verdict unlawful, then there would be no need to declare the statue incompatibility. (Section 3 can be used instead)

819) Q: Does HRA gives right for state to abode?

A: The HRA does not give right for member state citizen to abode. But article 8 can be used if the person has established a family in UK.

However refusing UK citizen is breach of international law.

820) Q: Which Article can be summoned when dealing with convention right?

A: Article 2 (Right of life) to avoid murder, GBH, manslaughter.

Article 3 (Degrading punishment)

Article 5 (Liberty of the person

Article 6 Fair trial and fair hearing

Article 7 Bands retrospective criminal liability is the most significant.

Article 1 protocol 1 Freedom of person and property.

821) Q: Name some of the legitimate aim for interference with EU Articles

A: 1) interest of the national security, public safety or economic well –being of country (Article 8).

2) Prevention of disorder (Article 8 and 10)

3) Protection of moral (Article 8, 10)

Protection of right and freedom of others (Article 8)

Protection of freedom of information (Article 8)

Protection of disclosure of information (Article 10)

Maintaining the authority and impartiality of Judicial (Article 10).

822) Q: Name the 4 elements in Article 8?

A: The right for private life, family life, home and correspondences

823) Q: What are the related rights?

A: Article 12 Right to marry and have family

Article 14 Right to enjoy convention right without discrimination

Article 1 protocol 1 Right to peaceful enjoyment of possession (property) both tangible

And intangible

824) Q: Give example of case laws?

A: 1) example Peck. V. UK (2003) 36 EHRR41—CCTV

2) Sand Marper. V, UK (2009) 48 E HRR 50 ECTHR this relate to DNA

3) Wood and metropolitan police commission (2009). This relates to police retained photograph of arms protestors. Lord Collins said "Never the less it is plain that the last word has yet to be said on the implication

for civil liberties of the taking and retention of images in the modern surveillance society"

4) Class. V Germany (1979-80)) 2EHRR 214 (telephone taping)

5) Hoffman. V Austria (1994) 17 EHRR 293

825) Q: What is the limitation or interference of qualified right such as Article 8, 10, 11?

A; There are three headings for interference;

Must be within the state or EU law

Must be necessary for the interest of democratic society.

Legitimate Aim; These include; security of the state, public order, protection of morals, protection of other reputation or right of others.

826) Q; Explain Article 10 of EU.

A; everybody has the right of freedom of expression which include freedom to hold opinions and receives and import information and ideas without interference by the public authority and regardless frontiers. It carries with it duties and responsibilities.

827) Q: How does Article 10 affect moral? Give supporting case law.

A; Protection of morals (R.V Handysde (1976) 1EHRR737. Some of the limitation or legitimacy of the qualified right can affect or support other articles.

828) Q; Give example of how Article 10 affect moral?

A; 1) Publication of members of security officers are for state security (confidential)

2) Business people, reputation of politicians etc will be breached of respect for private and family life (article 8)

3) Stop terrorist organisation broadcast direct to people (public and state security)

4) Injunction to newspapers trial while a case is being heard will breach Article 6 for fair trial.

829) Q; What Article direct or indirect relates to Article 10 (freedom of expression)?

A: Article 9; everyone has the right to freedom of thought; conscience and religion (include worship, belief, teaching, practice and observance.

830) Q; which section of the Article has restriction?

A; All qualified Articles have limitation restriction.

831) Q; Give example of the restriction of qualified right?

A; The first part of or section one of the Article carries the formal rights just as absolute right, but usually section 2 contain restriction or limitation. Examples are; Article 8(2), article 9(2). Article 11(2) e.tc.

832) Q How can EU members use the convention Rights?

A; State courts give effect to convention rights in the cause of any proceeding and can grant the relief against unlawful act of public authority.

833) Q: How is some of the member state court decision base?

A; Court decision in most cases will be based on more obviously moral basis in having to apply the principles of proportionality.

834) Q; what section support remedy?

A; Section 8 of the HRA enable court to award any remedy it considers just and appropriate in respect of an unlawful act of a public authority infringing convention rights (This include an award of damages if the award is necessary.

835) Q: What is the aim of award?

A; to afford just satisfaction. UK courts consciously applied the convention before incorporation (Sunday Times case)

836) Q: what is the recommended way to deal with answering legal question?

A; This depend on the question, but try to use "MISS" make it short and simple.

837) Q: When was EU laws incorporate to UK.

A: European Union community was incorporated into UK laws which cause implication of the doctrine of the parliament supremacy, since EU laws must override the UK law supremacy.

838) Q: Name the two approaches in interpreted the law in EU?

A: 1) International laws or teleological approach are used to interpreted EU laws. These are more detail than the method use in domestic.

UK approach is known as “Purpose Approach”

839) Q: What effect is EU treaties have on member state?

A: EU legist ration is made under name “TREATIES” and always have legal basis in the article of the treaties.

840) Q: What must member state do if EU law don’t have legal effect on member?

A: If EU treaty don’t have legal basis within member state or not compatible with EU, It can be declared invalid by the EU.

841) Q: How do member state interpreted EU laws?

A: EU laws don’t have “direct effect” on member state, so member state must use “indirect effect “to interpreted national legislation consistent with EU Directive, whether the national provision adopted before or after the directive (Marleasing SA v. La Comercial international de Alimentacian.

842) Q: What advantage is section 2(2) of EU?

A; Section 2(2) of the EU communities Act 1972 permits member state to make delegated legistration to implement EU obligation into UK laws

843) Q: What is the disadvantage of delegated legistration on UK ?

A: UK cannot use delegated legislation to make the following laws;

1) Impose taxation
2) Operate retrospective effect.
3) Sub delegate legislative powers.
4) Create major new criminal offence.

844) Q: What is the source of EU laws?

A: 1) Treaty provision set the aim and objective of EU and structure of institutions.

2 Set out the regulation which has legal force in member state.

3 DIRECTIVES—binding as to the result to be achieve but members have a choice of form and method use.

845) Q: What is directive using direct effect?

A: It means it can only be used against state and not individual (Marshal) but it can have direct effect if the time limit has passed that is individual can take (if the state fails to implement it (Van Duyn v Home Office.

846) **Q;** Explain section 2(1) of HRA?

A; Section 2 subsection 1 of the HRA make decision of the European court of Human Right persuasive in all member state court (in UK from lower to supreme court).But because these decisions is not precedent, UK court takes them into consideration but are not bound to follow them.

847) **Q:** Explain section 3(1) of EU?

A: Section 3(1) creates a specific new interpretative rule "that all UK statutes old and new have to be compatible with the Human Right act provision". If not compatible the court can declare it incompatible

848) **Q;** Explain section 3 (2) of HRA?

A; Section 2b, if the statute cannot be read then the court have to uphold the statute as written.

849) **Q;** Explain section 4 of HRA?

A: Section 4 gives member state power to make declaration of incompatibility with the Human Right. Parliament may repeal or review general the statue to make it compatible. The effect is mainly political.

850) **Q;** Which Article or section specifically formulated to protect freedom of expression of media?

A; Section 12 (4) of the HRA.but it is worth noting that there is mechanism built into all qualified Right to balance the right and respect of the other Article. Example this is specifically inserted to prevent unduly restriction of freedom of the press, journalist, artist, literary (but take into account public interest and code of conduct)

851) **Q:** how do we consider Right in EU?

A; In considering, we must always bear in mind to balance one right with other people right, especially where two Articles are engaged such as Articles 8 and 10 or 8 and 9. In such case the court apply proportionality test (Daly).

852) **Q:** Explain Article 8 and give supporting case law.

A; Article 8 is right to private life, the meaning is that, it covers physical and psychological integrity of a person. And a right to personal development and to establish and developed relationship with other human being and outside world. Dame Elizabeth Butler-slows (x.v.Netherland (1985) 8 EHRR 235. Botta.Itally (1998)26 EHRR 281- Mary Bell case.

853) **Q**: What consideration with regard to Article 8 and 10?

A; the special circumstances one has to take when Article 8 and 10 are engaged. Include the existence and protection of press\ media in section 64(4) for freedom of expression. Lord Woolf said “The existence of a free press is in itself desirable and so any interference with it has to be justified.

854) **Q:** What happen when Article 8 is breached? Give example

A: When article 8 is breached especially by press exercise their freedom of expression. The victim in Article 8 experience added potential harm in that he\she can't help thinking of being followed or betrayed, and deterring him\herself from going to the original place and affect him\her rehabilitation

855) **Q:** Give case law of press breached Article 8?

A; Campbell (in Narcotic treatment) v. Mirror Group and Von Hannover .v German in Ect HR are similar. Other cases are Princess Caroline of Morocco, Murray, Mary Bell.

856) **Q:** What happens if photograph is taken when the person is not in an official role?

A; When Paparazzi take photograph when the model is not in her official roll the Article 8 might be engaged.

857) **Q:** What about taken pictures of children?

A; if the press don't have the consent of the parent or guardian, Article 8 might be engaged and in most cases is winnable in court.

858) **Q:** What does engagements of Article 8 & 10 depend?

A; Engagement of Article 8 and 10 depend on the circumstances and subject to the facts of case. Example is the England captain John Telly injunction known as "super –injunction" but was overturned.

TORT

859) **Q**: How can Article 8 be used in Tort Claim?

A: Article 8 3ngage when individual has reasonable expectation of privacy (objective view)

Another term used for privacy claim in tort (as no claim in tort for privacy) is misuse of information.

860) **Q:** How can European directive be interpreted?

A: European directive can only have vertical direct effect that is action against state body.(Marshall v. Southampton)

861) **Q:** What is horizontal direct?

A; Horizontal direct is action against individual by a state.

862) **Q:** Compare ECA (European Community Act 1972) and HRA Human Right Act 1998?

A; Declaration of HRA incompatibility does not affect the validity of the offending legislation which the court must still enforce.

In contrast the ECA requires member state courts to give priority to directly effective EU law.

863) Q: What happen if there is conflict between the EU and UK laws?

A: If EU law conflict with UK laws, and despite incorporation, UK parliament retains supremacy as it can repeal the ECA and HRA, although there might be political difficulties, economic and social implication.

864) Q: What is the aim and how EU laws are abided by member state?

A; European community laws are enforced by national and European level., the aim is to outline the history of the European economic community identify the reasons why it was established, knowledge of the four main legal institutions

865) Q; Why was the EEC esblished?

A; The European community was established in the aftermath of the second world war in order to

1) bring stability back to the continent
2) To create a trading block with a large internal market

3) To establish a consolidated unit of countries which would provide a barrier between the communist powers to the east and American to the west
4) As well as being founded on a strong economic principle, it was also a product of a desire to ensure peace, a desired which has followed the first world war, but which had not been reality

866) **Q;** When was the first attempt of economic integration in EU?

A: This was in1951

867) **Q;** What happened?

A; In 1951 the treaty of Paris was signed, establishing the European coal and steel community (ECSC)

868) **Q;** Who were the countries involved?

A: The six member countries were France, Germany, Italy, The Benelux countries (Belgium, The Netherlands and Luxembourg)

869) **Q:** Who were the most influential in the formation of the first EEC?

A; The prime movers in this were the French foreign minister Robert Schumann and his compatriot Jean Monnet who became the first EU president.

CHAPTER 20
LEGAL RESEARCH

870) Q; How is legal research evolved)

A: In the last two decades, legal research skills have undergone a revolution compelled by communications technology, economic globalization and consistent alterations within tertiary education, legal education and legal profession sector. It can be argued that these alterations have impelled self-interrogation about the nature of legal education with the legal academy, the nature of methodologies and legal research involved. An argument can be made that legal research program has generally been consultant-driven and been largely confined and narrowly defined to doctrinal research (Sloan, 2018). Nevertheless, legal research incorporates a broader idea than meager doctrinal research skills. In particular, if a legal academic scholarship paradigm is considered instead of a legal practitioner paradigm (Sloan, 2018). With the predominant model established both in dialogues and praxis on the issue, lawyers have tried to conflate the doctrinal methodology.

To better understand the need for said development, many documents and traditional research methods will be critically analysed. Furthermore, any noticeable changes to the traditional modes of research will be overlooked to see any potential arguments that can be used for the paper.

871) Q: Describe Doctrinal Research Method with some argument

A: Looking from a critical perspective, all forms of methodology are in the process of transition and change. It is too constricting realizing the choice of doctrinal method (Richards, & Curzon, 2011). In their use of research method, academic lawyers are becoming diverse. In this transitional moment, legal intellectuals are progressively instilling evidence from other fields into their perceptive to strengthen their restructuring commendations (Sloan, 2018).

872) Q: How do you view doctrinal research historically?

A:Historically, the doctrinal examination has been a key legal technique in the world of law (Watkins, & Burton, 2013). Although additional research categories like theoretical, reform-oriented and essential have been recognized as crucial, the doctrinal research method has always comprised an interdisciplinary facet. However, legal academic achievement has been determined within the doctrinal organization outline, which involves the outlining of the legal model and judicial interpretation (Watkins, & Burton, 2013) .

873) Q: What is the main structure of doctrinal research?

A: The main structures of doctrinal scholarship include 'a perilous theoretical examination of all appropriate legislation and case law to show a declaration of the law important to the issue under investigation. On this kind of wider description, there is a consensus (Sloan, 2018). The case in which the conceptual analysis critique is based, involves an empathetic of the rules of guide between the court influences, statutory interpretation rules, the implicit castigation acquaintance like the variance between criminal and civil jurisdictions and different tests of obligation along with the recognized reasoning methods, rented from logic and philosophy, like deduction and induction. Thus, doctrinal research was the major disciplined know in all the discipline valuations for a law that occurred in the 1980s (Sloan, 2018).

874) Q: Has there been criticism of doctrinal research?

A: Since it has never been sufficiently explicated for lawyers or non-lawyers themselves, doctrinal research method has been broadly critiqued (Richards, & Curzon, 2011). Even with their scholarly work, legal researchers have not been in the exercise of telling their methodologies. Few theses in the past have shown a different narrative describing the level of the method. This technique is presumed gen within the field which is part of the grab-bag of abilities linked with the ability to reason like a lawyer (Sloan, 2018). The doctrinal technique is distinctive and qualitative, and the outcomes are often restricted to the explicit facts of the case in the courts and practice. In the early nineteenth-century, Christopher Langdell had tried to support the law as a legal science and the law library as a way of combating condemnation from the physical sciences (Sloan, 2018).

875) Q: How has the doctrinal process been defined?

A: Generally, the doctrinal process has been defined within an unruly context with a number of undeviating stages involving gathering the facts, classifying the legal issues, examining the issues with an opinion to probing for the law, carrying out background reading and then tracing the chief material, making all the matters in framework and coming to hesitant deduction. There is a need for a more stylish method to tease out the doctrinal method. Whether the doctrinal method can ever be given out in a prescribed way is challenging. At its soul is fluid. It is challenging to minimize to an algorithm.

876) Q: How has the doctrinal researched been supported?

A; However, the doctrinal fundamental of lawful scholarship stands unravelled, and the legal researchers are attempting to billet statistics, proportional viewpoint, social science proof and techniques, and hypothetical examination etcetera in the lawful research outline to give additional balance for law restructuring and legal system in the direction of the research growth. In the meantime, the political viewpoint of the law has been changed by doctrinal research. Now, it offers more crucial to sociological law since the main tools of legal scholars are employed sociological and experimental data (Sloan, 2018). Through the empirical data, sociological law always tries to examine the effects law and legal institutions have in society and on human attitudes. Nevertheless, the legal scholars are disturbed with experiential analysis, but the examination and influence based on the hypothetical ideas. Likewise, the law had a study model grounded mainly in the doctrinal approach. Because of the outline of locating collective law guide and legislative clarification, research model has been grounded in substantial theory and positivism. Law restructuring study, legal model study, and public strategy study are extensively used by the legal researcher in the doctrinal method (Richards, & Curzon, 2011).

877) Q: How is the doctrinal research carried out?

A: Consequently, that doctrinal study is carried out primarily distinct and qualitative according to established field guidelines and standards. However, it also needs to task into the study discipline for exact language and gen of skills. Conversely, it also needed legal study skills information in the research discipline to reform and remains to grow to more fully meet the requirements of students, occupation and various scholar people in the modern legal environment. In the doctrinal research approach, a high degree of appraisal and assessment as appropriate background are required. The principal bases for dóctrinal research are the focus for reading and the requirements to a managerial code for restructuring the law and legal scheme for study progress in legal research.

878) Describe Comparative Method of Legal Research and argument

For a proper critical argumentative paper, it is necessary that various legal research frameworks are evaluated. One of the frequently used methods of legal research happens to be depended on upon comparison as well (Richards, & Curzon, 2011). Comparison is an inductive and rational way of reasoning that allows unbiased merit and drawbacks identification of any kind, exercise, scheme or organization as equated to that of others (Van Hoecke, 2015). Comparative research is an instrument used in different fields, both in natural and social sciences. Its importance for the legal study involved in the relative assessment of human knowledge happening in legal fields of various jurisdictions and situations. From the eras of Aristotle to the present-day, laws comparisons, governance, legal structures and institutions have improved the empires of gen and permitted the growth of different legal systems (Samuel, 2014). The role of proportional research in the globalized world is developing with unlimited potentialities. The essay objects to know the nature, growth, significance, resolutions, procedure, contributions, opportunities and snags linked to comparative legal research. It claims that although there are broad potentiality and validation for comparative legal research, it is a resource or reserve not sufficiently tapped (Richards, & Curzon, 2011).

879) **Q**:How will one argue for comparative research?

A: To secure and enhance democratic values comparative legal research offers explanations of the viewpoints, the circumstances, and substitutes for all communities. It objects to understand how generally the premises of justice and additional standards are shared and what ethical conventions, cultural traditions, historical understandings, and financial deliberations are replicated in a specific society's assertiveness towards social control problem (Van Hoecke, 2015). It objects to research quality addition through providing the functionalist understanding and doctrinal contribution and by involving in law-society desertion. With a high number of applications of comparative legal research, it supplements solution supply, legal education develops healthier (Richards, & Curzon, 2011).

Comparative legal research can encourage serious indulgent of the individual legal system by combining various experiences and best present-day wisdom. According to Geoffrey Wilson, comparative researches have been widely indicated concerning the value they add to the national legal system (Van Hoecke, 2015). Both comparative legal research and empirical study have robust relations with the legal policy, and also create common relation with themselves. The examination of individual research is broadened by an eclectic approach (Samuel, 2014). It aids in resolving specific problems by giving substitute paradigm for a legislative designer or representative and by assisting understanding of national rule of law (Dickinson, 2016).

Courts and law commission find comparative legal study as a very beneficial instrument for their problem unravelling purpose. A comparative study in legal research for law restructuring is the utmost mutual element of multimodal research.

880) Q; How is comparative research helps advancement?

A: Comparative legal study permits advancement of knowledge amongst various communities and nation intending to minimize the world's tension. In the laws of individuals at related phases of economic and cultural growth, a comparative study must resolve the unintentional and discordant differences and minimize the number of discrepancies in law as well as support not to the moral, social and political merits of the various nations but conditional or momentary circumstances. Law amalgamation in the region of the law of responsibilities, rational property law, and conflict of laws will be potential through a comparative study by seeing to the mutual essential in various legal schemes.

881) Q: How has rules affected comparative research?

A: Under WTO design of legal rules after the development of TRIMS, TRIPS and GATS supposes research of the methodologies of different legal systems on crucial features of trade and commercial law. Through comparative legal research, organization of law and uniformity enhancement or minimizing the differences will be achieved. UNCITRAL and Hague-Visby were the yields of harmonization at the international level (Samuel, 2014). Legal norms transplantation and cross-fertilization, methods and organizations and common impact within various systems can be drawn and analysed from a social revolution viewpoint (Richards, & Curzon, 2011).

882) **Q:** What happen when international laws compare to domestic?

A: Nevertheless, when the foreign law or judgments are applied in domestic courts, research of imported law becomes unavoidable. If the judge is willing and ready to find out both variance and resemblance without prioritizing either of them, then the process of rule finding can properly work. Finally, comparative research enables choice between legal structures. Before beseeching the authority of the most suitable scheme or launching a new venture, the regulatory administration governing tax, investment, property, and the routine laws of various legal systems are regularly compared. According to H.M Watt perceives the tactical significance of comparative law seems in the assessment of the financial lure of specific regulations and their established setting

883) Q: How can comparative research be made more effective?

A: To make comparative legal research more effective the following should be invariably considered; theoretical commitment, inter-disciplinary commitment, willingness, and readiness to admit the variance rather than pursuing to work on the grounds of assimilationist methodology, and being serious at all moments (Richards, & Curzon, 2011). Posing basic questions, being content with the real nature of the exotic system and relating instead of meagre conflicting go a long way towards the comparative study success.

884) Q; When was the Crime and Disorder Act

A; 1998.

885) Q: In *Republic of Ireland when was* Children Act

A; 2001

886) Q: when was the Criminal Justice Act

A; 2006

Describe Historical Research Method with some argument

887) Q: What does historical research incorporates?

Historical legal research incorporates a series of prospects involving research of the historical progress of a given legal policy or the history of a legal establishment or legal profession (Peruginelli, & Faro, 2018). Legal history exceeds the study of the progress of material legal customs making it more conclusive. It also involves the examination of these guidelines in the light of the external legal history which includes the social, cultural, economic, political and religious development. The developmental progress offers responses as to why a legal scheme has specific features. The lawyer ought not only to be taught the use of legal history to look for the basis of the current day law, but he is obliged to use his understanding to come up with alternatives for legal growth.

888) Q: What is the objective of historical research?

A:The objective of legal historical research approach is manly to create what the progress of legal guidelines are and to suggest adjustments or clarifications to the prevailing law based on historical evidence (Vranken, 2011). This technique can be employed in segregation or can be joined with other techniques. Occasionally a transitory history of legal guidelines or legislation is provided afterwards the submission of the rule in the national law is debated or the guidelines likened to other legal structures or progress within those legal schemes (Dickinson, 2016).

889) Q: What is better way to understand historical research?

A:To better understand the legal meaning of the historical research, approach the following should be implemented whenever the model is being employed (Peruginelli, & Faro, 2018).

- Determining what moments in the legal history of the nation in the reference are and find out what the features, key writers and sources of every period are.
- Finding out what the present-day spot about the guideline in the national law is.
- Look at the footnote mentions in the nation guidebooks and get the mentions to old authorities.
- Determining what the court decision is and note down the referral sources given by the courts-old authorities and additional court rulings. Using these court judgments look for other references.
- Systemizing the ancient experts referred in the related time periods, for example, Justinian law, Classical law, Middle Ages etcetera.
- Determining the old authorities and look up the precise texts, beginning with the Roman law, check-in

the global record of these sources for other texts dealing with the same subjects, finding catchwords by checking in the index on the Corpus Iuris Civilis.

890) Q; What date was Abortion Act

A: 1967

891) Q: What date was Human Fertilisation and Embryology Act

A; 1990

892) Q: What date was Infant Life (Preservation) Act

A: 1929.

893) Q; What date was Malicious Shooting or Stabbing Act A; 1803.

894) Q: Mental Capacity Act

A; 2005

895) Q: What date was Offences Against the Person Act

A; 1828.

896) Q; What date was Offences Against the Person Act

A; 1837.

897) Q; What date was Offences Against the Person Act 1861.

Describe Social-Legal Method with argument

***898) Q:** Does socio- legal research only relate to societal facets?*

A: Socio-legal research approach does not only relate to law with societal facets adjacent it, however, as a result of the integration of those dissimilar social conditions, it unavoidably leads the study into a spot where comparative examination turns imperative. Thus, making it useful in its own right.

899) Q: What can socio-legal be link to?

A: For example, law societal characteristics may be equated to the socio-political aspects and assessed against the law guidelines an idea supported by Kahn-Freund who advocated that these features show, the contextual against which that law has established (Peruginelli & Faro, 2018).

This method of research approach has been termed as encouraging library-focused, experiential research comprising grounded theory (Vranken, 2011). Another reason it should be utilized is that it also recognizes the guidelines making practice and compares a multi-faceted methodology to legal sensations involving a collection of humankind-based categories, with key providers being the social policy development, with economics and sociology organized with various conditions. The result of this flexible method to legal research shows a hypothetical pragmatism which relates a gap of strategy-oriented tactics covering a wider range of circumstances from assenting deed for marginal groups to justice's failures (Richards, & Curzon, 2011).

How the socio-legal research approach is practiced out supports both its strengths and its flaws.

900) Q; What other method could be used in conjunction with socio-legal?

A: To enable a better understanding of legal meaning using a socio-legal approach that is a qualitative research method philosophy behind the classification of data should be organized and members' remark is incorporated. By doing this, organizations will be able to use this research approach on them to guide action and modify the change (Peruginelli, & Faro, 2018). The social scientist will also be able to study methods of delivering new knowledge that can be employed elsewhere.

901) Q: When was Children Act

A:1989

902) Q: Children, Schools and Families Act

A: 2010

903) Q: When was the Family Procedure Rules

A: 2010

904) Q; Family Proceedings (Amendment) (No.2) Rules

A; 2009 (SI 2009/857)

Practice Direction 27B (Family Procedure Rules), Attendance of Media Representatives at Hearings in Family Proceedings

905) **Q**: Human Rights Act

A; 1998

906) **Q:** When was the Mental Capacity Act

2005

907) **Q:** Name few cases to support social legal research

- **A:** *B v United Kingdom*; *P v United Kingdom* (Cases 36337/97 and 35974/97) [2001] 2 FLR 262
- *Doncaster Metropolitan Borough Council v Haigh* [2011] EWHC B16 (Fam)
- *Doncaster Metropolitan Borough Council v Watson* [2011] EWHC B15 (Fam)

Describe Feminism legal approach with argument

908) ***Q:*** *Does this involve more than feminist?*

A: This can be seen as a notable encounter to traditional and dominant legal doctrine together with Critical Legal Studies. Beside feminist legal theory sharing related apprehensions and obligations as Critical Legal Study, it differs therefrom in various important ways. Therefore, the feminist legal model has been approved by the feminist legal theorist to maintain feminist distinctiveness of feminist legal theory besides analysing and seeking reforms of existing legal methods (Richards, & Curzon, 2011).

Using the term 'feminist' does not mean that feminists share common concepts and models about restructuring the current legal system. Politically, feminist of different hypothetical viewpoint aims to endorse equality between men and women. On a practical level, the objective of feminist crucial agendas making 'gender an emphasis of scrutiny' is to 'restructure legal practices that have excepted, lessened or weakened women's concerns'. These critical frameworks on a methodological level seek to outline 'the world in means that match to women's knowledge' and also that 'recognize the basic social transformations crucial for complete equality among the genders (Richards, & Curzon, 2011).

909) **Q:** Has feminist theory been criticise

A; Feminist legal theory critiques conventional legal techniques for representing male power configurations, taking only a male opinion of the world into deliberation and abandoning a female opinion. This makes feminist have some qualms about the conservative legal models. Furthermore, they have strived to integrate the experience of women and their voice into jurisprudence. From this viewpoint, feminism has established its dissertation and approach to keep its uniqueness and to depict some structures of law that drawback women.

Describe Transnational legal method with argument

910) Q: *Describe transnational legal research*

A; Transnational law can be described as a non-state governance scheme. This suggests the variances and similarities between transnational law as a discrete legal field and conventional legal fields' resultant from the lawful orders of countries (Dickinson, 2016).

911) Q: What does transitional legal research consider?

A: Transnational law includes statutory element, functional elements, and a procedure element just like domestic law filed. Transnational law handles a large number of different authority societies prevailing concurrently and prepared past the rule commanding the power of states, unlike domestic legal orders (Dickinson, 2016). Furthermore, these authority societies are not automatically prepared in equal ways as the states with population and a definite physical boundary and an established structure exercising full authority. Thus, transnational law can be described as the study of the scheme of guidelines and values applied in place of or in addition to the nationally relevant law of a government, or of the group of states, to the associations among individuals and institutions both private and public, natural and lawful (Dickinson, 2016).

Describe Scientific Method with argument

***912) Q:** what does scientific method involve?*

A; Scientific research entails of setting up conditions in which visible action will be indomitable in a vibrant method by a small number of variables that can be methodically operated (Richards, & Curzon, 2011).

This approach is opinion and dimension loyalty to the general law of conduct. Positivist pragmatism aims to uphold the collective doctrines of science by giving theories to explain this elementary functioning. (,) (to) The theories could be either established or disproved consequently through research from which a set of distinct outcomes could be computed (Peruginelli, & Faro, 2018). This process is, of need, deliberated to be an impartial procedure with a distinct assumption which is tested impassively, and the outcomes got through measurement. These outcomes are then re-tested to guarantee rationality, after which an assessment of the information obtained either shows or disproves the suggestion.

913) Q: What else is considered in scientific research method?

A:Essential in this impression is the collectiveness of lucid and logical laws of conduct which require to be empirically considered through scrutiny, defined as a mathematical-logical model. He idea related with the scientific approach is not, conversely, essentially the most perfect method to assume self-governing legal research, shown in the Soft Systems Methodology which tried to integrate hazy adumbrate hitches into a research model and attain an outcome (Peruginelli & Faro, 2018). This shown the tenet of the scientific approach was inappropriate for considerable of the study being assumed in social sciences, as shown in the Hawthorne Research, the model of which explains the qualitative method in use by the social sciences (Richards, & Curzon, 2011). Distant more suitable for the different research frequently seen within the legal study is the suggestion amongst sociology and law, the common consequence of which was understood through an examination of its theoretical constructions, being both technical and rigid and worried with the whole series of substantial procedures of social relations.

914) Q: *How will one conclude legal research finding?*

A: The main scientific model advantages lie within its devotion to the unwavering laws of physics and the restricted number of variables. It is easy to get precise data grounded on mathematical examination and influence of provable statistics to arrive at a reliable end outcome and to expand upon the methodologies used.

Law is anticipated to be socially important and sociology gives an examination of law's theoretical structures. It would be more crucial to entirely reproduce this phenomenological simulation or socio-legal approach as each of them has advantages and benefits to being employed for this form of research whereas in some situations various restrictions undermine one from being the right choice. Concentrating particularly on socio-legal paradigm offers the sociological drive in law as, law-society relation with the object of the survey (Vranken, 2011). One of the major problems experienced when carrying out phenomenological research is that techniques come up and change as the research evolves. The importance and shortcoming of various research approach as tools for carrying out self-governing legal research would seem to be linked more to the significance devoted to the hypothetical position and association of this to the method in which legal study was to be implemented (Vranken, 2011). The right approach to be employed should be considered from theoretical grounds of a specific piece of research. Beside the consideration of both advantages and drawbacks of each methodology, most of the times the combination among the experimental method and socio-legal approach would be most suitable because each of these approaches can be modified as study progresses and changes, reacting more suitably to the many indefinite variables met in legal research when carried out from sociological approach.

Chapter 21
Agency/**contract/agreement**

915) **Q;** Defined Agency

A: Is when one person is authorised to enter into contract on behave of another person or business

916) **Q;** Name some typed of agency

A; special Agent, General agent, Commercial agent,, Universal agent,

917) **Q**; What is special Agent

A; Someone appointed to perform one specific act and when this is done, the agency role is terminated

918) **Q;** what is the duty of General agency?

A; A person who have powers over specific range of duties

919) **Q**; What is commercial agency?

A; Commercial agency as per commercial agent regulation 1993, is one who enter into individual for principal for the sale of or purchase of goods normally transacted in by that principal where the principal had an interest in in developing the particular market which the agent was working.

Employment protection (consolidation) act 1978

920) **Q;** what is universal agent duties

A; The person has the power to do anything which the principal is able to do, as he will have power of attorney

A; To obey lawful instruction of the principal

To exercise reasonable skill

To carry out the purpose of the agency

921) **Q;** What is Contract

A; Is a form of agreement which is legally binding

922) **Q;** Give example of agreement in business

A; purchase, sale price

923) **Q;** what is consolidation?

A; Consolidation is exchange of something intend that transaction is legally binding example contract of employment

Chapter 22

Companies/Business

924) Q; What are the statutory Books for companies

A; Register of members, directors, secretaries, charges, minutes books account records etc

925) Q; What must be done with company annual return

A: It must be submitted to the registrar of companies each year within 28 days of the return date, which is the anniversary of the company's incorporation

926) Q What must the annual return consist of

A; Type of company, Address of company, principal business particulars of company directors, Statement of capital company records
Etc

927) Q What is United Kingdom company Act 1985 section 349

A Where anybody enters into certain transaction on behave of company without identifying the company, then he or she is personally liable if the company default (include making of orders and the signing of cherub bills of exchange or money orders.

928) Q; What is company constitution.

A; This is made of memorandum

929) Q; what is company memorandum.

A It consist of ideal with the external of the company

930) **Q;** What is company association and article of association

A: It deals with the internal matter of the company

931) **Q;** What does section 14 of Company Act 1985 state

A: It states that the two documents (memorandum and article of association bind binds members of the company both to each other and to the company as if they had entered into a deed to this effect. This allows member to sue to enforce right of the memorandum and article

932) **Q;** What is non-contractual obligation

A; non contractual rules deals some legal obligation to bind the producers and sale of goods

933) **Q:** Name some categories of non-contractual obligation

A: liabilities to consumers impose by the Act of parliament or common law. Employment liabilities for the action of employee

Employers and employee acting negligently

934) **Q:** Do sellers have direct contact with customers?

A: Yes, but it is the producers who guarantee the products

935) **Q;** What Act govern these.

A: The sale of goods act or the supply of goods and services

936) **Q:** What is the rule of privet?

A; Is that only the person who is part of the contract if he or she suffers damages is protected by consumers protection. This is both under statute and common law

937) Q: What does negligence covers?

A; Proximity, Foreseeably, duty of care and neighbour

938) **Q:** Name four laws in business management?

A: Contract, Tort, Employment, Agency laws

939) **Q;** What must one look for in financial statements

A; manager's superior information on business activities, estimation errors, distortion from managers' accounting choices.

940) **Q** What do we mean by business environment?

A:These include; labour markets, capital markets, product markets; suppliers customers, competition, and business regulation

941) **Q:** What do we mean by accounting system

A; Measure and report economic consequences of business activities

942) **Q**: What is control test?

A; An employer controls how, where and when employee works.

943) **Q**; Give a case law in support

A; Yawens v Noakes1880 6 QBD 530

944) **Q;** What is integration test

A; someone is regarded as integral to a business and not just as an accessory to it.

945) **Q** Give a case in support of integration test.

A; Cassidy v Ministry of Health (1951)2 KB 343

946) **Q;** What is economic reality test?

A; This is where the court considers a number of factors in addition to control and integration to assess whether a person s employed, or self employed

947) **Q;** Give a case law to support this?

A; Ready Mixed Concrete (south East) Ltd v Minister of pension and national insurance (1968) 2 QB 497

Chapter 23

Employment

948) **Q**; What date is Employment Right Act

A; 1996

949) **Q;** what date was the working time regulation

A: 1998

950) **Q**: what date was Employment Act

A:2002

951) **Q:** What date was Equal pay Act

A;1970

952) **Q**:What date was National minimum wage

A;1998

953) **Q;** What date was unfair contract Terms Act (UCTA)

A: 1977

954) **Q** what date is Unfair Terms in consumer Contracts Regulations

A;1999

Chapter 24

BREXIT

955) **Q:**What is Brexit Relevant Legal Consequences

A: Members States enters into various treaties which are the source and basis of EU law. For as long as UK is EU party on the international plane, United Kingdom is bound by these treaties. The effect of EU laws in UK's domestic legal order is as result of Act of parliament saying it does. Under Article 50 of Treaty on European Union the UK's notifications has set in train a procedure by which the United Kingdom will stop being a member to the treaties, stopping the flow of EU law at its source.

956) **Q:** When did UK vote to leave EU

A; United Kingdom citizens on 23rd June 2016 held a vote on deciding whether their country was supposed to remain as a member of European Union.

957) **Q;** What was result of Brexit vote

A; The turn-out was 72.2% and out of it 51.9% voted to leave the European Union. After the referendum, the UK government promised to give effect to the vote result by following the stipulated process in Articles 50 of the Treaty on European Union.

958) **Q;** When did Britain serve notice to leave EU

A; On March 29, 2017, European Council was served with a formal notice by the Prime Minister acting with the parliament authority on the UK's intention to leave EU. Upon the agreement entering into force the UK will leave the EU or upon the notification entering into the second anniversary.

959) Q: What is the problem

A: Plentiful of the law that reinforces the United Kingdom's dispute resolution design is, directly or indirectly, European in origin. That law will stop to be effective in and to the UK when it exits the European Union. Practically, a mixture of autonomous action by the United Kingdom, provisional arrangements and in due course a new affiliation contract between the UK and the EU is likely to alleviate considerably the legal properties of Brexit in this area (Dickinson, 2016).

960) Q; What is the Legislating for Brexit

A: Just as the statute gave domestic effect to the UK's entry into EU's forerunner, the same will happen to the UK's withdrawal (Dickinson, 2016). European Union Bill in the House of Commons was introduced by government on July 2017. Legal continuity is some areas will be assured by enacting the Withdrawal Bill. The reason is that, while the UK parliament can enact to assimilate all EU law, it is unable to enhance all EU law work outside the setting of EU membership. On member state courts this is the mainly case where the law in reference imposes mutual rights and responsibilities to them if the United Kingdom is not a member state anymore.

961) Q: What is the consequences for Civil justice cooperation

A; According to the UK government position, existing administration should be sustained by EU27 arrangement where required. Generally, and as deliberated in more detail in the following sections:-

The European Union guidelines for governing law determination are very different and one of a kind which can easily be tamed and will remain to give out the same results in the UK and in the EU27 as they do today.

The European Union guidelines for determining which country's courts have authority over a disagreement and the implementations of resulting decisions are premised on Member State mutuality. UK wishes to discuss new bargain with the U27 that resembles to the fullest degree probable the prevailing European administration (Dickinson, 2016).

962) Q; What is likely to happen

A; Preserving the important essentials of the existing administration (on governing law) is the total impact of all this. In the area of influence and implementation one part of the modern administration can and will be conserved, but continuation of the residual parts of the scheme will need agreement between the UK and EU27. In areas where the present administration continuity is an issue for concession, the time on which Brexit will yield hard legal impacts is probably to be later that the already predicted exit day that 29th March 2019. According to the law as it is now, the transitional measures are probably to make sure that proceedings and agreements predating exit will continue to post-exit in the UK and the EU27.

963) **Q;** What Methods of legal research that could be used to research on Brexit

A; With Brexit, Historical and doctrinal and social legal research will be appropriate

964) **Q;** What is the purpose of research?

A; Generally, it can be said that all research involves gathering of information or evidence with a purpose of establishing a hypothesis or verifying some notion or assumptions. Therefore, research is an analysis for verifying a new theory or for supporting existing theories by new-knowledge. Since original discoveries for any research are an extension of the research already taken therefore there is no research that can be termed as purely new. The aim of the legal research is to protect the concerns of the society as whole by safeguarding its physical or mental health. Legal researches are meant for authority to prove some theories and are a field under a wide subject of enquiry about law. An enquiry is comprised of rules, ideas and institutes of the law and legal system in its entity.

965) **Q;** What is Legal Research in General

A; Research is any systematic inquiry, investigation or search for information. Any systematic investigation of issues and matters related with law is Legal Research. To obtain better understanding and knowledge of any delinquent of legal history, legal philosophy or any system of positive law, legal research may be carried out. In order for ascertainment of the correct guidelines bounded by their restrictions it is very crucial for writing text and teaching.

966) **Q:** What is the Objectives of research into Brexit?

A; Watkins & Burton, (2013) argues that scholars of the society are always motivated to inquire for the proofs of the empirical world and to show the truth right from the evaluation of human society. Every facet of human behaviours or evidences of life has a problem. Problems have always been there, are always there and will always be there in the society and thus we have to look for answers to those problems. Thus, this is the need of the society to carry out research.

A: In simple terms we can refer research as criterion for vibrant society. To get the answers of an issue and development of the society, research plays a major role. Each research is carried out with an aim for bettering the society and thus they are all socially oriented. Research may discover new facts or test old existing facts. The objective of the research is to determine the unknown or hidden truth, and which has not yet been revealed. The reason for conducting researches is to boost the efficiency of our systems, grow the size and quality of information adding to what that already exists. Thus, research is meaningful.

967) Q: Name one main reason for carrying out legal research

A: One of the main reasons for carrying out a legal research is to examine the law by reducing, breaking and separating the law into distinct components. It can be easy as explaining and examining new laws and legal schemes or as complex as interpreting, explaining and assessing given cases or bills. Another goal is to bring together the statutes and disparate elements of cases to come up with coherent or beneficial legal standards (Watkins & Burton, 2013).

968) **Q;** Why using Historical Research in Brexit?

A: In this method of legal research, it involves finding out the preceding law so us to know the reason behind the prevailing law and the course of its growth. There is an inscription on the Archives Building in Washington that state; “All that is past is prologue”. These words carry a lot of weight and meaning. The present is always explained by the past. Historical research in this juncture is not meant a debate of the past of each statute or each law provision for the purpose of simple rational delight. Just like all other methods of research needed for the law reform, historical research is crucial in law where the current law provision has highlighted significant queries and it becomes important to find out the situations in which the current position aroused.

969) **Q:** What is one advantage of using historical research in Brexit?

A; For the case of Brexit historical research will find out how the UK and Wales initially were incorporated in EU and the laws that governed all he member states. This will help understand the legal positions at this point in which the two-member states want to leave. Often, historical materials exploration provides a hint to the details why a given provision was outlined in the way in which it now appears. This gets rid of specific doubts or even provides the researcher with the explanations that proves the current provision- reasons that may not seem otherwise.

Moreover, historical research may frequently disclose the alterations in Brexit on specific issues which are currently under cautious considerations. Also, historical research would frequently show that a given existing establishment fully admissible at the time of introduction is no longer so admissible because the explanations that vindicated the original inclusion of that provision are no longer binding. Historical research helps in revealing the details which might remain unclear.

It is now well documented that in many scenarios there is specific logic in the way in which the Brexit evolves, though sometimes one may doubt, find that the statutory had earlier developed rather on random lines. One is not restricted to pure law when one speaks of historical research.

970) Q: What is the Effectiveness of historical research method in Brexit?

1. A: It gives information on present and future trends thus can tell everything that is involved in Brexit
2. It can give clear view of how a culture perceives a given idea like Brexit after interactions
3. It allows revaluation of data in conjunction to specific theories, hypothesis and generalization that are currently held about the past and present.
4. Compared to other methods it can make use of more categories of evidence and thus making it suit Brexit research more.

971) Q; Why using Doctrinal Research Method in Brexit?

A: In Brexit doctrinal research is supposed to be grounded in a descriptive premise that reasons and argues from doctrinal grounds actually explained judicial decisions. Doctrinal research in other words may be referred to as traditional research.

According to Vranken, (2011), doctrinal research involves severe systematic explanation, scrutiny and serious examination of legal rules, principles or doctrines and how they relate to one another. It assembles the prevailing law in order and gives thematic constraints for such an order. It also apprehends with serious review of decisional and legislation process and their fundamental strategy. For Brexit, doctrinal research will be employed in determining the explanations behind the need for leaving the EU as well as weigh it according to the EU laws so as to give out the constraints needed.

The legal research method thus involves organized analysis of constitutional provisions and of lawful principles convoluted therein, or derived therefrom, and coherent and logical ordering of the legal schemes and principles.

The conservative legal approach to the doctrine is all about law. Legal education knows that the language of judicial sentiments epitomizes the law. Doctrinal research was one of classical form of legal scholarship which a researcher evaluated the amount of legal opinion to determine whether it was reasoned effectively or to find out the impacts for future cases.

972) Q: What are the sources of doctrinal research?

A: Often conservative legal sources are used in doctrinal research. Each scholar having a task in doctrinal research takes relevant secondary data to his scheme. Sources include not only statutes but also committee reports, judgment and legal history. In Brexit the acts passed by parliament and state legislatures fall under this category of sources. They possess key authority. Journals, text books, and periodicals written highlighting the debate or the gap in the law can be used as sources for doctrinal research, but they have to be authentic (Vranken, 2011).

973) Q: What is the Role of Hypothesis in doctrinal research?

A: The main role of the hypothesis is to verify the commanding sources which are employed in the doctrinal research. It as well handles the identification of authoritative the source and how to employ the techniques to find the out. The gaps in law and the courts have led to the establishment of doctrinal principles, standards and norms. No field study is involved in doctrinal legal research. The aim for researchers to carry out the doctrinal legal research is not to prove or disprove the hypothesis. Sometimes the aim for the hypothesis is just to formulate the question for guiding the research as most of them are self-explanatory and descriptive in nature. The aim of raising questions in doctrinal legal research is to seek credible answer or solution to the problem.

974) Q; Describe effectiveness of doctrinal research in Brexit

A; This method of research involves analysis of legal preposition (Vranken, 2011). Brexit being a legal preposition doctrinal method can be applied is researching on the factors favouring the preposition as well as the one that does not support it.

Legal schemes from administrative tools, enactments or regulations, cases of courts can be part of doctrinal research. This makes it easier for the researcher to gather all the required data as all the sources are available and reachable. With the topic for Brexit being a UK national issue researching on it becomes easier as all sources want to be heard on their stand. Conventional sources are used; this kind of sources makes the research easier as getting the data and information is simplified.

975) Q: Name two prime ministers who resigned over Brexit

A: David Cameron and Theresa May

976) Q: Name other ministers who resigned over Brexit

A: Amber Rudd, home secretary, April 29, 2018 (Windrush scandal)

Phillip Lee, justice minister, June 12, 2018 (opposition to government's ...

Greg Hands, trade minister, June 21, 2018 (opposition to Heathrow ...

David Davis, Brexit secretary, July 8, 2018 (opposition to Theresa May's

977) Q: How is doctrinal research base on Brexit?

Doctrinal research will look on the following in Brexit research: the aim and values associated with Brexit, the problems associated with the gap between the UK an EU policy goal and the current state of achievement, availability of intent choice for implementation of Brexit goals, and finding the consequences that the Brexit might have on UK

Chapter 25

BUSINESS/ INCORPORATION

978) Q: Briefly explain the consequences of incorporation.

A; I propose to enlighten the significance, analyse the notion and evaluate any obligation on incorporate social responsibility and Human Rights.

Corporate is expected to be responsible legally, socially, economically for shareholders, stakeholders and society, be charitable and accountable of their action

979) Q: What terminology used

A; Internationally, terminology may differ for example Europe and many commonwealth countries use "company" whilst USA prefer "corporation" and others use "firm", but incorporation is globally accepted and are registered with unique number in their country of origin. "Corporation aggregate" is a term use for more than one-person example universities, charity, government institution

980) Q: What is the advantages of corporation?

A: Advantageous of Corporation include global protection known as "veil of incorporation" granted by House of Lords (Salmon v Salmon & co Ltd) (1897),which entitle them to be universally regarded as legal entity, or "artificial legal personality". shareholders and investors owe corporation who appoint board of directors and chief executive officer(Europe) or president (USA) and secretary to manage it for a period. They could have Limited liability to protect shareholder from losing their properties, but risk losing their investment if the corporate is liquidated. Corporate owns the asset, employ workers, borrow and lend money, buy shares in other companies or takeover other companies, and can enter into contract. Able to accumulate legal rights such as right to a fair trial Article 6 of HRA 1998. And may continue to trade regardless of any changes such as death of its directors, ownership can be changed by transferring of shares. Listed large corporate can issue shares and trade in the London, shanghai, and New York stock exchange whilst small company not permitted.

981) Q: What is the disadvantages of corporation?

A; The disadvantages of corporate include being sued under tort law for breach of established duty of care to society and employee causing damages due to negligence. Although corporate have protection, a court can still grant "floating charge" for individual to cover debt against its assets. Likewise breach of national and international laws could result, their objectives economically and reputation being adversely affected by stakeholders, creditors, local communities, organs of government, voluntary organisation, public sector. employee, suppliers, customers etc who can influence the direction of corporate.

982) Q: What happen to corporate fail to be honest.?

A: Corporation who breach fiduciary duties include false account and fraud have faced criminal liability, examples Mirror Group 1991 – Robert Maxwell, Polly Peck International 1990 – the Chief Executive, AIG 2004 – Maurice Greenberg, Chairman and CEO of AIG insurance, The Bank of Credit and Commerce International (BCCI) 1991, Enron 2001 – Kenneth Lay, WorldÇom 2002 – Bernard Ebbers, CEO, Parmalat 2004 – the CEO, (OU study Guild)

983) Q: How is criminal activities of corporation dealt with?

A: To combat criminal activities, there are international regulation in place such as Corporate Governance code (A.4, B.1, A.2. E.1 c.3 2016 and European union audit reforms (directive 2014/56/EU and regulation No.537/2014 applies to company accounting.

Corporate social responsibility could be summarise under four main headings legally, socially and economical (Carroll's 1979), but society expect corporate to have moral and act fairly, right and just.

Chapter 26

CSR (Corporate social responsibility)

(MNEs, verification, auditing)

984) Q: What are some objective of corporate?

A: Corporate main objective is to be economically sound for their shareholders whilst maintain stakeholders relationship before they are able to deliver their responsibility to society, However Society expect Corporate to implement national and international regulations and CSR codes in relation to environment, labour standards, pharmaceuticals, chemical and extractive industries, include clothing, production of food, services, finance and tourism, proactive in benevolence and to respect international Human Right treaties.

985) Q: What does CSR stand for?

A; Corporate social Responsibility

986) Q; How does CSR operate in corporation?

A: CRS is not compulsory although Roman Right laws could be if they are written into a constitution framework, but might not be specific for corporation because corporation takes advantage of various definition of CRS, and adopting easiest policies and ignore others.

Many small companies may adopt CSR policies for long term financial gain if it is requirement for tendering for public contracts include health and Safety, equal right, environmental issues etc., but others may not bother or may just include the easiest policy to increase perception to customers or tick boxes exercise as most of them do not adhere to policy. Example Apple Plc policy on CSR only have small write up on environment, and only indicated the role of responsibility of suppliers. UK diamond Plc with subsidiaries in South Africa don't specifically mention CSR on their website but have outline several initiatives they are involved in to help the local community. In Pakistan there are big companies with insufficient CSR policy.

987) Q: Do some corporate breach CSR codes?

A; There are some corporate who breach national and international laws and CSR codes include efficient healthcare, health and safety, good labour practice, reasonable wages and environment; example *Adams v Cape Industries Plc* [1990] Ch 433,

It is estimated that 24 million of Morden slavery yet there is no requirement for companies to have CSR on slavery in their document until 2016 when companies over certain size in UK require to publish modern slavery statement.

988) Q: How is breach of CSR code deals with?

A: To combat such abuse, international regulatory bodies are set up to monitor corporate activities, example Social Accountability International (SAI), UN Intergovernmental Working Group of Experts on International standards of Accounting and Reporting (ISAR) 1982,Coalition of Environmentally Responsible Global Reporting Initiative (GRI) 1997.

989) Q; What action did United Nation taken to avoid abuse?

In 1945, United Nation with 192 members issue a statement that directors of companies are obligated to manage impartially and to avoid abuse of their position, require directors to disclose their term of contract with some restriction include shareholders to approve director's numeration.

990) Q: Name some prominent people adhere with CSR?

A: It is encouraging that corporate social responsibility had been effectively demonstrated by prominent people like families of Camogie and Rockefeller in USA, Cadbury, Rowntree and Levers in Uk, and implemented "international treaties and convention which must bind corporate to respect human right.

991) Q; How are corporate involves in CSR?

A: It must be appreciated that corporate are obligated to implement the CSR code and human Right of their employee, society, environment etc., they also have considerable expenses for setting up and running business such as health and safety, minimum pay, level of staff on duty per shift, rise in inflation decrease their profit. Likewise modern technology such as voice dictation (reduce typist job), internet shopping, video and audio national and international conferences, employee taking business to tribunal and to court for breach of employment laws and human Right rules. All these have contributed to increase unemployment in most countries resulting more hardship for sections of society who would rather forego some of their rights in order to work/survive. The strict rules have resulted some corporate to close their business and the burden of supporting society falls on government in the form of benefit claims in Britain., but other countries without such scheme, people do suffer.

992) Q: Does Human Right plays part in CSR?

A:There is no doubt that human right is international norm in respect to social, political, legal, moral etc. Human Right must be respected and treated as obligatory(Nickel) 2006) and (Kinley 1998). It can be argued that Human Right existed when God created first human namely Adam and Eve and despite their disobedience, their Right of life, food, shelter, environment were respected. (Bible and Quran).This was supported by declaration of America independence dated 4th July 1776, the president said "We hold these truths to be self-evident, that all men are created equal, that they are endowed by their Creator with certain unalienable Rights, that among these are Life, Liberty and the pursuit of Happiness-"

993) **Q:** How is equality in terms of Human Right?

A; Equality in term of human anatomy and physiology, but there are class differences as not all human are brought up with same resources.

In1948, after the second world war, United Nations universal declaration of human Right state " a common standard of achievement for all peoples and all nations, to the end that every individual and every organ of society' are under an obligation to promote the ideals set out in the Declaration.." (OU study) since then many countries have acknowledgement human right in treaties include Declarations in Rio, The French 2001, European Convention 1950,1961and 1969, American Convention 1969, African Charter 1986, Arab Charter2008, The Asian human Right convention.

Some Corporate continue to violate human Right include; Slavery; bad service, Cheap labour, low pay, breach duty of care, mistreatment and discrimination towards employee, overtime become requirement, Health and safety avoidance.

Some political or military dictators include Hitler and Nazi German, Sadan Hussain, Ide Amin, Bin Laden, Gadhafi, Omar Al-Bashir, Mugabe etc. deliberately ignore international natural human right

994) **Q**: Can Human Right be enforced on Corporation**?**

A: However it is difficult to enforce international human right treaties violation on corporate because of individual government interest who may interpret treaties in line with their culture. Nations protect their sovereignty and do not want interference by other countries for infringement of human right .No code of conduct by a lot of companies on modern slavery. corporate have financial means to defend their action especially against individual. Until there is government protection through legislation to make companies accountable to international laws.it will be difficult to implement human right treaties.

995) **Q:** Why is Human Right important in CSR?.

A; Human Right is an essential part of corporate social responsibility to protect, respect and remedy the victim, therefore it must be made obligatory and legally compliance to its philosophies, otherwise corporate will breach fundamental human Right and profit will be their priority. Right and obligation go hand in hand and under the natural law, all human must be treated equal without discrimination of colour, gender, ethnicity or class.

996) **Q;** How do international treaties protect Human Right?

A: The national and international treaties declaration on human right were signed by government, after consulting corporate, business or employers, trade unions who represent employee, where broad agreement to accept, respect, duty bound and mandatory to implement human Right which include; protect society, freedom of association, recognition of collective bargaining, elimination of all force and compulsory labour and discrimination. However It is important to bear in mind that what is accepted morally or norm in one society, might be uncharacteristic in another, it appears that western countries try to impose their interpretation of human Right rules on other sovereignty countries expecting them to implement their ways and this has cause conflicts, and lead to some critics on natural Human Right notable Bentham (1843) said "natural right is simple nonsense". John Stuart Mill (1806–1873) dismissed natural rights in favour of legal definition; Thomas Hobbes(1588—1679) criticise human right.

997) **Q;** Is CSR obeyed by all corporate?

A: CSR is about responsible in its own action, operation and for its stakeholders and expected to implement Human Rights which is unconditional, undeniable, absolute, and universal include first, second and third generation of rights ;civil, political economic and social. It appears " " The social responsibility of business is to increase its profit" (Milton Friedman) 1970.

998) **Q:** Name example of how CSR been breached?

A; considering that in 2017, it is reported of 24 million Morden slavery and increasing. Evidence in Bangladesh reveal in August 2017; 18,083 children under 5 been treated for malnutrition, 424,000 children under 15 require diphtheria vaccination, 13,901 to 22,241 refugee, 37,215 temporary emergency toilets built by Bangladesh military, Massacre in Rwanda, and so many people on state benefit in UK, increase global unemployment and poverty. It is evidence that CSR and international human right policies have fail society.

999) Q: How do one relate business to CSR

A: CSR is the consistent commitment and dedication by business personnel to behave in an ethical way and contribute in the economic development of the workforce environment. The purpose is to understand the CSRs effect on brand image, implementation process involving verification and auditing phases in order to increase the understanding of CSR as marketing tool. This study has both positive and deductive approach with a cross sectional design. This study also incorporates with the International labour standards aimed to promote the opportunities for men and women to attain decent and productive working outcomes in conditions of freedom, security, equality and dignity.

1000) ***Q;*** What is important of CSR in MNEs (Multinational enterprise)

A; There is an increasing acceptance of a significant impact on the operations of private organizations on their employee's communities, environment, customers, competitors, shareholders, investors, government and so forth. CSR is important for many corporations, non-profits, and employees alike and helps companies to improve their domestic and global communities (Schwartz, 2017). It offers better brand recognition, easier access to the company`s capital, organizational growth, improves financial performance and contributes to operational cost savings with advanced capability to attract talent and retail employees. The CSR shows a strong contribution in all dimensions of the brand image. However, the ethical directions on brand image was rather strong. As both CSR and brand image are quite complex concepts, a qualitative research work is conducted in the paper. “Corporate,” “Social,” and “Responsibility” in general terms, relates to the responsibilities of corporations towards the society in which they existed and operate their function. It is the responsibility of any corporation for the effects of its decisions and operations on a particular society through sophisticated and ethical behavioral attributes.

1001) ***Q:*** Briefly discus branding

A; Branding has become a multi-billion-dollar business strategy and its success in creating profits has showed that it has been used widely. The authenticity and severity of CSR claims are checked by CSR verification. The auditing with reporting sources gives a basis for customers to verify that their goods can be sustainable by social life concerns. Verification and auditing are a part of CSR implementation which also involves CSR assessment, CSR strategy, CSR commitments and evaluation involved in the process. By integrating these elements, both economic and societal performance can be improved. The aim of the verification is to provide a clear viewpoint from a reasonable assurance of the information concerning with the company` products.

1002) Q: What is the rationale behind using CSR verification and auditing?

A: The rationale for using CSR verification and auditing to protection of brand image shows that the outright CSR plays a significant role to acquire appositive effect on brand image which is aligned with other processes as well. The verification and auditing of a company`s corporate social responsibility (CSR) policy is accomplished by the customer who uses particular goods and services.

1003) Q; What is the *reason for Verification?*

A; The reason for CSR verification is to examine their performance which enable organizations to present their products to their stakeholders. This impact on their operations and activities are having on society and sustainability. Furthermore, it improves data and accuracy for the various corporate decision, it contributes to setting the benchmark against the organization's competitors and helps in business improvement with shareholder support (Grayson, 2017). Verification also contributes to minimizing the risk factors and bring confidence in legal compliance.

1004) Q: What is the method for CSR verification?

A; The methods used for the CSR verification is based on the best practices. One way of verification is to evaluate corporation's CSR as the corporations are required to submit their internally generate report for external verification. The verification process can be delivered by for methods, and agencies which involve; external auditors, certification bodies, stock-exchange based verification, and NGO engagement. The verification process involves reviewing pertinent documentation, interviewing accountable personnel with responsibility for the preparation of Report and validating the chosen representative sample of data along with the relevant information integrated into the Report.

1005) Q: What is the Advantages of Verification?

A; The advantage for MNEs in verification and auditing process shows that it helps to promote ethical business. There are numerous MNEs, establish well-developed code of conduct gain success for social missions for operating their business operations ethically and reduce negative workplace effects through certain CSR processes. This paper will provide an overview of the verification of CSR and auditing resources to verify that their products are socially manageable., and strive to

1006) ***Q:*** What is the Reason for auditing CSR

A: Corporate social responsibility auditing process aims at recognizing the environmental, societal, and governance risk factors carried by the company and assessing managerial activities in respect of those. The importance or reason for CSR auditing process is to evaluate the applicable aims and objectives of the company that are designed to meet the business requirements and expectations of shareholders. Furthermore, the audit is concerned with the reliability of a company`s records and data available to the public and the protection of its assets.

1007) Q:What is the Method for CSR Auditing***?***

A: Audits and the method of auditing are mainly focused on the company`s success of its stated objectives; its compliance with rules, regulations, and legislation. The method of CSR audit requires the collection of a large number of documents to review before the auditing as it is an essential part of the auditing process (Liu, 2017). The collection of documents involves three types of review that are employee status documents review, Company tour, and employee interviews for the auditing process.

1008) Q: What document used in auditing CSR?

A; The documents review includes; business license, Labour laws, yearly payrolls and attendance record sheets, proof of retirement pays for employees, receipts and documents of employee and health insurances. Leave and annual leave records, staff association details, records of industrial waste.

1009) Q: What do we mean by company tour in auditing?

A: Company tour includes; list of fire equipment, first aid kits, proper labels of hazardous substances, the data sheet of material safety, environmental facilities details, floor, aisles, exits and stairs, electrical safety, guards, sleeves, etc.

1010) Q: What parts do employees play in auditing?

A: Employee interviews include; 25% of entire work facilities with over 100 employees and 25 records largely for the facilities with over 100 employees. These records are taken from different sectors of the organization and employee level associated with the company the sample should be constant and remain focus on the people of the organization.

1011) Q: What part do the auditor plays in auditing?

A: The auditor will be accountable to prepare the "Corrective Action Plan" after the auditing process. The CAP will help in summarizing the company monitoring visit observations along with a corrective action plan that both the checker and company manager belief is reasonable to confirm the client`s necessities and local laws. The risk factors of not considering the focused attention to the CST is clearly defined by the factors of loss of reputation, lawsuits along with the different scrutiny levels processed by relative government officials. Internal audit must consider such risk factors and support management to determine suitable action plans. This is known as a different approach to process the audit function that highly focused on health and safety issues.

1012) Q: How significance is CSR to business?

A; It can be concluded that in a recent informative world where information is readily available to the general public, CSR has been a significant measure for any corporation to be successful. Organization in today`s world cannot become successful without considering the social accountabilities. CSR has been a vital component for any organization to have perpetual succession and to create a brand. The information presented in the paper provides a structure, balanced and consistent demonstration of corporate social responsibility along with its implementation process involving verification and auditing methods. CSR aims to provide developing relationships among employees and customers while working in partnership with local companies where environmental protection and sustainability are highly focused concerns.

Chapter 27

ILO

1013) Q: What does ILO stand for?

A: International Labour

1014) Q; What does ILL stand for?

A; International Labour Law?

1015) Q: What is the Background of the formation and development of International Labour Law?

A; Global multinational enterprises (MNEs) are such organizations that work on a by covering a large global scale as opposed to MNEs that are considered on a regional basis — companies who generate sales and profit s in a different location across the world known as the MNEs. The MNE declaration provides a clear overview of a way by which enterprises can participate in their operations across the world to the realization of their efforts. Its implications stemmed from international labor standard which shows good and effective measures for numerous enterprises. Furthermore, it highlights the contributions of government in encouraging appropriate organizational behavior along with the complex roles of social dialogue.

1016) Q; What happen after the first world war?

A: Following the First World War, the Paris Peace Conference at the insistence of trade unions in April 1919 introduced a Commission on International Labour Legislation. Numerous representatives with their deliberated and persuasive arguments for social injustice that intimidates social peace, thus, they claimed, acting over such injustice represents the cause of peace. The operations of Commissioner introduces ILO as an agency for the League of Nations and serves as the clause of the treaty of Versailles. The first international labor law conventions and ILO`s governing body was firstly adopted by the International Labour conference held at Washington in 1919.

1017) Q: What happen after the second world war?

A; After the Second World War, the United Nations make ILO a part of its specialized agency. The ILC the adopted the Declaration of Philadelphia in 1944. This shows the particular objectives of ILO along with the acknowledgment of "poverty" is a dangerous element to prosperity in all parts of the nation. Correspondingly, "the war against want" was settled by ILO which enables several exhorted workers and employers to interrelate in building and employing certain measures associated with social and economic perspectives. Under the influence of "sentiments of justice and humanity along with the desire to protect the permanent peace of the world," actions were taken on standardizing several conditions of the labors and securing the rights of workers. These efforts result in the Noble price received by ILO in 1969 which shows great achievement.

1018) Q: What is ILO standard and legal considerations?

A; ILO standards are initiated by certain agreements among states for concerned matters. These are known for legally integrated international treaties which can be signed by ILO states members. This signing of agreements is found as volunteer operation but once it comes to pass to the country associated is then under legal obligations for the implementation of provisions of the signed agreement. On the other hand, recommendation and implications are comprehensively defined, non-binding procedures, which often supplement an agreement by offering advice on the way of implementation. One the ratification is completed; member states enable to make good on their ILO responsibilities often from domestic legislation. As in the case with any other provision based on international terms, it would be able of holding legal power and control; an ILO agreement should be clearly defined and within range of judicial interpretation. It should also be in the range of application by certain committees of ILO along with its member states, courts and by the UN Permanent Court of International justice.

1019) Q: What consist of International Labour Standards Framework

A: Once the legal considerations and historical interventions are interpreted then the major field of the task is ILO standard setting. The establishment of an international legal framework dealing with the area of operations in the world become a key consideration of action for ILO from the establishment of its foundation (Danieli, 2018). ILS requires legal considerations and recommendations to proceed in a proper way. However, the agreements of concerned towards the ILR are slightly different and relate with the core labor standard framework.

1020) Q: What is the first rule in the ILR?

A; Freedom of Association and Security of Rights to Establish Agreement, 1948 (Convention No. 87)

It creates the right of overall labors and workers to build and connect organizations of their selection with no authorization and establish a chain of guarantees for the free operations of corporations with no disturbance by the public authorities.

1021) Q; What is the second rule in the ILR?

A: Right for the establishment and collection of the bargaining agreement. 1949 (Convention No. 98).

It offers the security measures in opposition to anti-union segregation, for the security of labors and employers working for the organization over the acts of disturbance and for measures to support collective bargaining.

1022) Q; What is the third rule in the ILR?

A; Forced Labour Agreement, 1930 (Convention No. 29)

It uses the inhibition of forced or mandatory labor in all its forms. Numerous exceptions are enabled which normally includes military services, strict monitoring of criminal labor, and in the civil and military emergencies.

1023) Q; What is the fourth rule in the ILR?

A; Destruction of Forced Labour Agreement, 1957 (Convention No. 105).

It disallows the use of any document of forced or mandatory labor with the aim to education or political violence, punishment for the ideological viewpoints and political expressions, labor force movement, labor control, punishment for contributing in strikes or segregation.

1024) Q: What is the fifth rule in the ILR?

A; Segregation among employment and work agreement, 1958 (Convention No. 111).

It requires national policy to leave out the discernment in access to employment, training and working scenarios, on the basis of race, religion, sex, color, national extraction, political standpoints, and social origins and to support the equivalence of opportunity and treatment.

1025) Q; What is the sixth rule in the ILR?

A; Equivalent compensation agreement, 1951 (Convention No. 100).

It requires equality in the payment procedure for both men and women for the work of the same value.

1026) Q: What is the seventh rule in the ILR?

A: Minimum Age Agreement, 1973 (Convention No. 138) It aims to the purge the child labor, agreeing about the age factors for the admission to gain employment should not be less than the age of mandatory schooling completion. These rights have been must provide in ILO conventions and certain implications and also in the United Nations declaration on human rights which is important to workers working in different industries.

1027) Q: How can the activities of ILO be classified?

A: The activities of ILO in association with international labor standard framework can be classified into three different types which involves monitoring of the overview into national legislation and observing of monitoring along with the suggestion on carrying national legislation and practice In compliance with signed agreements.

1028) Q; What does these rules depend?

A; ILR firmly depends on the determination that the labour and other social concerns are not important issues for the nation-state. ILS is recognized to become an organic relation towards international trade and its impacts on a nation`s development. Since 1919, the ILO has created an extensive international code for the right of labor. On the other hand, different elements of international financial performance gained their regulatory regimes in which some are in the development process. On the global site, The ILO conventions and agreements are mainly focused on the concerned discussions on the issue of labor standards in trade agreements. Indeed the labor standards are still too different aims with ILO conventions.

Chapter 28

CORRUPTION (within Multinational enterprise)(MNES)

1029) ***Q:*** How will one describe corruption?

A; Corruption is a major problem which can be seen in all parts of the world. It does not matter that the country is prosperous or poor, dictatorial or democratic, gigantic or small, it will be unable to avoid corruption.

To analysis corruption at global platform, and emphasis on the monitoring and enforcing remedies. In this regard, there is a research work conducted which was initiated by scholarly journals and by the ways of combatting transnational corporate corruption for the analysis of different issues.

1030) **Q:** Defined corruption**?**

A; Corruption is found to be an abusive act which is often practiced by both public and private corporations for personal again. This involves the action of embezzlement, bribery, state capture or nepotism.

1031) **Q:** What is corruption linked?

A; It is generally linked and strengthened by different illegal practices which include; fraudulent activities, concealment of money, or bid activities.

According to the Transparency International, the corrupt activity is considered as a misuse of delegated authority to achieve personal gain (Ferguson, 2018).

1032) Q: How do one view Corporate integrity?

A: Corporate integrity is essential for displaying corporate social responsibility (CSR). This involves the values for honourable and principled standards, for example, trustworthiness, justice and honest apprises business plan.

The concept of corrupt activities accepted for a very long time where morally reprehensible is a significant factor since it decreases certain these values and standards (Harapan, 2016). Corruption has no domestic precincts and remains to be a significant problem for international corporations who are functioning in developing nations, where it is a general practice for both private and public regions. It could be viewed as a cultural aspect and a part of society.

1033) Q: What is the world bank view on corruption?

A: According to the Michael Hershman, official of World Bank Institute Working Group and founder of Transparency International; stated in Petkoski that the adverse influence of corruption is widely spread which shows that the global corruption outlays several industries billions of dollars from one year to the other. It is often obliging companies to decide between successful businesses through backhanders or mislaying the capability to work successfully or all the way in certain markets.

1034) Q: How thus corruption affect governance?

A: Corruption holds the ability to destabilize effective governance for both private and communal regions and it has the ability to effect on humanity rights. Corruption takes numerous forms and is deceptive by nature with certain complexities to exterminate. Corruption looks like a multinational organisation which pays a corrupt incentive to gain success and win a public contract for building the local highway, rather planning a sub-standard opportunity.

1035) ***Q:*** What was Lord Falconer view on corruption

A: In 2003, Lord Falconer, in his "Foreword to the corruption Bill" discusses the effect of corruption where he stated that "The corruption is a potentially devastating factor. It is important to check regularly. Otherwise it will result in serious damage in both governmental and private sector which causes the rise of major issues in economic and social life if the state. It requires constant observation as it is a major crime and it has insidious nature which causes a stretch in the international borders

1036)

Q: What effect of corruption?

A; The worldwide presence of corruption weakness democracy, damages economy, obstructs the developmental processes and also destroy respect for the rights of people by supporting the depraved government, with far-reached destabilising outcomes" (Hatchard, 2014).

1037)

Q; Who are involve in corruption?

A: Corruption embraces illegal beneficiation and embezzlement, where the funds from the public sector are misappropriated or moved for other`s benefit. The other form is related to the trading in control, where several public officials as well as politicians are persuaded to change their rules and regulations along with the implementation of certain laws. Such forms reflect corruption as a subverted democracy and also shows interests of justice. Numerous corrupt politicians, as well as civil officials, failed to serve the activities related with the electorate factors, but showed their level of interest's prior public value. The nature of corrupt and bribery is caustic as it impairs belief in several governmental institutions.

1038)

Q: What is the relationship among corruption, governance, and human rights

A; The relationship between human rights and corruption transgressions tends to become more delicate as compared with other types of breaches related to law practices. These type of breaches results in serious damages as their impact is readily ostensible. Even though, corruption is directly reduced by the principle along with the practice of powered government, its indirect impact on people of a particular community has become the main concern of certain scrutiny. The further consideration is placed on determining and evaluating the social effect of corruption.

1039)

Q: What is Julio Bacio Terracino view on corruption?

A; According to a well-known policy analyst Julio Bacio Terracino; corruption often abuses the right of human beings, and that is significant to differentiate certain cases where the role of corruption plays a direct part in violating the rights of human and also indirect where it shows an influential cause.

1040)

Q: How does MNEs (multinational enterprise) involvement in corruption?

A: where several MNEs favour illicit practices that often results towards the corrosion of established governance and shows a massive degradation for the rights of human being in the overall nation. The issue is related to the solutions that can be implemented to remove corruption which is the main cause of social abuse.

1041)

Q: Summaries International initiatives combat trans-national corruption

A: Corruption has certain implications aimed for different areas of the world, irrespective of the nation or a specific region where corruption is a regular practice. Where MNEs are found to be implicated, the concept of corruption appears to be international, which covers all national boundaries jurisdictions, international and financial mediums that are often considered to cover far-reached bribery. The international initiatives might become the reason of the most appropriate and eventually the reliable and optimal approach to ensuring that several states will effectively resolve the corruption problem.

1042)

Q: What other initiative taken to combat corruption?

A: The collaboration of "Convention on Combatting Bribery (OECD)" along with the "United Nations Convention against Corruption" is a particular combination in combatting corrupt and illicit activities as compared with others. From past 15 years, a series of conventions by different regions have been observed which took part in reducing corruption while covering different parts of the world including Africa, America and the European Union as well. They modify their aims but mainly aim to remove and combat corruption with a range of effective measures. This type of international effort has provided a host of the latest anti-corruption initiatives based on national levels or more in a significant manner (Symonides, 2017).

1043)

Q; What Role does the European Parliament Play to combat corruption?

A; In 2007, a new impulse emerges by the European Parliament in which certain initiatives were decided. The parliament decided that the corporations must be motivated to create a CSR report on an annual basis. It voted concurrently to approve the regulation on compulsory reporting. The report is based on the CSR activities relating to social and ecological influences of business industries. Later in 2014, the European Union took over Directive 2014/95/European Union which reflects the revelation of non-financial data by many industries who have more than 500 workers on a compulsory basis. It is important for the organisations to provide a detailed analysis in the form of a report on ecological, social and workplace matters including human rights, anti-corruption and some of the bribery cases as well.

Chapter 29

MNEs (Multinational Enterprise)

1044)

Q; How does corruption *Impact of Multinational Enterprises (MNEs) and Globalisation*

A; Corruption is the main problem in different part of the world`s economy. Corruption is found to be a complex and multifaceted strategy, which divides the global financial sectors. MNEs lie under large international financial entities whose marketing strategies and sales revenues are often high as compared with local enterprises and the GDPs of many countries where they are doing their business.

1045)

Q: What powers does MNEs have?

A; MNEs holds economic controls and political power authorities to influence both domestic and international regulations of their nations. The largest MNE obscures the size based on UN yearly budget of around $5 billion observed in 2014 to 2015 even in other foreign corporation such as "Organization for Economic Co-operation and development and the International Labour Organization". The political and financial control of MNEs eventually goes for the nature and effect of their operations that is important and holds the potential to influence the life of a large number of people for good and bad results. Therefore, the influence and behaviour of MNEs are very important for consideration and scrutiny (Foran, 2000). On the other hand, the global compact presupposes that the participants integrate a set of basic regulations voluntarily related to the area of human rights, labour standards and anti-corruption.

1046)

Q: How does corruption increase threat of imitate medicines?

A: According to the World Health Organization, the formulation of fake medicines hold certain terminologies which contains spurious, substandard, falsified, falsely labelled, and counterfeit (SSFFC) products for medical treatment. This shows a great corruption in the field of medical sector. The WHO fact sheet contain certain key points which were published in 2016, some of these points states that the SSFFC products used in medical treatment plans badly influence different regions across the globe ranging from North America to European states through different Africa, American and Asian regions as well. Furthermore, it states that, with the increase of internet connections those associated with manufacture procedure along with the distribution and supply of medical products which are termed as SSFFC have gained high accessibility towards worldwide marketplace (Silver, 1998) SSFFC products for medical ailments might contain no healthy ingredient which shows a clear corrupt activity around the globe.

1047)

Q: How is corruption combat in medicine?

A: To combat corrupt activities pharmaceutical companies must make medicines accessible at affordable process for lower income countries in the world. Meanwhile, such companies must ensure an effective and corrupt free supply chain process which does not contain SSFFC for medical products

1048)

Q; *What are stipulations against corruption to combat at the national level?*

A: In most areas of the world, there are different forms of legislation concerned with the practices of anti-corruption elements, and preferably, the cases of corrupt activities must be noticed at domestic level. According to John Hatchard the idea of Lesotho, the origins of corruption increased during the establishment of Katse and Mohal dams that addressed successfully by the actions of local government, which sentenced the officials of domestic nations and international officials who are linked with fraudulent activities. This type of case is not likely to address in states where the level of corruption is far-reached, and the government is poor.

1049) ***Q:*** Briefly describe The US (United State) Foreign Corrupt Practice Act 1977

A: The Foreign Corrupt Practices Act of 1977, as corrected, 15 U.S.C. §§ 78dd-1, et seq. ("FCPA"), was ordered to make it illicit for types of people and certain features to generate instalments for distant government authorities that are responsible to support in attaining or allotting business. In particular, the provisions for anti-bribery by FCPA disallow the intentional utilisation of certain emails or other methods for the usefulness of federal trade corruptly. Furthermore, to actuate the foreign power to do or overlook to complete a demo neglecting his or her reasonable obligation, or to anchor some inappropriate favorable position; can assist with acquiring or holding business for or with, or guiding business to, any individual.

1050)

Q: What has happened since the Act in 1977?

A; Since 1977, the opposing pays off arrangements of the FCPA has associated all U.S. individuals and some foreign guarantors of sanctuaries. Moreover, with the authorisation of specific changes in 1998, the counter pays off arrangements of the FCPA presently likewise applicable towards foreign organisations and people who became the reason, directly or by agents, a demonstration in assistance of such a degenerated corrupt payment to occur inside the domain of the United States.

1051)

Q: How does the FCPA control corruption in organization account**?**

A: The FCPA additionally requires organisations whose securities are recorded in the United States to fulfil its accounting arrangements. Such accounting arrangements, which were intended to work pair with anti-bribery for FCPA, involve enterprises associated with the provisions to; (1) make and save records and books that will reflect accurately and fairly towards the transactions of business organisations, (2) maintain and devise a proper system for controlling internal accounting factors.

1052)

Q: What is UK (United Kingdom) Response to organisational corruption?

A: In early 2010, the enforcement data collected, was published by OECD WGB for the first time. It has certain records of past ten years to 2009, the UK allowed on the person or a company for international bribery. This report gave a complete audit representing UK's reputation in the usage of the OECD Convention. Its discoveries can be abridged as follows. It argued the collapse of the UK laws regarding the bribery of open authorities and corporate obligation for international bribery. It focused on the requirement for the order of another foreign bribery crime, the formation of a successful corporate obligation regime and the selection of Article 5 towards domestic regulation. It assessed the job of the SFO in researching and indicating examples of bribery and international corruption and made certain recommendations for change. The last report was discharged in March 2017. The WGB noticed that a significant number of its implications had been actualised, and furthermore perceived that there had been an ongoing increment in the dimension of implementation procedures by the SFO.

1053)

Q: How is global bribery combated?

Bribery Act 2010

A; The Bribery Act settled in 2010 and came into action in 2011. This act became the most significant element for anti-corruption regulation in the United Kingdom, as is claimed to be one of the far-reached Acts across the world. It has four distinct offences which include; paying a bribe, receiving a bribe, bribing an international public official, and the corporate offence of failing to prevent bribery.

1054)

Q: Which sector is the bribery Act targeted?

A:This Act is designed for both public and private activities, and additionally for those who use business in collaboration with large companies as well as public authorities or operates in a country where a high level of corruption is present. UK courts hold the jurisdiction against bribery outside its nation in case if it relates with the person or any business which has some connection with the UK. This Act contains certain penalties which include up to 10 years conviction or an unlimited fine. Secondly, a company who has failed to prevent the bribery crime is punished with an unlimited fine or a company director might be disqualified.

1055) ***Q:*** How does corruption affect the world?

A: Corruption is a complex and pervasive form of crime. It has different types occurring at almost all levels around the world. It can be found at national government, local government or corporate sector and tends to spread where government and civil communities are weak. The globalisation factor increases commercial pressure towards securely profitable dealings in the establishing world along with the desire to protect the chance of bribery. This paper has discussed international initiatives in providing the potential for far-reached establishment. The need of all signatory regions taken broadly identical to anti-corruption practices offers significant assurance that corporations are not placed at a competitive disadvantage while deciding to not to spoil practising elements that are found to be corrupt

1056)

Q: Do all countries and MNEs help to combat corruption?

There are some major and established marketing nations have not yet associated with the OECD Convention and with UNAC as well.

1057)

Q;Is it easy to monitor corruption compliance?

A; The monitoring and effectuation of a nation's compliance with its foreign accountabilities have a significant role, which seems like penalties of corporations that violate national anti-corruption regulation. The establishment of certain principles for a well-maintained corporate government and adherence towards the rules of transparency, responsibility and reliability are important in this regard.

1058) Q: What has evolved in multinational corporation?

A: Global multinational corporations have come into existence in the last hundred years and have slowly gained dominance in society based on their power and influence.

1059) Q: What have MNEs influence?

A:Their ability to generate profit and keep the world's economy stable along with provided employment to millions of people have made them akin to superpowers. However with this level of influence, there are bound to be cases where power abuse is observed and how their influence have led to them gaining authority over the stake holders and communities, To that end many governments have also began to work with MNEs and with the new age of globalization, these corporations are able to contract third party suppliers form different parts of the country in order to boost their profit margin.

1060) Q: What should lawyers consider with regard to MNEs?

A;

1) To analyse and evaluate the influence of multinational corporations,
2) How lack of proper corporate governance can lead to the flouting of human rights and abusive practices.
3) Assess and attempt to explain the degree of political influence
4) How corporate authority that these multinational enterprises (MNEs) have in relation to their stakeholder along with the society at large.
5) To elaborate on the corporate social responsibility and its various factors that exist

for not just corporations in the US but everywhere in the world.

6) An attempt shall be made regarding the identification of gaps in governance that are created because of globalization that allows corporations the liberty to indulge in abusive acts without being held accountable.

1061) Q; What can corporate provide?

A; A corporation, in legal terms as a structure, provides a method for multiple individuals to combine their efforts to complete a goal. Being relatively benign, a corporation can demonstrate ethics, social responsibility and positive governance for social benefit if it is handled by similar minded shareholders and customers.

1062) Q: What is the negative side of corporate?

A: A corporation can be just as corrupt and devoid of ethical considerations if the internal governance disregard legal procedures in the pursuit of profit. Business corporation was an insignificant institution just over 200 years ago however today its dominancy extends to impacting animals, people and plants as well as water, food and resources and the overall shaping of the socio-economic system.

1063) Q: Can regulatory corporate prevent their negativity?

A: A major amount of regulatory corporate environment is focused towards public interest, however provides major economic benefits to MNE's who can afford the sponsorship and lobbying while dealing damage to small businesses and the public. An example of this is the study carried out by Sunlight Foundation which utilized tax data to assess corporate investment and their decreasing taxes, revealed that between 2007 and 2010 companies including Altria, Amgen, Boeing, Exxon Mobil and others invested $550 million into lobbying thus resulting in tax reductions of around $10 billion (George 2017).

1064) Q: With case evidence, what powers were given to MNEs

A; It was during the case of *Santa Clara County v. Southern Pac. R.* (1886), where MNEs were provided a major increase in power by the U.S. Supreme Court where their recognition under the Fourteenth Amendment lead to them having not only equal constitutional rights to individuals but superior rights because of the enterprise characteristics such as incorporating in jurisdictions with favourable laws, cheap labour and low taxes due to their long-term survivability, and wealth accumulation.

1065) *Q:* What are some influence of MNEs on stakeholders and community?

A; In recent years the influence and authority of MNEs have seen a remarkable increase regarding its stakeholders and society. With Supreme Court (United Kingdom) extending privileges such as political speech to corporations and religious liberty to enterprises such as Hobby Lobby, Love (2010) notes that MNEs have gained the power to sway the public to their side and be able to violate their rights without any fear of repercussion.

1066) Q; Do some of MNEs privileges experience in other countries?

A: The research also extends to other parts of the world such as Japan where MNEs termed 'Zaibatsus' are responsible for working with governments that regulate people on how to live their life. Furthermore, with Asian laws being unable to regulate and keep the corporations in check, the corporations can dictate their influence while blatantly ignoring civil procedures, one of which led to the infamous dumping of toxic waste in Korea in Misamis Oriental (Love 2010).

Another modern example is the BP Oil Spill incident where an explosion of the British Petroleum's oil rig caused the most massive oil spill in US history across the Gulf of Mexico. Under UK's constitution and corporate laws, the company should have had to pay major repercussions however lack of a severe legal reaction against them despite heavy community protest just goes on to show the abuse of human rights that corporates either intentionally or accidently indulge in (Locke 2013).

1067) Q: Is it fair to blame all MNEs for abusive practice

A: No, however, it cannot be said that abusive practices are a daily occurrence for MNEs as various US companies have taken an active part in using their influence to benefit the environment and society. Irogbe (2013) notes how corporate influence arises from corporate social responsibility. MNEs' engagement in social and environmental causes with multiple stakeholders is an attribute of the rising economic activity and globalization which has resulted in a larger environmental and social impact by corporate activities, by which they can thus be held accountable by an activist society. (Irogbe 2013).

1068) Q; Give some MNEs who contribute to public wellbeing

A; Many MNEs such as Tesco, Apple, McDonalds regularly launch initiatives that cater to their particular customers and the wider demographic. Green initiative that address environmental issues and proper disposal of waste is often at the forefront of these responsibilities. Companies like Microsoft gave over $900m to non-profits during the years 2012-2015 as well as announced their education in carbon emissions by 25 percent (Love 2010). Its moves like these that strengthen the influence and power of MNEs over communities (Irogbe 2013).

1069) Q: How do MNEs benefit from their good deeds to the public?

A:The number of companies voluntarily involving social and environmental policies in their business operations and models has seen a rampant increase in the last thirty years as they believe that enhancing performance in this sector would lead to higher financial performance however many theorize that indulging in CSR would actually result in the company to underperform. As noted by George (2017) that companies who cater to the community rather than focus on the profit shall be eliminated by competitors and can only survive by relentless focusing on profit (George 2017).

1070) Q; What can MNEs get away with due to their generosity to the society?

A; General consensus states that by catering to the beliefs and socioeconomic issues, and creating good services for the people, MNEs can generally get away with the consumption of natural resources, pollution of local and global environments at little cost as well as hurt the wellbeing of the employee if work conditions are less than stellar. Corporations have started impacting the development of constitutions and legislations and is shaping society and culture by creating hierarchies and thus imposing a power structure in the community. (George 2017).

1071) Q: Give an example of company who got away despite unethical activities?

A: Wal-Mart Stores, Inc. v. Dukes (2011) is a prime case where the company was called into question of using its positive image to conduct unethical activities however despite evidence, the company did not suffer from any major repercussion which goes no to show that CSR can be used as a front to keep the company's questionable activities in motion.

1072) Q; *What does Governance refer in relation to MNEs?*

A; Governance refers to the company's ability to ethically supervise its operations and take stakeholders interests in considerations when conducting business decisions. Corporate governance requires the business to not only conform to ethical standards in front of the public but also maintain a consistent and fair conduct of operations behind the scenes. However, with the recent expansion of globalization and a time where major companies are able to create their branches in other parts of the world, and outsource operations to third party companies, there remains a question as to what legal limits apply on them in order to stay within the boundaries of corporate law.

1073) Q: How do MNEs spread internationally?

A: Ruggie (2011) notes that globalization has provided companies to conduct their operations away from their home country and its legislations, thus being able to circumvent those laws and conduct actions that would have been highly illegal in their home country (Ruggie 2011). One such example is of the billion-dollar MNE Apple. Thus far Apple has refused to provide the statistics regarding their carbon emissions and is the one biggest global organization that has refused to join the

Carbon Disclosure Project which is a critical non-profit organization that assessed and reveals the environmental information of the company. By refusing to join them, Arnold (2010) states that the emissions of carbon must be high thus directly violating the rights of not only those civilians living near the vicinity of the plants but the population as a whole as carbon emissions lead to accelerated global warming thereby hampering the people's quality of life (Arnold 2010).

1074) Q; Name another gap in corporate governance**?**

A; Another gap in corporate governance is the lack of international laws that govern the conditions of workers at international off shore sites and the lack of legislations that determine a specific pay for these outsourced workers. This gap is fully taken advantage of by Apple as they have a history of ignoring the standards and working conditions of their international suppliers.

1075) Q: What is the consequence of MNEs harshness on some workers?

A: It was revealed that over 50% of Apple's supply chain workers have to work over 62 hours per week and that many of these suppler companies do not even follow normal safety protocols. After a four-month investigation underground at Foxconn Factory in Taiwan, a third-party supplier of Apple revealed to the Students and Scholars Against Corporate Misbehaviour (SACOM) group that working conditions there is akin to a "life without dignity".

Furthermore, there is also a history of suicide among the young workers who could not withstand the harsh working environment.

1076) Q: How do the public view on MNEs breach of corporate governance and CSR?

A; These issues made its way to the public resulting in many questionings the lack of corporate governance and CSR practices of Apple. The progress report of Apple in 2012 showed that over half of the workers of Apple's suppliers have worked over 60 hours per week and 40% of the suppliers have not provided the basic safety standards to them.

Wettstein (2010) provides information as to why or how this occurs and what gaps in governance allow these abusive practices to continue. Foxconn is located in Taiwan where governance and supervision of corporations are not strict thus companies can get away with stricter working hours and paying their workers extremely low wages. The workers themselves hail from poor families and are often uneducated about their rights. Compounded with the fact that their only choice is to work at low wages or not work at all, they often have to give in thus allowing the rule of these corporations to flourish (Wettstein 2010).

1077) Q; What other MNEs abuse their position?

A: Apple is not the only company that has seen such controversy. Nike has a lot of its football gear outsources to third world countries such as Pakistan and Inia. In fact, Ramasastry (2015) mentions how the soccer balls used in world cups are created in Sialkot, Pakistan where the workers are mostly underage children working 16-20 hours per day at about 5$ per day. These inhuman conditions and abuse of human rights are possible due to Pakistan's non-existent enforcement system to ensure workers get their basic rights (Ramasastry 2015).

1078) Q: How has globalization help MNEs to abuse their power?

A: It can be ascertained that globalization has given these multinational corporations access to establish or outsource work to companies in third world countries, by which they can not only get away by paying the workers measly wages but also don not have to care about providing them adequate working conditions.

Research conducted by Ramasastry (2015) states that Pakistan and Taiwan indeed have laws that dictate the workers granted their basic right and adequate wages however, lack of implementing them does not incur any scrutiny since no one actively enforces these legal limitations on the companies.

1079) Q: What evidence that some MNEs are hypocrite?

A; By explicitly making sure that their suppliers or outsourced work is handled by companies in these countries, the MNEs are able to assume plausible deniability in the case, this was ever traced back to them. By keeping their hands clean in front of the public they are able to demonstrate a positive image of their company while undertaking schemes that would take advantage of workers in third world countries, and all this is a result of globalization that has allowed MNEs to form relations with overseas suppliers and companies.

As a result, it can be said that governance gaps no only exist due to the lack of proper law implementation in their party companies but also the fact that international laws and corporate laws in US do not restrict these MNEs from working with these third-party supplier companies.

1080) Q: What measures for effectiveness of Monitoring and Enforcement methods***?***

A: International Labour Standards (ILO) as set forth by the United Nations is a viable way of ensuring the MNEs adhere to the labour standards and laws as well as keep in check the working standards of their supplier companies.

1081) Q: How can enforcement be implemented?.

A: One method to enforce conformance to ILO standards is to hold the government accountable. Many governments bend the labour and environmental legislation to allow MNEs to operate freely. Thus, it is critical to bring states to assume their responsibilities as that would put pressure on the companies. This can be done by leading civil cases against them and independent lawyers investigating these companies.

1082) Q; How difficulties to hold MNEs accountable?

A: Holding MNCs to account directly in their home state is difficult in many countries such as in South Africa where employees cannot sue their employers. And relatives of dead claimants cannot launch claims against

MNEs. However, having recourse to MNEs' home states puts their sovereignty into play. Host government's laws cannot be ignored blatantly. Many third world countries including Nigeria are launching their own civil government that aims to hold companies accountable for their actions. Similarly, in countries like Pakistan, there is a need to establish governance and public bodies in order to monitor the companies since in many third world countries the government themselves collude with the MNEs.

1083) Q: How can third party be monitored?

A: MNEs actions can also be monitored in regards of third-party contractors or suppliers under the OECD Guidelines for Multinational Enterprises that holds details regarding the treatment of such contractors. Furthermore, the Alien Tort Claims Act (ATCA), in the United States allows US courts to listen to cases regarding abuse of human rights occurring anywhere in the world given the courts have jurisdiction. The case of Burmese people v. UNOCAL of California is one such example. In UK, The European Union legal drafts allow compel the companies to ensure the upholding of human rights both of workers and civilians. However, the question rises to what extent are all these monitoring and enforcement systems effective?

1084) Q: What has resulted due to lack of universal monitoring of MNEs?

A: While there is no universally monitoring method and detailing all the local methods of enforcement it can however be established that these tools leave a lot to be desired since it was under the supervision of these enforcement systems that Apple was able to work with Foxconn for such a long time and even today countries like India, Pakistan and Nigeria has a lot of companies that claim to adhere to the ILO standards yet do not implement them at all since there is no actual body capable of enforcing them. Kennedy et al. (2017) states that despite the United Nations existence and the ILO being a major forefront of how corporations should function, they ultimately do little to combat the abuse of human rights that is being done by the companies thus leading to the conclusion that these methods are not effective at all (Kennedy et al. 2017). However, such a situation can be combated by launching public and non-profit bodies that would be able to overrule the governmental regulations of providing these MNEs with privacy and aim to investigate their labour practices.

Such a conduct is already being conducted in Bangladesh and has reduced MNE influence by 32% and has highly impacted the working standards of the workers and can thus be implemented in countries such as US, Brazil and Canada as well (Wieland and Handfield 2010).

1085) ***Q:*** *How I reflect on MNEs?*

A; Working on this research article has enlightened me of the harm that MNEs can do in terms of violating human rights, if left unchecked, there certainly needs to be a universal monitoring and enforcement method established in order to hold all the MNEs globally accountable for misconduct. The research also helped me learn about the criticality of corporate social responsibility and how it can be used positively by multinational companies in order to benefit the environment, and those living in it. By indulging in CSR, the companies also are able to create a positive image of themselves thus leading to an increased financial performance.

I was able to observe that the initiatives that are being undertaken around the world including UN interventions as well as The Alien Torts Claims act along with public intervention from bodies such as Students and Scholars

Against Corporate Misbehaviour have been able to keep the MNE behaviour in check, however to a certain extent. It must be noticed that these bodies only have so much influence and cannot regulate and monitor every single aspect of every single corporation 24/7. There are cracks in the surveillance systems which is taken full advantage of by the corporations. Nigeria's construction of a public body that would work independently alongside the government is certainly a step in the right direction, one if successful can set an example for other countries in the future on how to handle and ensure accountability by the MNEs.

1086) Q: What is my conclusion on MNEs research?

A: This research aimed to analyse the conduct of MNEs and their power and influence globally as they conduct operations on a multinational scale. The aspect of globalization has awarded them a lot of opportunities to benefit the world however many use unethical standards in the pursuit of profit such as working with third party suppliers who provide haphazard working conditions to their works also with meagre wages. In many parts of the world governments actually violate their own laws and collude with the corporations actively. While western countries do enjoy the privilege of enforcement methods primarily due to an activist and aware society, such is not the case with other countries.

Research Diary

1087) Q: Although argument is blood line of law. How do one carry out research by using diary?

A; I have use the research when compiling questions and answers on MNEs(multinational enterprise)

A: I conducted a primary research which entail the usage of data gathered from interviews, surveys and questionnaires. I believe that carrying a primary research result in more accurate data collection.

I also used secondary research strategy which allows me to research previously published research papers and use them to derive conclusions. An interpretive approach was used that enabled me to come to my own conclusions based on the research free of any biasing factors. I planned my search strategy by isolating the requirements of the question. It required me to search for MNEs and corporate governance and how they abuse human rights and the various methods of monitoring them. By using keywords in databases, I was able to adhere to the topic without deviating from the subject matter

1088) Q: What were the sources?

A: The sources were moistly research articles that were published in the last 10 years. The year limit was kept from 2008 to date. This allowed access to only the most recent and up to date information. The databases that was used were EBSCO database, JSTOR Library database and Google Scholar to get access to the relevant research papers. The reason why these sources or databases were used is that they have access to a large variety of research articles, not to mention they have a very strict system of only holding verified articles. Thus, the authenticity of the research is never in doubt resulting in the accuracy of my own research.

1089) Q; Give an example of how you will carry out research to write assignment in law?

A; In my opinion my research was successful. I was able to access a lot of research data from which I isolated 500 research papers regarding the topic and utilized their data to answer the questions of the assignment. However, I was unable to find any data regarding lack of corporate governance in the early 20th century. Due to this I was unable to link my theories and research with historical evidence.

1090) Q: Give example of you would outline research in a table form?

A:

Details of the search:

Database	**Keywords**	**Year Limit**	**Research Paper Results**
EBSCO	1. Multinational Enterprise 2. Corporate Governance 3. Abuse of corporation authority	2008-2018	8
Library JSTOR Library Database	1. MNEs violation of civil laws 2. Monitoring and enforcement of MNEs 3. Lack of corporate Governance	2008-2018	5
Google Scholar	1. Internal corporation violations 2. Abuse of corporation	2008-2018	7

	authority 3. Monitoring and enforcement of corporations		

1091) Q: Give conclusion of the research?

A; Out of 19 useful research articles, I utilized the ten most critical ones in this research. The major problem in undertaking this research was to carefully select and analyse what data must be included in the paper and what must be omitted. Since the limit was only 3000 words, a lot of critical information had to be removed in favour of other important information. This project taught me how to research data and material in order to write up a research article. It also taught me the criticality of crediting those whose data has been used in the research.

1092) Q: What is the difference between secondary and primary source research?

A: A secondary source is an interpretation of another period by one person, so there is no guarantee that their interpretation is accurate and can be relied upon. Some secondary sources have more authority than others. Care must be taken when rely on secondary source. Primary source have documentation to support and therefore reliable

Chapter 30

WOMEN

1093) Q; How can one argue equality for men and women?

A: Argue for equality of women and men, but risk ignoring vital differences between them (Rothenberg: liberal feminists would argue that, if men can donate sperm, so women should be allowed to donate eggs, but also that sperm and egg donation are not truly analogous)

1094) Q: What actions might be used as male dominance over women?

A: There is possible restrict choice for women by arguing that certain actions should be avoided because they reinforce male dominance although some women might like to take those actions (Rothenberg refers to views that IVF is a male-dominated technology that has been used to control women's sexual lives),

1095) Q: Are all women the same?

A: Might emphasise that there is no objective reality for women, and that each woman's circumstances are different, but this risk ignoring concerns common to women when it comes to reproductive technologies (e.g. are their bodies being controlled by men, generally speaking?)

1096) Q: Do the law favours women?

A; There appear to be inconsistencies in the law – granting women equal rights on the one hand by allowing egg donation, but making compensation for them on the other, for example by offering more money for egg donation. Similarly is feminist viewpoints alone are pertinent – what about the rights of men, for example to know the children born using their sperm, or the donors without parental rights?

1097) Q: How do men and women differ

A: Could be argued that women's – and men's – experiences differ based on their cultural backgrounds, and that the effects of reproductive technology differ from one country to another, for example, might argue that the law reflects the realities of power relations in society, and that the law has the potential to change those power relations

Chapter 31

ABORTION

1098) Q: Define abortion

A: Abortion – this is the 'separation of a non-viable human foetus' (Richards and Curzon, 2011) from the pregnant woman. Various terms that are used in everyday language also occur in medical and legal documents. Miscarriage is often used as a colloquial term for spontaneous abortion, i.e. the unwanted loss of a pregnancy. However, older legal documents use the same word to mean both a deliberate abortion and a termination of pregnancy. The term abortion is used throughout this block.

1099) Q: What is the difference between foetus and embryo?

A: Foetus – strictly speaking this refers to the later stages of development of an unborn child, from about the eighth week of conception to birth. Prior to the eighth week, it is correctly referred to as an embryo. In this block the term foetus is used to refer to the fertilised ovum, the embryo and the foetus, i.e. throughout the whole pregnancy. It is used as an alternative to the terms unborn baby or child.

1100) Q: What is quickening

A: The modern view is that quickening occurs when the pregnant woman notices movement from the foetus.

1101) Q: who made that decision?

St Thomas Aquinas, study saw quickening as the point at which the soul entered the foetus.

1102) Q: when was abortion criminalised?

A: the ecclesiastical courts in1800 to 2000 first 'criminalised' abortion, and prosecuted those who performed abortion. The Church took the view that abortion was unacceptable after quickening, but acceptable before quickening.

1103) Q: What was the punishment for abortion?

A: The punishment for committing abortion after quickening was a period of penance, which could be private or public, involve the reciting of prayers, or corporal punishment, or mortification with the wearing of religious artefacts such as the cilice, a garment or device worn to induce discomfort and could last for a number of years.

1104) Q; Why were women have to undergo penance?

A: The objective of requiring people to undergo penance is for them to make amends for their sin.

1105) Q: What power had the church in people lives?

A; The Church was the central point of people's lives. Committing a crime against the laws of the Church was seen as being more severe than committing a crime against the laws of the land. the ecclesiastical courts had tremendous influence and power.

1106) Q; What was the punishment for abortion when the church power deteriorated?

A: When power and influence of the ecclesiastical courts declined in the seventeenth century, During the reform, the common law courts still prosecuted those charged with abortion, but followed the principles of the ecclesiastical courts, and the quickening distinction remained but punishment for committing abortion was a fine or period of imprisonment

1107) Q: When was Lord Ellenborough's Act

A: The Act received Royal Assent on 24 June 1803. It is known as the Malicious Shooting or Stabbing Act 1803 or, more commonly, Lord Ellenborough's Act. (offence against person Act)

1108) Q: How was the punishment for abortion under Lord Ellenborough's Act

A: Section 2, however, provides that undertaking or attempting to undertake an abortion prior to quickening shall result in the person being:

liable to be fined, imprisoned, set in and upon the Pillory, publicly or privately whipped, or to suffer one or more of the said Punishments, or to be transported beyond the Seas for any Term not exceeding fourteen Years, at the Discretion of the Court before which such Offender shall be tried and convicted.

1109) Q: How do one compare the changes in the law?

The severity of the sentence for performing an abortion post-quickening. Under ecclesiastical and common law this was penance, a fine or a period of imprisonment, whereas under the provisions of Lord Ellenborough's Act it was now the death penalty. Also, note that performing an abortion pre-quickening became a criminal offence

1110) Q: Give summary of Offence against person Act 1837

A: Section 6 of the Offences Against the Person Act 1837 reads:

And be it enacted, That whosoever, with Intent to procure the Miscarriage of any Woman, shall unlawfully administer to her or cause to be taken by her any Poison or other noxious Thing, or shall unlawfully use any Instrument or other Means whatsoever with the like Intent, shall be guilty of felony, and being convicted thereof shall be liable, at the Discretion of the Court, to be transported beyond the Seas for the Term of his or her natural Life, or for any Term not less than Fifteen Years, or to be imprisoned for any Term not exceeding three Years.

1111) Q: What happened to the quickening

A: The result of this section is that the distinction between offences committed pre- and post-quickening has been removed, because the 1837 Act refers to 'the miscarriage of any woman'. In addition the death penalty has been abolished for all abortion convictions.

Under that Act, there is now no distinction between attempting an abortion on a woman who is pregnant and one who is not. Therefore an attempt at abortion is sufficient for a conviction to succeed rather than the previous need for an abortion to have actually occurred.

1112) Q: When were Offence Against person's Act

A: the four Acts (Lord Ellenborough's Act 1803, Offences Against the Person Act 1828 and Offences Against the Person Act 1837 and 1861

1113) Q; Why was the Act of 1861?

A:This was to overcome the loopholes in the previous Acts against the person and to remove the harshness of punishment whilst at the same time given clarity of the abortion laws.

1114) Q; When was the infant life preservation Act

A;1929

1115) Q: What did the infant Act 1929 sought?

A: Section 4 of the Infant Life (Preservation) Act 1929 sought to prevent possible circumventing of the abortion laws outlined in the previous section by creating an offence of child destruction.

1116) Q: Why was the abortion Act 1967 introduced?

A; Public outcry and severe punishment couple with right of women prompted politician to think that from the 1930s until the passage of the Abortion Act 1967 there was a period of uncertainty regarding the lawfulness of abortion, so the 1967 Act attempted to address most of the concern.

Chapter 32

FGM (Female Genital Mutilation)

1117) Q; What do you think of FGM

A; In my opinion, FGM is barbaric way to prevent young girls having sexual feeling. Yes, it must be painful as they are backstreet procedure (because is illegal) without local anaesthetic. I guess women with FGM are ashamed and would like to keep it secret, hence lifelong anonymity section within the Serious Crime Act 2015

Using doctrinal approach alone, leaves gap in the law because prior to 2003 Act and 2015 Act, there must be social-legal consideration as well.

1118) Q: What does the term FGH means in law?
A: Female Genital Mutilation (FGM) is a collective term for a range of procedures which involve partial, or total removal of the external female genitalia for non-medical reasons. It has also been referred to as 'female circumcision', or 'female genital cutting' (CPS, 2017).
1119) Q: How does it affect the victim?
A: The practice is medically unnecessary, is extremely painful and has serious health consequences, both at the time when the mutilation is carried out, and in later life

(Riesel, 2015). It appear to be a barbaric procedure to reduce female sexual desires.

FGM has remained a taboo subject, hidden behind euphemisms or is “excused as a cultural tradition” (Author, 2001, page 13)

1120) Q: How is it classified by WHO?

A: Female Genital Mutilation is helpfully classified by the World Health Organization (WHO) into four major types (World Health Organization, 2019);

Type I: Clitoridectomy: partial or total removal of the clitoris;

Type II: Excision: partial or total removal of the clitoris and the labia minora, with or without excision of the labia majora;

Type III: Infibulation: narrowing of the vaginal opening through the creation of a covering seal:

Type IV: Other: all other harmful procedures to the female genitalia for non-medical purposes, e.g. pricking, piercing, incising, scraping and cauterizing the genital area.

1121) Q: What is United Kingdom Law on FGM

A: In England the main legislation to address FGM is The Female Genital Mutilation Act 2003 (Great Britain. Female Genital Mutilation Act 2003) and was amended by sections 70 to 75 of the Serious Crime Act 2015 (Great Britain, Serious Crime Act 2015).

1122) Q: Give some details of the 2003 Law. Section 1

A: The Female Genital Mutilation Act 2003 makes it a criminal offence to excise, infibulate or otherwise mutilate the whole or any part of a girl's labia majora, labia minora or clitoris, although not if the procedure is undertaken by an approved person on the basis of it being necessary for her physical or mental health or connected to child birth (s. 1).

1123) Q: Give some details of the 2003 Law. Section 2

A: Section 2, makes it an offence of assisting a girl (or woman) to mutilate her own genitalia, with Section 3 identifying that assisting a non-UK person to mutilate overseas a girl's genitalia is an offence. The Serious Crime Act 2015 (Serious Crime Act 2015 s. 70(1)(a), 88(4), s. 86(10))

1124) Q: Give some details of the 2003 Law. Section 3

A: s.3 of Female Genital Mutilation Act 2003 to include when an offence is committed outside the UK, proceedings may be taken, and the offence may be treated as having been committed anywhere in England, Wales or Northern Ireland

1125) Q: How was it amended in 2015 Act in sec.70

A: Additional elements were introduced and updated with the Serious Crime Act 2015 with Sections 70 to 72 extending the scope of extra-territorial offences, granted victims of FGM lifelong anonymity and introducing a new offence of failing to protect a girl from risk of FGM.

1126) Q; what is section 73 of the 2015 Act

A; Sections 73 of the Serious Crime Act 2015 inserted section 5A (and schedule 2) into Female Genital Mutilation Act 2003, which provided for FGM Protection Orders and also section 5B which introduces a mandatory reporting duty for professionals, in girls under the age of 18. These civil orders have been used in the following cases; Re B & G [2015]; Re X [2017]; Re E [2015] and; Re F & X [2015].

1127) Q:What is section 72 of the Act

A: The Serious Crime Act 2015, at section 72, provided for an inserted section into the Female Genital Mutilation Act 2003 at section 3A, which made an offence of failing to protect a girl from risk of genital mutilation.

1128) Q: When was a woman first convicted in United Kingdom?

A:On the 1 February 2019, a woman became the first person to be convicted under the Female

Genital Mutilation Act 2003 (Summers, 2019). This law has been in place for over 14 years.

Chapter 33

Family Law

1129) Q: How will you describe the media in relation to family court

A; The law on media in family court had been like roller-coaster, depend on the judge or the Lord chancellor at the time

In 1950s under lord K--, judges could disclose any case to the media, however in the 1980s. the lord chancellor Lord Macke overturn this and in 1990s Lord Taylor allow media access (OU Professor Gary slapper interview Frances Gibbs)

1130) Q: When was family proceeding amended

A: Family proceeding was amended in 2009 to allow the media to report (No 2 rules 2009) and it is governing by r27.11 family procedure rule 2010.

Children, Schools and family Act 2010 and the New Law Journal Wolanski and Wilson (2011)

The continue bar on the press in family court (family division) (2011)

1131) Q: Should media be allowed in family court

A:No.The European court of human right allow Uk to have family hearing in private.

There are opposition of media reporting from;

Children and parent, (their right under the human right Act 1998 must be respected).

Allow media will increase vulnerability of the children and the parent.

Also, from the professional such as the social service, probation service, the police (who sometimes misuse EPO)

It may be possible for further research to allow restricted reporting, i.e. not to reveal the names and address, school of the children.

Chapter 34

SILENCE

1132) Q: Why will individual be advised to remain silence when being interview by police?

A: Because the police and the court might wrongly interpreted the terminology used in answering question.

1133) Q: Can remain silence be construed as guilty?

A: It should not be because individual has the right to remain silence. However it might be advisable to let the court aware the reasons of silence to avoid any doubt.

1134) Q: In what situation might one choose to be silence at interview?

A: If the person feel depressed, anxious or have any symptoms of mental disorder or neurosis.

1135) Q: Can individual stop police interview at any time?

A: Yes, especially if one feel pressurised.

1136) Q: Can police interview be void and why.

A; if one claim that evidence had been given under duress or pressure, or police bargaining.

Chapter 35

ASSAULT (By people in power)

1137) Q:What happen if government servant, employer, or people in higher position say something during interview that resulted one develop symptoms of neurosis such as reactive depression, anxiety, phobia what can one do?

A: You might be able to claim assault occasional/ psychiatric injury. However you need to see your doctor as soon as the symptoms develop;

1138) Q: What happen if the symptom developed after a week.

A; as long as you might have flash back of the events or post tremor stress disorder as result of the assault, and evidence of some treatment such as counselling or medication etc, then you stand chance of claim under tort as long as you satisfied all the requirement of tort claim as stated in earlier questions and answers in this publication.

1139) Q; Personal injury claim stipulate that it must be claim within three years, is there any way round it.

A; Yes the three years might be when you got the evidence that support the injury was caused by the defendant. Also under the limitation Act !980, if you have psychiatric diagnosis at the time or developed as result of the injury, You can claim at any time up to when you are cured, within tort rules.

1140) Q: What happen if you have chronic Psychiatric diagnoses.

A; Yes you might be able to claim at any time during your life.

Chapter 36

CLASSIFICATION OF THE UNITED KINGDOM COURTS

1141) Q: DESCRIBE SUPREME COURT

A:SUPREME COURT: The Supreme Court is the highest court in the hierarchy, and in every country including the UK. The courts below the Supreme Courts are bound by the decisions of the Supreme Courts; whereas the Supreme Court is not bound by the decision of the courts below but is bound by the decisions of the European Court of Justice. Prior to the existence of the Supreme Court, the Lords of Appeal/Law Lords (12 most senior judges) sat in the House of Lords. In the House of Lords, the Law Lords, the Law Lords will partake in the debate.

1142) Q:DESCRIBE **COURT OF APPEAL**

A: COURT OF APPEAL**:** The court of appeal is an appellate court, and it's the second highest court in the hierarchy. In the Court of Appeal, there are two divisions and they are criminal division and civil division. In the Royal Courts of Justice (in London), cases are heard by

Lady Justices and Lord Justices of Appeal; and other cases will be heard by judges of the high court.

1143) Q: DESCRIBE **CIVIL DIVISION**

A:CIVIL DIVISION: The civil division hears appeals which are from the High Court, County Courts, and certain Tribunals. These cases will be based on the infringements on the rights of an individual.

1144) Q; DESCRIBE HIGH COURT

A:The High court is a court of first instance, an appellate court. The High court is bound by the decision of the court of appeal, the supreme court, and the European court of justice. It is not bound by the decision of the court below it, the three divisions that are below the High court are bound by the division of the High court. Appeals made by judges in the High court is sent to the court of appeal then send to the supreme court

1145) Q; DESCRIBE FAMILY COURT

This deals with cases concerning divorce and children, inherent jurisdiction is applied to cases that are connected with children

1146) Q; DESCRIBE THE QUEEN'S BENCH

It deals with cases associated with contract laws, personal injury cases, negligence, etc. Discrete specialist handle cases in their individual areas

1147) Q; DESCRIBE CHANCERY COURT

This handles cases associated with business, land, insolvency and probate.

1148) Q;DESCRIBE TRIBUNALS

A: Tribunals work together and in cooperation with courts. It has two tiers =; the first tier has to do with the chambers for tax, property, mental health, immigration etc.

The second-tier deals with the chambers for tax, immigration land and appeals.

1149) Q;DESCRIBE COUNTYCOURT

A: County court deal with cases like landlord/tenant disputes, injury compensations, recovery money owed to business, etc. In each county court there is only one circuit judge and one district judge

1150)

Q;DESCRIBE APPELATE COURTS

Appellate Court; decision made in this court is binding.

1151)

Q; DESCRIBE DUAL JURISDICTION

A; DUAL JURISDICTION

This jurisdiction handles both civil and criminal division law.

1152)

Q;DESCRIBE COURT OF FIRST INSTANCE

A: COURT OF FIRST INSTANCE

The Court of First Instance is a court that hears a case for the first time.

1153)

Q; DESCRIBE SINGLE JURISDICTION

SINGLE JURISDICTION
They handle either criminal law or civil law.

1154)

Q; DESCRIBE CRININAL COURTS

CRIMINAL DIVISION: The criminal division hears appeals from verdicts in the Crown Court, sentences given by the Crown Court and Confiscation of commands set by Crown Court. The Attorney General will take certain cases to this court if the judgement/sentence was very lenient

1155)

Q; DESCRIBE CROWN COURT

A; CROWN COURT: The Crown Court is an appellate court, and it handles offences like rape, murder, etc. In the Crown Court, there are the Jury (those that will make their judgements on the case, if the defendant is guilty or not guilty) and the Judge (who makes the ultimate and final judgement/sentence. The sentences that are set are broad; for example prison, community, etc.

1156) Q:DESCRIBE MAGISTRATE COURT

A: MAGISTRATE'S COURT: The Magistrate's Court handles Summary Offences, and they handle all criminal proceedings including more intense cases like drug crimes. After the crimes that are more intense are first heard in the Magistrate's court, they will be sent to the Crown Court. The Magistrate's Court will decide if the defendant should be retained in custody or if they should be allowed a bail, under certain conditions of which the defendant must accept or obey. The Magistrate's Court has the power to give sentences that are up to 6months in prison or fines that are up to £5,000.

1157) Q: DESCRIBE ADR (ALTERNATIVE DISTE RESOLUTION

A: alternate methods of dispute resolution (ADR) is communal name given to different techniques that are used to settle dispute without involving the court.

1158) Q:DESCRIBE TRIBUNALS

A;**TRIBUNALS:** The motive behind the making of tribunals is to make sure that time is not misspent on resolving little disputes when courts need ample time to deal with sizeable cases simultaneously.

1159) Q; DESCRIBE ARBITRATION

A: ARBITRATION: In the arbitration process, there is a third party involved, and he/she is called an arbitrator. The two opposing parties will make a mutual agreement to make sure that the cost/price of the dispute being resolved will be low and affordable.

1160) Q; DESCRIBE SUMMARY OFFENCES

A: SUMMARY OFFENCES: Summary Offences are cases that are not as intense and are tied by the Magistrate's Court. In this, three magistrates on a bench will decide what the sentence will be after evaluating the intensity of the crime. The highest period of imprisonment is 6 months; however, this is normally less. It has been set by an essential rule utilized for this offense that prosecution must start within 6 months after the offense has been carried out. For example; minor criminal damage, being drunk/disorderly, most driving offences and common assault

1161) Q; DESCRIBE CLASSIFICATION OF OFFENCES

A: This is triable either way offences.

This is offences that can be examined and determine as an indicatable offence or a summary offence. The offences will be tried in the magistrate court or in the High court at a mode of trial hearing, based on the intensity of the damage created. For instance, the magistrate's court will hear the case and will make decision on whether it should be case to be tried as an indictable offence. Some examples will be theft, bigamy, assault, etc.

1162) Q; DESCRIBE INDICTABLE OFFENCES

A: INDICTABLE OFFENCES: They are the most intense crimes committed, which will normally result in long periods of stay in prison. The first hearing is held at the Magistrate's Court, yet, crimes that are more intense are taken to the Crown Court for trials. (Cases that are handled in the Magistrate's Court are normally for bail). Some examples are murder, robbery, manslaughter, rape and more.

Part 4

REFERRENCE

TORT

STATUTE

Compensation Act 2006

This is civil liability (c) Act 1978 and is joint liability.

Civil liability (contribution) Act 1968 section 11 defendant convicted of careless driving and causing injury is tort claim.

Corona and Justice Act 2009 section 54

Aggravate damages Act 1971

Test

First test=Donohue. v. Edward son (1932) AC 562 (owe duty of care)

Second test; **Caparo** industries Plc. V. Dickinson (1990)2 AC 605 involve foreseeable, proximity and fair, just for the court to impose duty of care. (Duty of care)

Marc Rich and co.AG.v.Bishop rock Marine Co Ltd (1996) AC 211 (court decided not to impose Caparo fair, just (third arm of the Caparo) duty of care because the defendant is charity (another policy decision.

Bonnington for material contribution

McGee for material contribution to risk

Precedence cases tort of negligence

1) Caparo industries Plc. V. Dickinson (1990)2 AC 605
2) **Donoghue.** v. Edward son (1932) AC 562
3) **Wisher** .vessel Area Health Authority (1987) QB 730 CA (5 causes of loss, but none satisfy balance of probability (must be more than 50%)
4) **Bolam**. Frien hospital management committee (1957)2 ALL ER 118 (**doctor** to show degree of skill as "reasonable doctor"
5) **Blyth** .v. Birmingham waterworks (1856)11 EXCH 781 society expert defendant **conduct to be measured against expectation** of a "reasonable person" objective test." But for"
6) **Hull.**v. Chief Constable of West Yorkshire (1989) AC 53 (police negligence cannot be liable as they only have **duty to the public and not to individual**. (causation test) but for
7) X(Minors) .v.Bedfordshire county courts council (1995) AC 633
8) **winny.**v. Chief Constable of Northumbria (No1) 1997 QB 464 (in a very rear occasion the **court allowed duty of care owe** by police to individual.(causation test) but for
9) **Capital** and Counties plc. V. Hampshire CC (1997) QB 1004 **fire brigade failure** to maintain fire hydrant
10) Highway authority aware of dagger to pedestrian in a junction but did nothing about it and accident kill pedestrian. Court said they were not liable as they have **no duty of care to the individual.**

11) **Smith**'s. Lee Brain & co (1962) 2 QB 405 claimant had pre cancerous lips which made worse due to the defendant conduct (To be used as contributed factor).

12) **Paris**.v.Stepney Borough Council (1951) AC 367 Defendant was not aware of the defendant have partial blindness so they were not liable for causing injury to the other eye. This could also be used for **contribution** claim. (causation test) but for

13) **Mc farlane**.v. Tayside health board (1999) 3WLR 1301, (causation test) but for

14) **Hall.v. Broke land** auto racing club (1993) 1KB 205,

15) Polemis.v.Furness,Withy & Co Ltd (1921) KB 560 (once causation is established, defendant **label for all loss**

16) **Thompson**'s. Metropolitan police commission (1997) 2 ALL ER 762 (Claimant requested the court to award **aggravated damages**.

17) **Bonnington Casting Ltd.v. Wardlaw**

18) **McGhee.v.NationalCoal Board**

19) **Fairchird** (mesothelioma cancer).v. Glenhaven funeral services Ltd (2003)1 AC 32

20) Baker .v. Corus (2006)2 AC 572 since the other employers have disappear the defendant was asked to pay the full loss. THIS PROMTED THE PARLIAMENT TO INTRODUSE THE COMPENSATION ACT 2006

21) **Holtby**

22) **Performance Cars .v.Abraham (1962) 1 QB 33**

23) **Holtby to pay proportion of what defendant cause**

24)) Polemis .v. State that once the claimant can show that once causation is satisfied, the defendant is liable for all the loses which flows from the conduct whether or not that damage was foreseeable by the defendant. (This is culpability and compensation.

25) Rule of remoteness is Wagon.v. Mould (no 1) (1961) AC 388 Reasonable foresee ability of the damage or a reasonable person would have foreseen or "If a reasonable person cannot foresee the damage, it cannot be recovered.

25) **From .v. Buther (1976)2 QB 286** claimant was not wearing seat belt so the claim was reduced.
26) Thompson. Metropolitan police commission (1997)2 ALL Er 762 in which the claimant request award of aggravated damage.
27) The claim to be dealt with on "egg-shell-rule" Robinson's. Post office (1974) 1WLR.
28) Johnson v. Tennant Bros. Ltd (1954) not to criticise emergency team.
29) M x 3 % In Baker v.TE Hopkins (1959)1 WLR 966-the law state that emergencies team (fire, ambulance, police) must not be criticised when they act to save life in dramatic manner. Per Lord William LJ's
30) Danger Haynes v. Harwood (1945) 1 KB 146 (police rescue people from imminent life danger

JUDICIAL REVIEW

REFERENCE

1) "Failure by decision maker to understand correctly the law that regulate his decision power and to give effect" by Lord Dip lock example Misinterpreting legislation (error of law) example (Ainsminic Ltd .v. Foreign Compensational commission (1969)2 AC 147) Appendix A

2) Ultra vires; Decision maker exceed the power conferred on him McCarthy and stone v. Richmond upon Thames LBC ex –parte McCarty and Stun development Ltd (1992) 2AC 48 appendix B

3) Error of Law or Juridition questions of fact i.e. factual error whereby the decision maker exceeds his powers. (R.V. secretary of state for the home department, ex part kawaka (1984) AC 74.) Appendix C

4) Improper purpose is used where discretion power result mistake as to the relevance of factors\improper purpose Associated provincial picture house ltd Eynesbury corporation (1948) 1 KB 223 or Robert s.v.Hopwood (1925) AC578.) Appendix D

5) Unauthorised delegation with discretion power given to decision maker must not appoint anybody else Barnard .v.National Dock labour Board (1953) 2 QB 18.) Appendix E

6) Acting under the direction of another person or implement some body's else police. (H. Lavender and son Ltd.v. Minister

of housing and local Government (1970) 1 WLR 1231.) Appendix F

7) Fettering of discretion- Must not be restricted by rules

8) ("In considering South African, Canada and Zimbabwean authority if measured is proportionate; The legislative objective is sufficiently important to justify limiting fundamental right 2) The measure designed to meet legislative objective and rationally connected to it 3) The means used to impaired the right of freedom are no more than is necessary to accomplish the objective") appendix

PROPERTY LAW

REFERENCE

R.V.GRAHAM (1982) 74 DR.APP R 235

R.V.HASAN (2005) 2 AC 467

R.V.SHARP (1987)1QB853 (ARM ROBBERS

R.V.HUDSON AND TAYLOY AND ABDUL HUSSAIN

2006) CRIM.L.R.2006,FEB,142 -146 PROFESSOR DAVID ORMEROD

ERIE C.J.IN R.V.CHALLOTTE SMITH (1865) 10 COX 82

LORD HALSHAM. L. IN R.V.HOWE (1987) 1 ALL E R 77 AT 777 (1987) A C 417 AT 429

LORD STEYN IN R.V.BURSTOW (1997) 4 ALL E R

PSYCHIATRIC CASES

R.V.CHAN-FOOK (1994) 1.W.689.CA (LORD HOBHOUSE.L.J

R.V.MILLER (1954) 2 QB.282) LYNSKEY.J)

MCLOUGHLIN.V.O'BRIAN (1983) 1 AC 410 418

ATTIA.V.BRITISH GAS PLC (1988) Q.B.304

ALCOCK .V.CHIEF CONSTANBLE OF SOUTH YORKSHIRE POLICE (1992)1 AC. 310

R.V. ROBERT,56 CR.APP.R.95

FAGAN .V. METROPOLITAN POLICE COMMOSSION (1969) 1QB. 439

R.V.SAVAGE AND R .V. PARMENTER.

a) Jonathan (ends) (2015) *oxford dictionary of law* (6th edition) Oxford university press, Oxford press.

Waite. And Hawkins.S (Edn) (2009) *Oxford paperback dictionary* thesaurus (13th edition

Statute

(s. 29 TA 2000). s. 36 (60 Trustee act 1925 1 Ta 2000). (s.32 TA 2000

Cases

Re Denley's Trust Deed (1969), Megarry & wade's "The law of Real property

Peace and Stevens, Trust and equitable Obligation. OUP 6th edition, at P791

(Gray & Gray), Land law, 7th edition, OUP 539. (Prudential assurance (House of Lords)

(Lace v. Chantler (1944) 1 All ER 305. (Street v. Mountford).

(Ashburn Anstalt v. Arnold) and s.205 (1) (xxvii) LPA 1925 to have absolute possession.

Leave Robson v. Hallett (1967) 3 WLR 28. Lord Diplock LJ said a licence can be withdrawn but the person needs to be given reasonable time to leave the premises by appropriate route.

; Hardwick v Johnson (1978) 2 ALL ER 35, a woman living in a house with a child, the husband left her. Court of appeal ruled that she had licence to occupy the property.

Court of Appeal in Ashburn Anstalt v. Arnold (1090) Ch 1

Antoniodes v. Villies (1990) 1 AC 417, Street v. Mountford (1985) AC 809.

Act 1954 for business (part 11), Tenancy example; Act 1977

A G Securities v. Vaughan (1990) 1 AC 417. (Street v. Mountford),

(Markou v. Slaves). (Howyler v. Ruddy (1996) 28 HLR 550

Westminster City Council v. Clarke (1992) 2 AC 288

Burton v. (LQHT) landlord and Quadrant Housing Trust (1998) QB 834.

Gilliam v. Breiden Bach (1982) RTR 323,

In Morice v. Bishop (1805) 10 Ves JR 522 Sir William Grant MR said "Every trust must a definite object. There must be someone in whose favour the court can decree specific performance".

(Tonley v. Sherborn; Styles v. Guy) Mcphaul v. Doulton, CF, Re; Barlows

1. . Dishonesty test in Royal Brunei Airlines v. Tan
2. Barlow Clowes v. Vaurghan. (BCCI v. Akindele) Foskett v. Mckeown
3. Schmidt v. Rosewood (2003) 2 AC 709

Goff J's reference to Re Boyes. Saunders v. Vautier (1841) 4 Beav 115

McPhail v. Doulton (1971) AC 424 (Re Dean (18890

(Pirbright v. Salwey (1896) Astor ST (1952) Ch 534.

1957) 1 WLR 729, Leahy v. A-G for New South Wales (1959) AC 457

STATUTE

The prescription Act 1832 Law of property Act 1925 Land Register Act 200 Trust of land and appointment of trustee Act (TOLATA) 1996

Will Act 1837 Trustee Act 1925 S.52 LPA 1925

s.1 (2) LPA 1925. (s.52 (1) LPA 192 S.27 LRA

2002 Section 62 LPA 1825

s.1 (2) LPA 1925. s.53 (1) (b) LPA1925.

TOLATA 1996 s. 6(1)

s. (34) (1) trustee Act 1925. s. 27 LRA 2002 s. 34 (4) LPA 1925.

WILL

STATUTE

Will Act 1837

The inheritance (provision for family and dependants) Act 1975

The Mental capacity Act 2005

Cases

Execution

(Barry v. Butlin 12 ER 1089, Wintle v. Nye (1959) 1W.L.R 284 applied.

Supple v. Pender (2007) EWAC 829 Sherrington v. Sherrington (2005) EWCA Cave 326

(Wyniczenko v. Plucinska (2005) EWHC.

Lack of mental capacity

(Coventry v. Coventry).

(Parker v. Felgate).

Walker v. Baldwin (2004) EWHC,

Parker v. Felgate

Bank v. Good fellow 1870) LR 5 Q 549and

Burns v. Burns (2016) EWA

<u>LACK OF KNOWLEDGE</u>

(Strong v. Bird), Simon v. Byford, Bank v. Goodfellow and Parker v. Felgate,

Sherrington v. Sherrington (2005) EWCA Cave 326

Greave .v. Stolkin (2013) EWHC

<u>UNDUE INFLUENCE</u>

Daniel v. Drew (2005) EWCA Civ 507. (Edward v. Edwards 92007) EWHC 119.

Wingrove.v.Wingrove (1885) 11 PD 81. (Shomberg v .Taylor)

Conventry v. Coventry (1980) Ch 461. Corduroy v. Cranfield (2011) EWHC.

Edwards .v Edwards (2007) EWHC 119

ROYAL BANK OF SCOTLAND V. ETRIDGE (No 2) (2001) 4 ALL ER 499.

INHERITANCE

liott v. Mitson   Fisher v. Diffley (2013 EWHC

Berry v. Buttlin

CASES

Wright v. Macddam (1948)2 All Er 565 (1949) 2KB 74 (Ward v. Kirkland) (1967) Ch 194.

Wong v Beaumont property trust Ltd (1965) 1 QB 173.

(Ellenborough Park (1956) ch 131. Wheelor v. Burrows (1879) 12 Ch D 31.

Payne v web (1874) LR 19 E9 26   (Re; Fullers contract (1933) ch 652. (88 Berkeley road NW9 (1971) Ch 648. (Re Draper's Collis v. Home and Colonial stores Ltd (1904) AC 179.

Harris v. Goddard (1983)1 WLR 203.   Goodman v. Gallant (1986) Farm 106.

Constitutional law

REFERENCES

Thompson, B; andGordon.M. (2014) (11th edn)."*Cases and Material on Administrative and Constitutional*

Law" Oxford University press, UK

Constitutional law in United Kingdom in

Thompson, B and Gordon, M. (2014)

Hutton, s; Tayler,T; (3rd edn 2015) *"Law;the individual and the state "The university of law* " Oxford university press UK

Fundamental values, Constitution and core constitutional principle, in Hutton, s; Tayler, T; (3rd edn 2015)

The sources of the UK constitution.p76 in Hutton, s;

Tayler,T; (3rd edn 2015) and p187-188 in Thompson,B; andGordon.M.(2014) 11th (edn)."*Cases and Material on Administrative and Constitutional Law"*

The sources of the UK Constitution P76-77 in Hutton, s; Tayler,T; (3rd edn 2015) Parliamentary supremacy;

P 133-140 in Hutton, s; Tayler,T; (3rd edn 2015)

Parliamentary supremacy;P 122-125in Hutton, s;

Tayler,T; (3rd edn 2015) *"Law;the individual and the*

state "and P 402 in Thompson,B; andGordon.M.(2014) 11th (edn)."*Cases and Material on Administrative and*

Constitutional Law"

Dickinson, A. (2016). "Back to the future: the UK's EU exit and the conflict of laws." *Journal of Private International Law* 12.2. 195-210.

Law, J. (2015) 8th edn. Oxford Dictionary of Law OU Library

Peruginelli, G., & Faro, S. (2018). Research quality evaluation: The case of legal studies. In *the Evaluation of Research in Social Sciences and Humanities* (pp. 103-129). Springer, Cham.

Richards, P. & Curzon L.B. (2011). *Dictionary of Law*, 8th edn, London, Longman.

Samuel, G. (2014). *An introduction to comparative law theory and method* (Vol. 11). Bloomsbury Publishing.

Sloan, A. E. (2018). *Basic legal research: Tools and strategies*. Wolters Kluwer Law & Business. TGF (Tutor Group Forum) and posts for W820

Van Hoecke, M. (2015). Methodology of comparative legal research. *Law and Method*, 1-35.

Vranken, J. BM. (2011). "Methodology of legal doctrinal research: A comment on Westerman." *Methodologies of Legal Research–Which Kind of Method for What Kind of Discipline*.

Waite. M. Hawker, S (2009)3rd edn Oxford Paperback Dictionary & Thesaurus

Watkins, D. & Burton, M. (eds) (2013). Research Methods in Law, Abingdon, Routledge

Historical research

References

Cases

- *British Pregnancy Advisory Service v Secretary of State for Health* [2011] EWHC 235 (Admin).
- *R v Bourne* [1939] 1 KB 687.

Other

- *Alfie* (1966) film, directed by Lewis Gilbert, Paramount Pictures.
- *Daily Politics* (2011) BBC1, 4 February [online], http://www.bbc.co.uk/ news/ uk-politics-11913228 (Accessed 10 September 2012).
- Hansard (2005) Parliamentary Debates (House of Commons), vol. 439, col. 67w.
- Hansard (2008) Parliamentary Debates (House of Commons) vol. 476 col. 258.
- Richards, P. and Curzon L.B. (2011) *Dictionary of Law*, 8th edn, London, Longman.
- *This Week* (1965) ITV, 4 February [online], http://www.screenonline.org.uk.libezproxy.open.ac.uk/ tv/ id/ 475063/ (Accessed 10 September 2012).
- *Up the Junction* (1965) BBC 1, 3 November.
- *Vera Drake* (2004) film, directed by Mike Leigh, New Line Cinema.

REFERENCE

he Irish Statute Book website

he World Legal Information Institute's website

the European convention of Human right(ECHR,2010)

, united nations convention on the Rights of the child (UNICEF, 2005),

f the Criminal Justice Act 2006,

Other

- ECtHR (2010) *European Convention on Human Rights: as amended by Protocols Nos. 11 and 14*, European Court of Human Rights, Council of Europe Treaty Series No. 5, Council of Europe Publishing; available at http://www.echr.coe.int (accessed 10 September 2012).
- UNICEF (2005) 'Convention on the Rights of the Child' [online], United Nations International Children's Emergency Fund, http://www.unicef.org/ crc/ (accessed 14 September 2015).
- UNICEF (n.d.) 'UN Convention on the Rights of the Child: In Child Friendly Language' [online], United Nations International Children's Emergency Fund,

http://www.unicef.org/ rightsite/ files/ uncrcchilldfriendlylanguage.pdf (accessed 10 September 2012).

- BBC (2009) 'Young brothers admit boys' attack' BBC News, 3 September, http://news.bbc.co.uk/ 1/ hi/ england/ south_yorkshire/ 8233822.stm (accessed 10 September 2012).
- Buckley, M. (2010) 'How Edlington case follows course paved by Bulger trial' BBC News, 22 January, *How Edlington case follows course paved by Bulger trial* (accessed 10 September 2012).

SOCIAL LEGAL RESEARCH

References

Other

- BBC (2007) 'Our Missing Children', *Panorama*, BBC 1, 6 July.
- Cownie, F. and Bradney, A. (2013) 'Socio-legal studies: a challenge to the doctrinal tradition', in Watkins, D. and Burton, M. (eds) *Research Methods in Law*, 2nd edn, Abingdon, Routledge, pp. 34-54.
- Economic and Social Research Council (ESRC) (1994) *Review of Socio-Legal Studies: Final Report*, Swindon, ESRC.

- Epstein, L. and King, G. (2002) 'The Rules of Inference', *University of Chicago Law Review*, vol. 69, no. 1, pp. 1–133.
- Children's rights director Roger Morgan
- ECtHR (2010) *European Convention on Human Rights: as amended by Protocols Nos. 11 and 14*, European Court of Human Rights, Council of Europe, Treaty Series No. 5, Strasbourg, Council of Europe Publishing; available at http://www.echr.coe.int/ Pages/ home.aspx?p=basictexts&c=#n1359128122487_pointer (accessed 10 September 2012).
- Fink, A. (2005) *Conducting Research Literature Reviews: From the Internet to Paper*, 2nd edn, Thousand Oaks, California, Sage.
- Harris, D.R. (1983) 'The Development of Socio-legal Studies in the United Kingdom', *Legal Studies*, vol. 3, no. 3, pp. 315–333; available at http://www.heinonline.org.libezproxy.open.ac.uk/ HOL/ Page?handle=hein.journals/ legstd3&collection=journals&index=journals/ legstd&id=323 (accessed 10 September 2012).
- McConville, M. and Chui, H.W. (eds) (2010) *Research Methods for Law*, Edinburgh, Edinburgh University Press.
- Mahadevan, J. (2011) 'Children in care oppose media access to family courts, says children's rights director' [online], *Children & Young People Now*, 15 February, http://www.cypnow.co.uk/ cyp/ news/ 1045001/ children-

care-oppose-media-access-family-courts-childrens-rights-director (accessed 4 July 2012).

- Masson, J.M., Oakley, M.W., and Pick, K. (2004) 'Emergency Protection Orders: Court Orders for Child Protection Crises' [online],
- Law Lords (Paterson, 1982)
- Harris (1983)

Twining,1967).

Emergency Protection Orders (EPOs).

- http://www.nspcc.org.uk/Inform/publications/downloads/EPO_wdf48137.pdf (accessed 4 July 2012).
- Melville-Brown, A. (2012) 'Practice Points: The Leveson Inquiry', *The Law Society Gazette*, 13 April 2012, p. 17.
- Ministry of Justice (2011a) *Family Justice Review: Final Report*, London, Ministry of Justice; available at http://www.justice.gov.uk/ downloads/ publications/ moj/ 2011/ family-justice-review-final-report.pdf (accessed 8 August 2012).
- Ministry of Justice (2011b) *The Family Courts Information Pilot*, London, Ministry of Justice; available at http://www.justice.gov.uk/ downloads/ publications/ moj/ 2011/ family-courts-information-pilot.pdf (accessed 8 August 2012).
- Paterson, A. (1982) *The Law Lords*, London, Macmillan.
- Research Excellence Framework (2015) *Overview Report by Main Panel C and Sub-Panels 16-26*; available at

http://www.ref.ac.uk/ media/ ref/ content/ expanel/ member/ Main%20Panel%20C%20overview%20report.pdf (accessed 8 July 2016).

- Rights4Me (2011) *Children on Family Justice*, Manchester, Ofsted; available at http://www.lgcplus.com/ Journals/ 3/ Files/ 2011/ 2/ 15/ Children%20on%20family%20justice.pdf (accessed 14 September 2015).
- Rozenberg, J. (2012) 'Balancing Exercise', *The Law Society Gazette*, 19 April 2012, p. 6.
- Schon, D.A. (1983) *The Reflective Practitioner: How Professionals Think in Action*, New York, Basic Books.
- Twining, W. (ed) (1997) *Law in Context Enlarging a Discipline*, Oxford, Oxford University Press.
- Vick, D.W. (2004) 'Interdisciplinarity and the Discipline of Law', *The Journal of Law and Society*, vol. 31, no. 2, pp. 163–93.
- Wolanski, A. and Wilson, K. (2011) *The Family Courts, Media Access and Reporting*, available at https://www.judiciary.gov.uk/ wp-content/ uploads/ JCO/ Documents/ Guidance/ family-courts-media-july2011.pdf (accessed 11 July 2016).

Danieli, Y., Stamatopoulou, E. and Dias, C., 2018. International Labour Organization (ILO) Standards and Human Rights: Lee Swepston. In *The Universal Declaration of Human Rights* (pp. 59-66). Routledge.

Schwartz, M.S., 2017. Corporate social responsibility. Routledge.

Liu, L., Carey, P. and Qu, W., 2017. Voluntary Corporate Social Responsibility Reporting and Financial Statement Auditing in China.

Grayson, D. and Hodges, A., 2017. Corporate social opportunity!: Seven steps to make corporate social responsibility work for your business. Routledge.

CORRUPTION

REFERENCES

Ferguson, G., 2018. *Global corruption: Law, theory & practice*.

Foran, N.J. and Theisen, B.A., 2000. The business of charity. *Journal of Accountancy*, *190*(6), p.77.

Harapan, H., Anwar, S., Bustaman, A., Radiansyah, A., Angraini, P., Fasli, R., Salwiyadi, S., Bastian, R.A., Oktiviyari, A., Akmal, I. and Iqbalamin, M., 2016. Community willingness to participate in a dengue study in Aceh province, Indonesia. *PloS one*, *11*(7), p.e0159139.

Hatchard, J., 2014. *Combating corruption: legal approaches to supporting good governance and integrity in Africa*. Edward Elgar Publishing

Law, J. Oxford dictionary of Law 2015 eight edn

McCorquodale, R.The Business of human Rights 2011 Zed books (the Reader).

Open university Library;-e-Journals, database

OU, "Study Guide 2 & 3 W822 Business, Human right law and corporate social responsibility.

Postgraduate Open university website

Silver, J.K. ed., 1998. *The business of medicine*. Hanley & Belfus.

Symonides, J., 2017. *Human rights: international protection, monitoring, enforcement*. Routledge

MNEs

References

Arnold, D.G., 2010. Transnational corporations and the duty to respect basic human rights. Business Ethics Quarterly, 20(3), pp.371-399.

George, S., 2017. Shadow Sovereigns: How global corporations are seizing power. John Wiley & Sons.

Irogbe, K., 2013. Global political economy and the power of multinational corporations. Journal of Global South Studies, 30(2), p.223.

Kennedy, E.T., Welch, C.E. and Monshipouri, M., 2017. Multinational corporations and the ethics of global responsibility: Problems and possibilities. In Human Rights and Corporations (pp. 123-147). Routledge.

Law, J. Oxford dictionary of Law 2015 eight edn

Locke, R.M., 2013. The promise and limits of private power: Promoting labor standards in a global economy. Cambridge University Press.

Love, M.C., 2010. Beyond sovereignty: Issues for a global agenda. Nelson Education.

McCorquodale, R.The Business of human Rights 2011 Zed books (the Reader).

Open university Library;-e-Journals, database

OU, "Study Guide 2 & 3 W822 Business, Human right law and corporate social responsibility.

Postgraduate Open university website

Ramasastry, A., 2015. Corporate social responsibility versus business and human rights: Bridging the gap between responsibility and accountability. Journal of Human Rights, 14(2), pp.237-259.

Ruggie, J., 2011. Report of the special representative of the secretary-general on the issue of human rights and transnational corporations and other business enterprises: Guiding principles on business and human rights: implementing the united nations 'protect, respect and remedy'framework. Netherlands Quarterly of Human Rights, 29(2), pp.224-253.

Santa Clara County v. Southern Pac. R. Co., 118 U.S. 394 (1886)

Waite, M. & Hawker, S. Oxford dictionary and Thesaurus

Wettstein, F., 2010. The duty to protect: Corporate complicity, political responsibility, and human rights advocacy. Journal of Business Ethics, 96(1), pp.33-47.

Wieland, A. and Handfield, R.B., 2010. The socially responsible supply chain: An imperative for global corporations. Supply Chain Management Review, 14(6).

Abortion

Reference

- Abortion Act 1967.
- Human Fertilisation and Embryology Act 1990.
- Infant Life (Preservation) Act 1929.
- Malicious Shooting or Stabbing Act 1803.

- Mental Capacity Act 2005.
- Offences Against the Person Act 1828.
- Offences Against the Person Act 1837.
- Offences Against the Person Act 1861.

FGM

Reference

Great Britain. The Female Genital Mutilation Act 2003 (Commencement) Order 2004*: Elizabeth II. Chapter 10* (2004) London, The Stationery Office Limited.

Great Britain. Prohibition of Female Circumcision Act 1985: *Elizabeth II.* (1985) London, The Stationery Office Limited.

Great Britain. Serious Crime Act 2015: *Elizabeth II. Chapter 9. Section 70-75, 86, 88* (2015) London, The Stationery Office Limited.

Office for National Statics. (2018) Population of England and Wales: 2001 – 2011. https://www.ethnicity-facts-figures.service.gov.uk/british-population/national-and-regional-populations/population-of-england-and-wales/latest (Accessed 23 February 2018)

Summers, H. and Ratcliffe, R. (2019) "Mother of three-year-old is first person convicted of FGM in UK". The Guardian, 1 February 2019, https://www.theguardian.com/society/2019/feb/01/fgm-mother-of-three-year-old-first-person-convicted-in-uk (Accessed 17 February 2019).

The Female Genital Mutilation Protection Order (Relevant Third Party) Regulations 2015 (2015) No.

1422. London, The Stationery Office Limited. https://www.legislation.gov.uk/uksi/2015/1422/pdfs/uksi_20151422_en.pdf (Accessed 23 February 2019).

World Health Organization (WHO) (2019) Sexual and reproductive health: Classification of female genital mutilation [online]. Available at https://www.who.int/reproductivehealth/topics/fgm/overview/en/ (Accessed 17 February 2019).

SOME TERMINOLOGY WORTH KNOWING IN LAWS

Tort, criminal, public law, Judicial revues, Property law, Constitutional, Contract, Equity and Trust Equity, Family, Business, Agency, Employment, Tax, European Human Right, Pure economic loss, Vicarious Liability Licence, Easement, Rules, Drive way, Co-ownership, Tenancy in Common, Contract, Implied terms, Express Terms, McLaughlin, Alcock, Actus reus, Mens rea, Homicide Theft Arson, Reckless, Attempt, Intoxication, Voluntary intoxication, involuntary intoxication, strict liability, Duress Dishonesty, Insane, coward, Criminal damage, Suicide pacts, Non-insane Automatism, Diminish responsibility Defence, Sexual offences, Negligence, accomplice, Attempt, making off without paying, Robert Manslaughter, murder, exception clauses, unfair terms, Express Terms, complex structure, judgement reasonableness, undue influence, remedies, gratuitously bare trust, execution, mental capacity, knowledge inheritance, accomplice, counsel, procuring, Albert, Aid insanity, guilty conduct, rape, sexual assault, basic Intent Dutch Courage, Absolute liability, rule of law, Omission mistake, force, innocent agent, inchoate, mercy killing, Euthanasia, gracious bodily harm, coroners, terminology parliament, penalty, bizarre, outlandish, But for burden of peeve, direct, objective, subjective, infanticide attempt, substantive offence, Attempt impossible, conspiracy, justification, Arson, self-defence, consent, Criminal gangs, presumption, children fraud, police, Instan, Dobson, stone, intention, stone, intention, comment, court, Psychiatry PTSP, employer, employee, unfair terms, duty of care, breach duty, nuisance, personal injury, causation, pragmatic test, shock sudden occurrence, consequential, restrictions, policy establish rules, test, terminology electric cable, exclusive factors, lessor, periodic lease, patrol lease, necessity legal, beneficial principle, trust, monitoring, maxim, shares, chattels, procedure impropriety, remedies proportionality, irrationality, mixed case, appeal, respondent locus stand, hybrid authority, offer, acceptance, agreement, certainty, offeror, rejection, consideration, adequacy, sufficiency, UCTA, custom, condition, Warranties, innominate, Will, legacy, test or, attestation, witness authencity, jigsaw, police protestors, convention assessment, professor Glanville, Constitutional, Article Magna Carta, elements, characteristics, supremacy, monarch, European Convention, authoritative, persuasive, House of Lords, international law, UK, Human Right, member state, Royal prerogative, House of Lords, House of Commons, Legislation, Supreme Court, European treaties, statute, books, reference, damages.

INDEX

www.ingramcontent.com/pod-product-compliance
Lightning Source LLC
LaVergne TN
LVHW100246210926
848480LV00003B/837